CRISIS

1918

By the same author

They Never Had It So Good
A Matter of Morals
Adventure Underground
Bridges and Men
Wonders of the Modern World
Harry S. Truman, A Pictorial Biography
Franklin D. Roosevelt, Portrait of a President

—with Frances Gies

Life in a Medieval City
Merchants and Moneymen:
The Commercial Revolution, 1000–1500

CRISIS
1918

The Leading Actors, Strategies, and Events in the German Gamble for Total Victory on the Western Front

JOSEPH GIES

W · W · NORTON & COMPANY · INC ·
NEW YORK

Maps by Anne Marie Jauss

This book was designed by Margaret F. Plympton.
The type is Caledonia and Perpetua.
The book was manufactured by Vail-Ballou Press, Inc.

FIRST EDITION

Published simultaneously in Canada
by George J. McLeod Limited, Toronto

Library of Congress Cataloging in Publication Data

Gies, Joseph.
Crisis, 1918.

Bibliography: p.
1. European War, 1914–1918—Germany.
2. European War, 1914–1918—Campaigns—Western.
3. Ludendorff, Erich, 1865–1937. I. Title.
D531.G5 1974 940.4′0943 73–14861
ISBN 0–393–05493–4

PRINTED IN THE UNITED STATES OF AMERICA
1 2 3 4 5 6 7 8 9 0

To *Tac P. Gies*
Sergeant, Company A, 1st U.S. Engineers,
First Division, A.E.F., and to all the
other survivors of the battles of 1918

CONTENTS

Illustrations appear between pages 128–129 and pages 192–193

Maps

The author wishes to express his appreciation for the help given by the personnel of the Imperial War Museum, London; the Wehrgeschichtliches Museum, Rastatt, Germany; Mlle. Véronique Blum, Chief Conservator of the Bibliothèque de Documentation Internationale Contemporaine of the University of Paris; the Northwestern University Library, Evanston, Illinois; and finally, Frances Gies, whose contributions included research, translation, and practically everything except writing the book.

I

LUDENDORFF CHOOSES WAR

1

WAR OR PEACE

On the morning of November 26, 1917, three Russian soldiers with a white flag appeared before the German lines in Courland. They identified themselves as emissaries of General Krylenko, the new Russian commander in chief, and stated their mission: to obtain an armistice for peace negotiations.

On the same day, Leon Trotsky, commissar for foreign affairs in the new Soviet government, circularized the foreign embassies in Petrograd with a call for a peace conference of all belligerents, to end the war on a basis of "no annexations and no indemnities."

Krylenko's request and Trotsky's summons created consternation in London and Paris by confirming the western Allies' fears that Russia was dropping out of the war. Yet among the masses of people in Great Britain and France it brought a surge of hope that more than three years of unparalleled suffering might come to a close. A peace of no annexations and no indemnities would mean that France must forgo recovery of Alsace-Lorraine and reparations for her devastated territory, but to most French people peace was worth it. In Britain, which had no Alsace-Lorraine and no devastated territory, there was even less reason for resisting peace. On November 29, three days after Krylenko's mission, a letter appeared in the London *Daily Telegraph* over the signature of Lord Lansdowne, a former British foreign secretary, architect of the Entente Cordiale with France, and one of Europe's most distinguished statesmen. Lord Lansdowne proposed that all the combatants accept the Bolshevik lead by publicly stating their peace terms. Certain questions, according to Lord Lansdowne, could be left to negotiation at the peace table, e.g., Alsace-Lorraine. Certain others, on the contrary, had to be agreed on in advance: evacuation of occupied French and Belgian territory. What did Germany have in mind in respect to Belgian independence, the one irreducible British war aim?

In Berlin a new chancellor had just taken office. Dignified, old-fashioned, conservative seventy-four-year-old Count von Hertling, a former professor of philosophy, had confided to his friends that he wanted to go down in history as the "Reconciliation Chancellor." He hoped to be remembered as the leader who had succeeded in bringing peace to a Germany that needed it desperately, a peace both "of honor," as the German nationalists demanded, and "of understanding," as the liberals and socialists insisted. Besides ending the outpouring of blood on the battlefield, peace would damp down the rising class antagonism that was threatening to turn, as it had in Russia, into violent revolution.

The "Turnip Winter" of 1916–17 had brought privation to nearly all segments of the German population. Germany's normal sources of food imports—Russia, Rumania, and Austria-Hungary—had all been shut off or thrown out of gear by the war, and the British blockade stopped imports from overseas. German bread was rationed and was composed largely of potatoes. Carrots and beets, once spurned as fodder, had become luxuries. Ham and pork, the German meat staples, were limited to one meal a week. The only really plentiful food was turnips, which were even replacing acorns as the basis for coffee. A good middle-class Berlin dinner featured "vegetable beefsteak"—cornmeal, spinach, potatoes, and peanuts bound with egg. The emaciated appearance of many Berlin mothers showed where their food ration had gone, yet hungry children spent their days and often their nights begging and stealing potatoes or bits of butter.

The food situation was better in the countryside, but this only exacerbated relations among Germans, the Bavarian farmers refusing to share with the *Sau-Preussen* ("Prussian hogs"). But Bavarians suffered too. Their houses were searched for brass and copper utensils, doorknobs, and curtain rods; even their lightning rods were confiscated. Their beer, once Bavaria's pride, had turned pale and watery. Munich's famed beer halls remained closed all day, opening only at six o'clock to customers standing in line, tapping tunes on the door with their mugs.

Universal hatred was vented on the *Kriegsgewinneren* ("war profiteers"), who ate and drank their fill in certain restaurants that served meat dishes under deceptive names and were popularly dubbed "speak-easies." Honest businessmen took care not to look like profiteers. A new fur mantle or a new pair of shoes was an invitation to assault and robbery. Teen-age crime was rampant, but even more disconcerting was the unprecedented freedom of expression of the older workers. A lady-in-waiting of the Kaiserin, forced by bad roads to take a tram, found herself amidst workingmen openly reviling the Kaiser. When she undertook his defense, she was so menaced with abuse that she felt forced to quit the tram.

A particularly alarming sign had appeared in the form of a strike by sailors of the idle High Seas Fleet at Kiel (June, 1917), brought on by discrimination in favor of officers in the allotment of rations, and suppressed with courts-martial and executions.

Under the heavy pressure of the nation's war-weariness, the normally passive Reichstag had surprised everyone in the midsummer of 1917 by adopting a "Peace Resolution" that called, exactly like the Bolsheviks' subsequent proclamation, for "no annexations and no indemnities." A reaction followed promptly, as if the conservative Reichstag was shocked by its own act, and the Peace Resolution was interpreted out of all meaning by a new, right-wing chancellor named Michaelis. Nevertheless, a genuine movement had been set afoot, and Michaelis was presently overthrown in favor of von Hertling, while a new foreign minister, a career diplomat named von Kühlmann, though wary of committing himself publicly, was correctly believed to favor a negotiated peace. At the same time it was widely recognized that an obstacle to peace was the undemocratic makeup of the Reichstag itself, the result of the weighted, three-class Prussian franchise, which awarded political representation on the basis of property ownership. A proposal was introduced to modernize and democratize Germany's parliamentary body by franchise reform. Socialists and liberals united for franchise reform and a negotiated peace, while reactionaries and nationalists rallied for the Prussian franchise and victory on the battlefield.

Hertling and Kühlmann agreed with the patriotic conservatives that Germany's great sacrifices should be richly rewarded. But in General Krylenko's white flag and Lord Lansdowne's letter they perceived the heaven-sent opportunity to end the war on a resounding note of German victory. Helpless Russia could be freely robbed, and a satiated German imperialism could afford to be magnanimous, or at least moderate, in the West.

The root of the problem of negotiating peace in the midst of war lay in the universal terror every government had of showing a sign of weakness. The initiative had to come from somewhere else, and had to come in a form that forced a response. The Pope's heartfelt peace attempt of 1917 had lacked the power of the Bolsheviks' proposal because the Pope had nothing to offer except the benefits of peace. The Bolsheviks, however, had vast stretches of the Czar's territories, on which, by a variety of means, Hertling and Kühlmann meant to lay hands. Since Russia was defecting from the Allies, thereby breaking the Treaty of London, they felt that Britain and France could find no grounds for objecting to German gains at Russia's expense.

To make the opportunity perfect, it came when the fighting

season on the Western Front was just over. For four months there would be a lull along the vast belt of devastation in France.

It was as if the war that had begun in 1914 was now over, with Germany victorious. All that was needed was to offer Britain and France terms that they could accept.

It was felt that they would certainly accept a peace of no annexations and no indemnities, a simple return to the *status quo ante bellum* of 1914. But Hertling and Kühlmann were convinced that there was no need for so extreme a degree of magnanimity. They envisioned the annexation of the Grand Duchy of Luxembourg and of at least the Longwy-Briey iron-ore basin from France. On the matter of Belgium they thought of some sort of special relationship which would be to Germany's advantage. All that was really necessary to bring the western Allies to the peace table was to promise the restoration of Belgian independence, without going into details. Britain would be unable to resist, and France would be compelled to go along.

Only one thing remained to be done before putting the peace project into action. The acquiescence of the Army had to be secured. A message was sent to Field Marshal von Hindenburg, chief of the General Staff, at his headquarters at Kreuznach, in the Rhenish Palatinate. What did Supreme Headquarters think of this providential opportunity conferred by the events in Russia?

Supreme Headquarters was prompt in its answer. The Bolshevik Revolution did indeed present an opportunity—an opportunity for total victory. Not by peace resolutions and peace negotiations was this immense war, the greatest in German history, to be ended, but by *Friedensturm* (a "Peace Offensive") that would impose terms on the beaten adversary.

Give up Belgium, when the German Army at last had in sight a superiority in numbers on the Western Front? Certainly not, said Hindenburg. "Since our military situation has developed especially favorably," the Field Marshal wrote Hertling, "I can no longer see the necessity for a partial renunciation of the military demands." This was a reference to an earlier concession by Supreme Headquarters, made in September when events in Russia were not so clear, and consisting of a willingness to substitute for outright annexation of Belgium (or *Anschluss*, as it was called) a combination of partition, occupation, and customs union that would lead to *Anschluss* later. Now even that concession was retracted. The Flanders coast, of critical importance to Britain, must be German as "an imperative condition of peace with England." Liège, gateway to the invasion of France by Germany or of Germany by France, must belong to the German Army.

Despite all the propaganda about Belgium in the Allied camp, Allied statesmen and editors had little notion of how German intentions toward Belgium had metamorphosed in the course of the war. At the outset German Chancellor von Bethmann-Hollweg had protested that the violation of Belgian neutrality was only a momentary necessity dictated by the military need. But as the war lengthened into stalemate, German leaders came to think of occupied Belgium in one of two ways: as a trump card in the diplomatic game—Kühlmann's view—or as a German conquest to be added to the growing Empire. Where the Prussian Junker landlords were eager for acquisition of agricultural land in the East, western German businessmen's appetites were stimulated by the industrial regions across the western border: Belgium, Luxembourg, and the Longwy-Briey basin. At prices well below the market level, Fritz Thyssen, Hugo Stinnes, and other barons of the Ruhr took over former French and British interests in Belgium, with payment postponed until six months after the war, and found the arrangement so gratifying that they quickly extended it to purely Belgian firms.

By an irony, British public opinion had in the course of the war come around to a more lenient view of the German transgression of 1914. In 1916 Ramsay MacDonald, a prominent leader of the Labor party, had indicated that a simple reaffirmation of Bethmann-Hollweg's pledge of 1914 would now be enough for Britain. By that time the German position had evolved into something very different, one version of which Kaiser Wilhelm privately summed up in piquant language: "Albert shall keep his Belgium, since he too is king by divine right. . . . Though of course he'll have to toe the line. I imagine our future relationship as rather that of the Egyptian Khedive to the King of England."

That was in 1916. Now, after the Russian Revolution, even an Egyptian Khedive arrangement was out. Hindenburg's note to Hertling made no mention of King Albert at all.

Hertling made one more effort. If nothing could be done in respect to Belgium, perhaps the demands on France might be moderated somewhat. He asked his liaison officer at Spa to bring up the question of the Longwy-Briey basin—might the generals relent a little there?

The liaison officer answered by telegraph on December 14: "I do not want to pass on the suggestion about Briey at present as conditions are unfavorable for a good reception of it and the impression would be created that Your Excellency wishes to be very lenient toward France. They are feeling very big here at present and are entertaining ideas of smashing the enemy. . . ."

So far from forgoing the Longwy-Briey annexation, Supreme Headquarters was thinking of annexing all of northern France, as far as the Somme, and adding an indemnity mammoth enough to shift the German war costs to the French. "They" were indeed entertaining thoughts of "smashing the enemy." The plural pronoun was universally used in referring to the Supreme Command, because it was well known that the Army was led not by Hindenburg, but by the team of Hindenburg and Ludendorff, and by all knowledgeable people it was also well understood which of the two was the real guiding genius.

2

LUDENDORFF-SIEGFRIED

The two military chiefs of Germany were a familiar sight to Berliners. On their frequent visits to the capital for conferences the pair habitually took a morning stroll in the Tiergarten. Invariably the two massive, solemn, gray-overcoated figures were followed by a respectful, even reverent crowd. The reverence was for the seventy-year-old Field Marshal Paul von Hindenburg, a monument of a man, with a large square face and a white moustache, the visual embodiment of the old German virtues of character—courage, patience, patriotism. The respect was for Erich Ludendorff, who represented the less appealing virtues of the mind. The crowd's view notwithstanding, Ludendorff was by far the more exceptional man.

One of a very few German officers to achieve a high rank without having a "von" to his name, Ludendorff was a non-Junker Prussian, a parvenu who had joined the army after the bankruptcy of his businessman father, and had risen on merit alone, with considerable abrasion among his colleagues. Stocky, thick-necked, round-headed, he was noted in the army for his brusque manners and lack of humor. Less well known was his mystical side, suggested in his strong, square-jawed, high-foreheaded face only by blue eyes of a dreamer's depth. Behind them flourished Wagnerian fantasies of the German race. Ludendorff was not satisfied to be another Blücher, or another Moltke, titles of glory that sufficed for Hindenburg. His taste ran rather to a reincarnation of Siegfried, the ancient Germanic hero of the Nibelungen legend.

The tradition of bestowing high commands on princes and dukes had given the German Army an organizational quirk: each titled commander had a professional chief of staff who actually ran the show. Hindenburg and Ludendorff represented an extension of the system; Hindenburg, though a professional soldier of long standing (he was actually living in retirement in 1914), was basically a figurehead; in their successes in the East, Ludendorff had done all the thinking. Since Hindenburg had assumed the post of chief of the General Staff when they were appointed to the Supreme Command, Ludendorff had had to find a special title to denote his role, and had settled upon a tradition-laden Prussian rank from Napoleonic days—First Quartermaster General.

His actual function was all-encompassing; he took charge of strategy, operations, supplies, morale, everything to do with the Army. The indefatigable executive, he drove his staff as hard as he did himself. He received his first reports while still in bed, and his last telephone calls just before retiring at one in the morning. Between, he labored incessantly, permitting himself only a short walk and rest after the noon meal. An endless stream of subordinates reported to him, and he insisted in every case on assuring himself that his minutest orders were carried out with precision. "All his muscles were in constant motion," reported one observer. He had the patience to be an avid listener as long as his interlocutor spoke to the point, and he did not interrupt contrary opinions. Information gained, he invited no discussion.

With Hindenburg he had a relationship that the old Field Marshal described as that of a husband and wife, an apt metaphor: elderly husband Hindenburg commanded the obedience of the family and approved all decisions, but ambitious wife Ludendorff did the planning. From the beginning of their association, Hindenburg succeeded in achieving a benign and profitable partnership, as a husband wise enough to listen to his cleverer wife.

The Kaiser, on the other hand, tried in vain to adjust to Ludendorff. The lack of a "von" was not the problem; the Kaiser felt at home with bourgeois businessmen, even Jews. The trouble went deeper. By an exquisite irony the war had robbed the Supreme Warlord of all his power. A fifty-eight-year-old adolescent, jealous of Hindenburg and loathing Ludendorff, Wilhelm had been forced by public opinion to give the pair the top command, and had at once sunk even further into insignificance. The arrogant sovereign who had dismissed the mighty Bismarck was now a Merovingian *roi fainéant* to Ludendorff's Mayor of the Palace. Ludendorff barely took the trouble to be courteous. Appearing at the Kaiser's headquarters to report on the military situation, he snapped out short, pithy sentences, as if in a Cadet School classroom. The Kaiser asked a question; Ludendorff clapped his monocle to his eye, marked off distances on the map with his compasses, and returned the answer. The lesson over, the schoolmaster clicked his spurs, about-faced (no backing out of the room for Ludendorff) and returned to his own headquarters, leaving the Supreme Warlord frustrated and humiliated. To get even, the Kaiser invented a derisive nickname behind Ludendorff's back—*der Feldwebel* ("the Sergeant Major").

Only a man with overpowering confidence in his own judgment could have put forward and carried through the daring maneuver that Ludendorff executed shortly after his arrival on the Western Front in the beginning of 1917—the withdrawal to what the Allies named the Hindenburg Line, though Ludendorff christened it the *Siegfried Stellung* ("Siegfried Position"). A system of defense in depth, it consisted of several well-spaced lines of trenches, covered with barbed wire and fortified with concrete bunkers. The surrender of conquered territory went against the grain of the Kaiser, the upper Army officers, and the nationalist press, but it gave

Germany the best casualty ratio of the war in 1917, first against the recklessly attacking French in Champagne, then against the persistent British in Flanders.

But the retreat to the Hindenburg Line was purely a chess move for Ludendorff. His view of the war was in reality more aggressively imperialist than the Kaiser's or Hindenburg's. Where they conceived of territorial acquisitions in the nineteenth-century sense of war booty—win a battle, gain a province—Ludendorff envisioned the war as the foundation of a new Germanic super-empire, stretching from the Atlantic to Asia, a military-naval-industrial colossus capable of dominating all the lesser nations and races of mankind. This was the German destiny foreseen by the great racist prophets—Heinrich von Treitschke, Paul de Lagarde, and Houston Stewart Chamberlain. It was confirmed in Ludendorff's eyes by the unheard-of scale of the war. Germany's narrow escape in 1916, when the Army found itself compelled to battle simultaneously the French, British, Russians and Rumanians, seemed to him less a warning signal than a guarantee of ultimate fulfillment. Ludendorff destroyed the inviting possibility of a separate peace with Czarist Russia early in 1917 by insisting on the foundation of a German-dominated Kingdom of Poland. Far from giving up part of his vast eastern scheme to remove one major antagonist from the battlefield, he unhesitatingly drew another, even more formidable, onto it. One of his first and most momentous decisions on arriving at the Supreme Command was to cast the decisive vote in favor of unrestricted U-boat warfare, bringing America into the war. Siegfried could not be hobbled by legalists' quibbles over neutral rights.

Ludendorff shared his dream of German racial glory with an army of writers, editors, professors, and schoolmasters. The term *Herrenvolk* ("Master Race") had been invented by Dr. Heinrich Class, chief spokesman of the Pan-German League, to describe the Germanic brotherhood of Germans, Flemings, Dutch, and Balts destined for future rule. War itself was "a bracing educational experience," according to leading editor Maximilian Harden, and "a beautiful and splendid thing," in the words of novelist Thomas Mann, who lived to retract this opinion. Literary critic Karl Toth, reviewing in the *Deutsche Rundschau* the latest volume of Romain Rolland's *Jean-Christophe,* was outraged by the French pacifist's vision of a democratic union of the western peoples: "The union of the holy Germanic race, with its pure blood, with that of corrupt, degenerate peoples!"

Albert Einstein wrote Rolland that "[Germany has arrived] at a sort of religion of force [that] dominates nearly all the intellectuals." Einstein was struck by the large number of educated Germans who led private lives of unblemished altruism but foamed with impatience over the restrictions on U-boat warfare.

The Allied countries had their extremists too, but compared with the German superpatriots they were few in number, limited in influence, and lacking in the emotional force that racism gave the German ideology. Apart from that, no Allied leader, civil or military, could hope to play the role that Ludendorff by 1918 played in Germany. In Britain and France the tradition of democracy was too encompassing, too well established, to permit a general such power even in wartime. On the contrary—prime ministers Lloyd George and Clemenceau both freely intervened in military matters, and often treated generals with cavalier contempt. The defeats at the Marne and Verdun had brought the successive downfall of two chiefs of the German General Staff, but the elevation of Hindenburg, laden with glory, had restored and enhanced its prestige. The deepening crisis of the war, making Hindenburg more and more the hope of Germany, provided an opportunity that Hindenburg was not suited by temperament to exploit. Capable, ambitious, neurotically driven Ludendorff was.

Hindenburg conceivably could have been won over to a peace of large but limited profits along the line proposed by Hertling and Kühlmann, but Ludendorff never. Throughout the war his career had been meteoric, as he moved from personally leading the assault on Liège in 1914 to planning the huge offensive operations by which the Russian giant had been felled. He could even claim to have foreseen and warned against the major German reverses. The Marne defeat in 1914 had resulted from a weakening of the left wing that Ludendorff had vainly opposed (suffering a temporary career setback for his obstinacy), and Verdun from a frontal-assault concept that he had condemned. Now, in the winter of 1917–18, he had a plan for victory to match the resources available, a new battle tactic tried out in Russia and Italy with spectacular results, and a strategy that would defeat the Allies in four months. The time consideration was crucial because of the Americans. Ludendorff hardly shared the newspapers' fantasy that the U-boats could prevent the Americans from coming over. But he was certain they could not be in France in serious numbers before midsummer, and by midsummer he would have won the battle.

The Master Race was a greater, more inspiring, more modern concept than the medievalistic German Empire to which Hindenburg was so devoted. To the service of his ideal, Ludendorff dedicated himself heart and soul. He promoted a vast expansion of German arms production, putting the nation for the first time on a total-war footing. For the sacrifices involved in total war, he promised the reward of total victory. That promise gave Ludendorff his supremacy. Against it no one could hold out—not Chancellor, Reichstag, or Kaiser.

At a Crown Council at Bellevue Castle (January 2, 1918), the Kaiser produced a map showing the future boundaries of Germany and Poland, to be presented to the Russian representatives at Brest-Litovsk. The Kaiser had been listening to Hertling and Kühlmann, who objected to the huge outright annexations of Polish-inhabited regions demanded by Hindenburg and Ludendorff, and who had found unexpected support from General Hoffmann, senior commander in the East and a formidable military tyrant himself. Hoffmann had told the Kaiser that only small pieces of Polish territory around sensitive military installations, such as the railway center of Thorn, needed to be annexed. The rest could be erected into a semi-independent Polish state under the Habsburgs, a plan known as the "Austro-Polish solution" and naturally much favored in Vienna.

But Hindenburg, and especially Ludendorff, had no use for the Austro-Polish solution. The German Army, under their leadership, had played the main role in beating the Russians; the Austrians had merely helped. Therefore the profits should go to Germany. Ludendorff minced no words in expressing his fury over the Kaiser's map. To the shock of the assembled notables, he asserted that the Kaiser had no right to ask the opinion of another general. The frontier as drawn by the Kaiser could not be considered final. He himself would have to study the matter.

It was a critical moment. The Kaiser might have declared his independence and rallied Hertling, Kühlmann, and the Reichstag. But the Kaiser could not bring himself to act without Hindenburg's support, and Ludendorff had made sure of the old Field Marshal. The ambitious wife was habitually at pains to guide and manage the slower-witted husband, going to the length of screening visitors to headquarters before admitting them. Now Hindenburg did not fail him. "We had better study this matter further," muttered the hero of Tannenberg, and the Kaiser hastily gave in. "Very well, I will wait for your report."

A few days later (January 7) Hindenburg wrote the Kaiser a letter, unmistakably dictated by Ludendorff. The letter did not merely press for an annexationist settlement in the East; it connected such a peace with the coming offensive in the West.

> Your Majesty has made it our right and duty to cooperate in seeing that the results of the peace [in the East] are in proportion to the sacrifices and performances of the German people and the German Army. . . .
>
> In all the conferences with the Imperial Chancellor over which Your Majesty presided we pointed out the importance of secure frontiers. . . . It is

doubtful whether such frontiers will be obtained, and this causes me the greatest anxiety.

In Alsace-Lorraine, where we could achieve something independently of the enemy, nothing fundamental has yet been done; the Imperial Government has not yet entirely rejected the idea of autonomy. [Hindenburg and Ludendorff wanted repressive rather than conciliatory measures taken against the Alsace-Lorraine separatist movement.] In the discussion with regard to Belgium I have encountered nothing but the greatest reserve on the part of the Imperial Government with regard to military demands.

In the East . . . we have cooperated as in duty bound. . . . On 2nd January . . . Your Majesty laid down a line which reduced our demands to a great extent and renders the solution of the question of the Austro-Polish frontier no longer acceptable to me and General Ludendorff. . . . I do not know whether it will be possible to find another solution which would suffice to allay our serious objections to handing over Poland to Austria. The creation of a Ukrainian state would certainly moderate the danger. . . .

I am unable to suppress the apprehension that the manner and result of the negotiations in Brest have an unfavorable influence on the frame of mind in the Army.

This frame of mind is at present being subjected to the greatest test. In order to secure the political and economic situation in the world which we need, we must defeat the Western Powers. For this purpose Your Majesty has ordered the offensive on the Western Front. This means the very greatest effort that we have made in the whole war; the very greatest sacrifices will be demanded. Whether we would then obtain for Germany, in concluding peace, the profit which our dominant position demands and

> which our sacrifices are worth seems doubtful to me after what has happened at Brest. The inevitable consequence would be a terrible disillusionment of the returning Army and of the people who would have to bear an insupportable burden of taxation [i.e., if a sufficiently merciless indemnity were not imposed on France].
>
> . . . Your Majesty will not order honest men who have served Your Majesty and the Fatherland faithfully to attach the weight of their names and authority to proceedings which their innermost conviction tells them to be harmful to the Crown and the Empire.
>
> The difficult task which Your Majesty imposes on the men who have to prepare and conduct the operations in the West in accordance with Your Majesty's directions demands that they should be assured of Your Majesty's unlimited personal confidence. In fulfilling their task, they and the Army must be sustained by the feeling that the political result will correspond to the military result.

That was the Hindenburg-Ludendorff viewpoint spelled out, with *t*'s crossed and *i*'s dotted. The new partition of Poland must be in Germany's, not Austria's, favor. A separate Ukrainian state should be erected under German tutelage. Alsace-Lorraine must be ruthlessly Germanized in preparation for the absorption of more French territory and of Belgium. The weakness being shown by the German side at Brest must be corrected, and must not be allowed to affect war aims in the West, because the Army could not fight properly unless assured of large territorial and financial gains. Unless the government bowed to their wishes, the two hero generals would have to resign.

Ludendorff had already leaked his threat of resignation to the press, causing what Hertling, in a supplicating letter to Hindenburg, called "the greatest agitation in all patriotic circles." In reply Hindenburg coldly emphasized that "not only

General Ludendorff but above all I myself must consider the question" of resigning if things did not go as they wished. But in accepting Hertling's implied surrender, he stated his approval of the decision "to speak to the Russians in the language of the conqueror," especially as the agreement on a hard line for the East would be "a good lesson to us for the later and much more difficult negotiations with the Western Powers."

Before assuming the role of spokesmen for the Army, Ludendorff and Hindenburg did not trouble to consult the rank and file. Rudolf Binding, a conservative monarchist staff officer who published an interesting war diary, noted at this moment that sentiment among the soldiers was distinctly opposed to "any German demands which are likely to impede or delay the conclusion of peace," and that patriotic enthusiasm for annexations was in direct proportion to distance from the front line. The front-line men had no more to say about it than the Kaiser. On January 9 an article planted by Kühlmann appeared in the *Berliner Börsenzeitung*, couched in veiled language, insinuating that the First Quartermaster General had assumed dictatorial authority. The Kaiser read it, and in accordance with his long habit, wrote observations in the margin. But where once his marginal comments had carried the imperious tone of authority—"Who does he think he is?" This must be stopped at once,"—now he wrote only, "Quite right," "Yes," and "Very true."

The same day's newspapers carried the news of a speech by President Wilson replying to the Bolshevik call for statements of peace aims. Wilson enunciated his Fourteen Points, including restoration of Belgium, return of Alsace-Lorraine, a corridor to the sea for Poland, and cession by Austria-Hungary of Italian-inhabited regions. The Fourteen Points were a bonanza for Ludendorff because they lumped the Belgian question in with demands for annexations of territory from the Central Powers. Hertling, replying in the Reichstag, was able to imply that Germany was ready for a non-annexation peace but had to keep fighting because Wilson and his Allies wanted annexations.

Allied statesmen were too little aware of the real German intentions on Belgium to call the bluff, even though the Social Democrats in the Reichstag criticized Hertling, pointing out that an outright declaration on Belgian independence could have been made conditional on an Allied guarantee against loss of Alsace-Lorraine and the Polish Corridor. Such a German declaration would have forced the hands of Wilson and Lloyd George. Lloyd George, it was noted, in his own reply to the Bolsheviks, had maintained the circumspect position of the British government on Alsace-Lorraine stipulating only for a "reconsideration"—something Germany could easily accept.

But Ludendorff and the Pan-Germans brushed aside the critics. From the Reichstag they demanded and got credits to finance the great offensive on the Western Front, along with the call-up of half the Class of 1920, the boys who reached their eighteenth birthdays in the first half of 1918. At Brest-Litovsk they imposed on the Russians a peace that was annexationist beyond the accusations of Germany's enemies. So enormous were the territories torn from Russia—Finland, Estonia, Latvia, Lithuania, Poland, White Russia, the Ukraine, Kars, Ardahan, and Batum, some 386,000 square miles with a population of 46 million—that Lenin and Trotsky, antipatriotic internationalists though they were, refused to sign. After a stormy meeting in Petrograd, the Central Committee of the Communist party agreed to a plan of Trotsky's to procrastinate on the negotiations in order to put pressure on Ludendorff, known to be impatient for the release of German troops. Returning to Brest-Litovsk, Trotsky proclaimed the end of the war without signing the treaty.

That Bolshevik eccentricity brought a new Crown Council at Bellevue, in which Ludendorff demanded immediate military action against the treacherous Reds. Backed as ever by Hindenburg, and furiously overriding the objections of Hertling and Kühlmann, Ludendorff called for operations to support the German minorities in Latvia and Estonia, and the anti-Bolshevik independence movements in Finland and the Ukraine. Ludendorff left no doubt that if only the troops could be spared, he would root out Bolshevism completely.

The Kaiser, wanting to contribute a thought to the discussion, observed that international Jewry was part of the problem.

The subsequent German offensive against the unresisting, practically unarmed Russian Army brought a new violent debate in Petrograd, ending with a decision in favor of peace at any price carried in the Central Committee of the Congress of Soviets by the margin of the solid vote of the soldier delegates. On March 3, with the Germans a hundred miles from Petrograd, the Russians signed the treaty.

The mood in which they signed it was vividly expressed six days later by Kamenev, one of the leading Bolsheviks in exile, interviewed by a correspondent of the Paris journal *L'Illustration* on a steamer from Scotland to Norway. "Germany is wrong if she believes she has obtained peace," Kamenev said bitterly. "We have only signed an armistice. The idea of revenge is henceforth going to reach enormous proportions in Russia. . . . We need time to organize ourselves [and] our new Red Army . . . [But] we too will have our Alsace-Lorraine. Our whole people will clamor for revenge!"

Within Germany there were indignant protests at the vast territorial theft imposed at Brest-Litovsk. The orthodox Social Democrats, who supported the war, abstained from voting ratification in the Reichstag, while the Independent Socialists, who opposed the war itself, voted Nay. Perhaps the most significant denunciation came from the Spartacus Union, an angry new party of the streets that had just led a wave of munitions strikes. Brest-Litovsk confirmed the Spartacist leaders in their view that only a violent social revolution could restore Germany to health.

But in the Reichstag the moderates of the Center joined the nationalists in overriding the opposition and ratifying the treaty. Matthias Erzberger, Bavarian leader of the Catholic Center party, pivot of the Reichstag, had personally drafted the Peace Resolution of a few months earlier. He had shown considerable prescience in warning his colleagues about the danger of prolonging the war, and had shrewdly put his finger on the problem of Belgium, which he had characterized as "the darling of the world."

Yet now Erzberger backed Ludendorff to the hilt. The fact that he was on steelmaker Fritz Thyssen's payroll made Erzberger a dubious peace advocate at best, but the glibness with which he reconciled Brest-Litovsk with the Peace Resolution was a clear indication of the way the wind was now blowing among the German middle class. One enemy had been knocked out, now for the others. Ludendorff had the blessing of the Reichstag majority for *Friedensturm.*

3

DESPERATION IN VIENNA

In addition to the embittered radicals in Berlin, Ludendorff was aware of another dangerous peace party in his rear—the government in Vienna. For Germany's only major ally, Austria-Hungary, peace on the Eastern Front had hardly come too soon. A month earlier a shocking message had arrived in Schloss Baden, on the edge of the Vienna Woods, where young Emperor Karl and Empress Zita had nervously settled. Sailors of the Austro-Hungarian Navy, at the Adriatic naval base of Cattaro, had hoisted the red flag on their destroyers, seized control of the port, and locked up their admirals and officers.

Mutinous acts in the Austro-Hungarian armed forces were scarcely news; decimated by casualties, weakened by bad rations, undersupplied with everything, the Austrian army of 1918 bore little resemblance to the fighting force of a century earlier that had proved itself a worthy adversary of Napoleon. "The Austro-Boche is much less tough than the Boche," noted the French General Fayolle on the Italian front. War resistance in the Austrian army took many forms. Malingering was a universal art. Jaroslav Hašek's "Good Soldier Schweik," who en route to the front disingenuously loses his train, his officer, his papers, and his sense of direction, and marches off toward the rear, had real-life counterparts by the thousands. Soldiers forged furlough papers, falsified orders, roamed behind the front in search of distant or fictitious regiments, openly refused to return to the front, rioted, shot officers, seized control of towns. Prisoners of war released from Russia, instead of reporting for duty, assembled in the forests of Hungary and Transylvania and lived by banditry.

Thirty-year-old Karl had unexpectedly fallen heir to the ancient Habsburg throne through the assassination of Archduke Franz Ferdinand that had precipitated the war, and two and a half calamitious years later, amid food riots and strikes, had quit Schönbrunn Palace for Schloss Baden in an effort to dodge the fate of Czar Nicholas, now ominously missing in Siberia. A loyal Austrian Tyrolese regiment had been withdrawn from the front to guard him. His attempts to conciliate disaffected Czechs, Serbs, Croats, and Slovaks in the Army had had no effect except to irritate his generals. Hearing of fresh desertions Karl burst out, "I should like to know what the men's idea is," whereupon his Army chief, Marshal Conrad, retorted caustically, "That they will be pardoned, Your Majesty!"

That soldiers should malinger and mutiny at this stage of a frightful war, in which they had nothing to look forward to but death as an end to misery, was not surprising. But the sailors at Cattaro had hardly fought at all; the red flag raised by these little-embattled men was disturbing indeed. Yet as he approved orders to seal off Cattaro, suppress all news, and by threats, force, or trickery overcome the insurrection, Karl knew as well as anyone that Cattaro was merely one more symptom of impending catastrophe to his Empire. In Russia at this moment a "Czech Legion," formed of men who had fought unwillingly for Austria, was preparing to fight enthusiastically against her. The redoubtable Czech intellectual Dr. Thomas Masaryk was in the United States promoting a Czech-Slovak independent nation. Serbs, Croats, and Slovenes were busy in Washington, Paris, and Rome with plans for a South Slav (Yugo-Slav) state.

Intensifying all the other problems was the terrifying food shortage that had Central Europe in its grip. Normally Austria-Hungary was not only self-sustaining in food, but an exporter. The war had turned normality inside out. Even more damaging to food production in Hungary, Slovakia, and Bulgaria than the loss of muscle power drafted into the armies or the destruction inflicted by invaders and defenders, was the rapid erosion of the transport system. Of 14,000 locomotives belonging to the overloaded Austrian rail network in 1914, only 5,000 were operational in 1918. As in Germany, the food-raising regions refused to share; Austrian boys and old women smuggling sacks of potatoes were fired on by Hungarian police. Meat was hardly to be had at any price; the much-reduced rations for the army (200 grams—less than half a pound—per week for the front line, 100 grams for the rear echelons) could not be supplied by the quartermasters. Among civilians the death rate rose, especially for infants and old people. The strikes and riots were not confined to Vienna but exploded in cities and towns throughout the Empire. Here and there the popular fury against profiteers and the frustration at shortages was expressed in pogroms.

Karl was fortunate to have an able minister to turn to. Tall, angular, dry-humored Count Ottokar Czernin was a clear-headed conservative, a loyal stalwart of the Habsburg monarchy who had reluctantly concluded that almost any peace was better than a continuation of the war. Twice Czernin had succeeded in kindling secret negotiations, once between a pair of professional diplomats, Count Revertera of Austria and Count Armand of France, in Switzerland, and again between Count Mensdorff, a former Austrian ambassador to London, and General Smuts, the old Boer hero who had become a pillar of the British empire. On the face of it, the information gained in both contacts was encouraging; Armand stated that the Alsace-Lorraine question alone stood in the way of France's making peace, while General Smuts gave assurances that he himself, and presumably other members of the British establishment, wanted the Habsburg monarchy preserved as a bulwark against the specter of Bolshevism. Smuts added that he wanted to get rid of Hindenburg and Ludendorff, a formula that suited Czernin, who had just experienced Ludendorff's influence on the negotiations at Brest-Litovsk. Czernin had been astonished at the obstinancy with which Ludendorff insisted on his exorbitant demands for territory while all Central Europe waited hour by hour for the "bread-bringing peace" with Russia, and despite Germany's own terrific problems with Turnip Winters, black markets, and peace protests. For an anxious day or two following the Bolsheviks' call for a general peace conference based on "no annexations and no indemnities," Ludendorff was in a panic lest Paris and London accept. Czernin noted acidly in his diary, "He could not think of ending the war in this unprofitable fashion," adding, "It is intolerable to have to listen to such twaddle." Czernin was not even sure he liked the prospect of German victory in the West, which he foresaw would leave "no bounds to their demands, with the difficulty of all negotiations . . . still further increased."

Emperor Karl had been kept fully informed of the 1917 Revertera-Armand and Mensdorff-Smuts talks, in which he had taken the liveliest interest. He had even initiated a peace feeler of his own in 1917, through his wife, Empress Zita. Zita had invited her brother Prince Sixtus of Bourbon-Parma, a French prince serving in the Belgian Army, to pay a clandestine visit to Vienna. There Sixtus had long talks with his sister and brother-in-law and much briefer ones with Czernin, who took little stock in a peace overture through this route. Consequently Czernin was not aware of the dangerous fruit of the discussion. At Sixtus' suggestion, and with Zita's strong backing, Karl had penned a letter addressed to Sixtus but meant for the eyes of President Poincaré of France, in which he volunteered a rash promise: "I will use all my resources and influence upon my allies to support the just claims of France in respect of Alsace-Lorraine." The prince had carried the letter off to Paris. It astonished Poincaré, who showed it to Lloyd George, but it led to nothing, as Czernin could have foretold, for the simple reason that Alsace-Lorraine was not Karl's to give away.

German opinion, Czernin knew from his own experience, was practically unanimous against giving back Alsace-Lorraine. That solidarity did not, however, extend to Belgium. Like Hertling and Kühlmann, Count Czernin perceived that Belgium, not Alsace-Lorraine, was the key to peace.

One week before the insurrection at Cattaro, Czernin had sought to seize an opportunity afforded by a speech in Parliament by British Foreign Secretary Balfour which had frankly alluded to the Mensdorff-Smuts talks. In replying, Czernin had the courage to give favorable mention to President Wilson's Fourteen Points. Czernin had taken special note of Point Ten, in which Wilson had called for "the freest opportunity of autonomous development," rather than independence for the Austrian subject peoples. Czernin was prepared to make serious concessions to the Czechs and Slavs, and he was ready to bring all the pressure he could to bear on Berlin over Belgium. President Wilson commented publicly that "Count Czernin appears to envisage the basis of peace with clear eyes." Czernin and Karl were encouraged to get off a message by way of the King of Spain expressing agreement with the Fourteen Points. They demurred over Trieste and the Trentino, but for bargaining purposes only, Czernin having fully convinced Karl that "painful sacrifices" were going to have to be made. The alternative to peace, both men realized, was revolution and the end of Austria-Hungary.

That prospect at least could be utilized. It gave them the only weapon they had against their ally, because the collapse of Austria would unquestionably be militarily fatal to Germany. But Ludendorff, after rescuing the Austrian Army with his brilliant Caporetto operation (October, 1917), felt confident that the Italians were too badly hurt to undertake anything serious in the first half of 1918. All he asked of the Austrians was that they stay in the ring for one more round, just as all he asked of the Americans was that for one more round they stay out.

4

REVEILLE IN WASHINGTON

Far different from the mood of Vienna was that of Washington. Stefan Zweig described Austria-Hungary as "a whole country which, its emperor at its head, wants nothing but peace and is . . . forced to fight." In America in 1918 hardly anyone longed for peace, and some even feared it might come too soon.

Enthusiasm for the Allied cause had been strong from the beginning, and had from the start been accompanied by material factors. Charles M. Schwab of Bethlehem Steel had set the tone by bringing back from London in 1914 what was admiringly described as the largest single order for artillery shells ever placed. In the years just before 1914, national and personal income levels in America had stagnated, but from 1914 to 1918 they doubled. A striking indication of both the popular enthusiasm and the prosperity level was the public response to the Liberty Loan drives, by which the Treasury borrowed 21 billion dollars from the nation in eighteen months, averaging two hundred dollars for every man, woman, and child.

To the surprise of many, the enthusiasm for Liberty Bonds

did not carry over into another area of recruiting, that of manpower. Despite the flood of patriotic rhetoric in the press (only maverick publisher William Randolph Hearst favored neutrality), young American men appeared at the recruiting centers in quite modest numbers. In the first three weeks after the declaration of war, only 32,000 signed up, a far cry from the spirit of '61. Many if not most Americans thought that America's role would be limited to financial and of course moral support of the Allies. In Washington, however, it was realized that an expeditionary force had to be sent to France for two reasons: first, to make sure the Allies won the war, and second, to give substance to America's claims at the peace table.

Paradoxically, though America wanted nothing in the way of annexations and indemnities, the highest levels of the American government were exceptionally occupied with the peace settlement. America's very isolation from territorial interests focused Washington's attention on larger issues, especially the Society of Nations, or League of Nations, a European idea that had won a warm reception on the banks of the Potomac. In the spring of 1918 Secretary of State Lansing was arguing for a "League of Democracies" on the ground that "if the principle of democracy prevails in a nation, it can be counted on to preserve peace and oppose war." If that notion contained a certain amount of naïveté, it also contained a certain amount of truth, and Lansing would have found fascinating support for it could he have read the recent correspondence between the German Supreme Command and the government in Berlin over Belgium and the Peace Offensive. The simple and eloquent words Wilson used in asking for the declaration of war—"The world must be made safe for democracy"—would have rung more convincingly to sophisticated skeptics if they had had fuller knowledge of the intimate connection in Berlin between democracy and peace.

The size envisioned for the American Expeditionary Force was about 500,000, backed by a million more men at home. The draft law passed by Congress on May 18, 1917, therefore authorized expansion of the Regular Army to 488,000 men, and of the National Guard to 470,000, figures believed attainable with volunteers, while another 500,000 men were to be recruited by draft lottery for a "National Army." As in Britain, the draft aroused little opposition.

Despite the prolonged brink-of-war period of 1915 to 1917, the country's actual entry into the conflict took Washington largely by surprise. General Tasker Bliss, acting chief of staff, rummaged in the War Department for the "contingency plan for war" and found the pigeonhole empty. He had no subordinates to order to prepare one because despite his title there was actually no general staff. There was no army organization worth mentioning, and no unit larger than a regiment. General John J. Pershing was directed to remedy this last deficiency by collecting four Regular Army regiments of infantry and one of artillery, scattered along the Mexican border, and forming the First Division. That, Pershing could take to France at once (June, 1917) as a sort of pledge to the Allies, and the rest could follow some time later.

Pershing no sooner landed in France than he cabled home that he needed at least a million men in his Expeditionary Force. From the point of view of procurement, the exact number hardly mattered, since it was a question of starting from scratch and getting maximum production going as soon as possible. But quantities had to be put down, and those the War Department settled on were dazzling—21,700,000 blankets, two and a half times what the whole American population bought in 1914; 30,700,000 pairs of shoes and 131,800,000 pairs of stockings; 85,000,000 undershirts and 83,600,000 pairs of underdrawers; 13,900,000 coats and 8,300,000 overcoats. Some orders were rather imaginative. Perhaps mindful of the Cuban campaign, somebody called for 20,000,000 mosquito nets, while another procurement officer, possibly bemused by the Indian wars, ordered 1,000,000 horse blankets, 2,000,000 feed bags, and 945,000 saddles.

Fierce competition developed among agencies for scarce supplies. Secretary of War Newton Baker found a basement in the War Department piled ceiling-high with boxed typewriters the Adjutant General had bought to forestall the Surgeon General and the Navy Department.

The one serious problem in procurement, rather surprisingly in the light of America's war production for the Allies, was weapons and ammunition. Arming American infantry required no more than the adoption of the British Enfield rifle, being turned out in great numbers by U.S. factories, to supplement the Army's own excellent Springfield, but artillery and machine guns were something else. The French military mission, headed by Marshal Joffre, came to the rescue with an offer to equip the Expeditionary Force with French 75-mm. guns, 155-mm. howitzers, trench mortars, machine guns, and ammunition.

One element of a modern war machine proved to be highly congenial to the American genius—propaganda. An ex-journalist and born public-relations man named George Creel, appointed by Wilson to head the Committee on Public Information, put out so overpowering a stream of reports and forecasts of American war preparations that they became almost self-defeating. A throng of war correspondents raced off to France and sat around awaiting the arrival of the American Army.

Europeans watching the American performance were so far not impressed. Prince Max of Baden, an intelligent German conservative and cousin of Kaiser Wilhelm, concluded that "the American war machine gets going with an immense to-do, but very, very slowly, for American prestige appears to demand that America must learn not by the mistakes of the Allies but by bitter experience of her own."

General Robert Lee Bullard, commander of the U.S. First Division, echoed Prince Max's sentiments in his diary in October, 1917: "We cannot beat Germany. She has beaten Servia, Russia, Belgium, and Rumania. She is now beating Italy [at Caporetto]. France and England are now practically alone in the war and will be until next summer, when we may be able, if England does not starve this winter, to come into the war to a scarcely appreciable extent. . . . So far as we are concerned, the war is practically lost." Bullard blamed America's tardiness on the "hope that we needed only to give our moral and financial support."

A month later, after the Bolshevik Revolution, Clemenceau and Lloyd George held a conference at the Quai d'Orsay. The British Prime Minister raised the question of whether it might not be a good idea to try for a separate peace with Austria-Hungary, to balance the defection of Russia. Clemenceau doubted the possibility of prying Vienna loose from Berlin, but pointed to the alternative: "We may be losing one ally, but we await another. The essential thing is to hold on until he arrives."

No one on either side of the Atlantic any longer doubted the necessity of America's battlefield participation. The whole question was whether the American Army would get trained, uniformed, equipped, and ferried across the Atlantic in time to do any good.

The key problem had been identified early as shipping. Space was needed not merely for the men, on a one-time basis, but for their continuing food and supplies. American ingenuity made some interesting contributions to space saving in the form of dehydrated vegetables and boned frozen meat, but in 1918 shipping remained a critical bottleneck. Congress had long tried to get a government shipbuilding program started, but private interests had lobbied so tenaciously that in the end the program had to run on a crash basis. "Appalling prices were paid for everything that had to do with a ship," according to Secretary of the Treasury McAdoo, and in early 1918 hardly any of the new ships were afloat. That American blunder compounded a more long-standing and more puzzling British blunder, the tardiness in adopting a convoy system. In 1917 the rampaging little U-boats sank more than double all the tonnage built by British, American, French, Italian, and neutral shipyards. U.S. Admiral Sims, a dedicated anglophile who had told the British before the war that if ever their Empire was threatened, they could count on "every ship, every dollar, every man, and every drop of blood" of their "kinsmen across the sea," could not for the life of him figure out why his kinsmen were so obtuse. Not only the Admiralty but the British merchant shippers refused to try convoying. Only the invincible determination of Lloyd George at last overrode the admirals and magnates and brought about an experiment with a convoy from Gibraltar to England that proved completely successful. Convoys were then adopted for the Atlantic; in June, 1917, Pershing's First Division sailed safely in convoy to St-Nazaire. The availability of a large number of American destroyers was most helpful; their construction had been pushed vigorously by the war-hawk Assistant Secretary of the Navy, Franklin D. Roosevelt.

Roosevelt also promoted an American scheme for shutting off the U-boats completely by mining the entire North Sea entrance; the British objection, that this would require a fantastic number of mines, Roosevelt waved aside with airy American confidence in quantity production. He was justified by the subsequent development of the project in 1918, but in the winter of 1917–18 it was nowhere near completion. The convoy system, though effecting a radical improvement in ship conservation, did not solve the shipping problem. There were now far fewer ships, Britain still had to be fed, and the Allies needed even more munitions from America. Only one potential new source was found for American troop convoys, the 500,000 tons of German shipping that had lain in U.S. harbors since 1914. The German skippers had been ordered by their embassy in Washington to anticipate seizure by sabotaging their ships, and they had reported the job done. But either the skippers were reluctant to wreck their ships or their technique was poor, because American repair crews rapidly put most of the vessels back in commission. Some, such as the giant liner *Vaterland,* at 56,000 tons the largest ship afloat, made ideal troop carriers; renamed the *Leviathan,* she sailed in December, 1917, with five thousand doughboys.

Not all the conversions were as successful. The Iowa boys of the 168th Infantry, Forty-second (Rainbow) Division, were packed like sardines aboard an 18,000-ton ex-German liner renamed *President Grant.* Rough weather the second day out made everybody seasick, not only the doughboys, few of whom had ever seen the sea, but the equally inexperienced sailors. Heads were soon out of order, measles broke out, water was so short the Iowans paid the sailors fifty cents for a canteenful, quarters below were unlivable and there was no room on deck. Then the *Grant*'s main boilers quit, and she had to turn around and limp home.

The Rainbows eventually made it to England, and on December 8, after a sobering wait watching the unloading of British casualties from the recent battle of Cambrai, boarded the Channel ferries. Along with the First, Second, and Twenty-sixth divisions, which had preceded it, the Forty-second suffered through the severe 1917–18 winter, with frostbite added to scarlet fever, mumps, and malaria, while learning from French instructors how to assemble, disassemble, and fire the Chauchat and Hotchkiss machine guns. American uniforms and shoes were found deficient in quality; a contingent of the Forty-second marching to its training area in Lorraine left bloody footprints from its rag-wrapped feet, like Washington's army at Valley Forge.

The Forty-second followed a routine worked out with the bellwether First Division. After a month's training, the soldiers of each new American division were given an initial trench exposure in small groups. Half of a French (or British) G. C. (*groupe de combat*) moved out and a like number of doughboys moved in, so that each American had an Allied veteran as a coach. Officers were similarly paired off at the P.A. (*point d'appui*, or support point), of which there was one behind each two G.C.'s. The trenches of Lorraine were a little different from what the Yanks had been led to expect. Instead of the neatly revetted models displayed in training camps at home, these were half-ruined ditches, eroded by rain and disfigured by bombardment, with shallow, wet, bad-smelling dugouts cut into their rear walls. Trenches and dugouts alike were often ankle-deep or deeper in mud and water. The dugout roofs dripped, and their inhabitants were habitually wet through from head to toe. Lice were universal and inescapable. But the food, brought up in iron pots carried on a pole by two men, if barely warm, was good: slum (stew), coffee with sugar and condensed milk, white bread with butter, boiled rice, molasses or jam, occasionally even a pudding. The German soldiers opposite were much less lucky.

After this initial trench exposure in small groups, the men of a division received a month's training together as a unit, and the division was then pronounced fit for combat in a quiet sector. In February, 1918, the First Division led the way into this important stage. In the interval since its coach-and-pupil training, the First had made good its various deficiencies in field kitchens, winter clothing, horses, and officers. It had discarded the broad-brimmed campaign hats brought from the Mexican border for small French caps ("overseas caps" to Americans) and British steel helmets. The day it started for its assigned combat sector on the southern face of the St-Mihiel salient in Lorraine, the ground was covered with snow that had melted and refrozen, turning the roads into sheets of ice, onto which rain had fallen during the night. Neither the feet of animals nor the wheels of vehicles could take hold. Falling men and horses continually broke up the long column. Whole teams went down, struggling, panting, tangling harnesses. The weight of gun carriages and ammunition wagons pulled the horses backward, pitched them forward, or racked them sideways into the ditches. Men standing up to their knees in slush had to right overturned wagons and reload soaked boxes of ammunition and rations. By nightfall the tail of the train had made about a mile and a half. General Bullard figured that much of his division might as well have slept in the houses from which they had started in the morning.

It was an awkward beginning, in keeping with the American war effort in general, but it was a beginning, and deserved more notice than Ludendorff gave it.

5

NEW WEAPONS

If large America found herself in the odd position of depending on small France for her army's artillery, (and as the event proved, for many other things besides) this was no fault of American technology, which was well represented on the astonishing and appalling battlefield of 1918. American-invented airplanes roared above a devastated landscape strung with American-invented barbed wire, where millions of men had to live in trenches and dugouts to avoid being slaughtered by American-invented machine guns.

By 1918 the proliferation of weapons systems had reached a point where, according to a Paris newspaper, it cost 75,000 francs to kill an enemy soldier. (Romain Rolland observed that for the same sum one might pension the man off for life.) Besides airplanes and machine guns there were high-angle heavy artillery (howitzers) and light artillery (trench mortars) firing high-explosive ammunition (TNT or ammonium picrate); rockets (used primarily for signaling); grenades hurled by hand or fired from rifle attachments; and finally, two weapons never before used in warfare, poison gas and tanks. These last two were critical question marks in Ludendorff's preparations for *Friedensturm.*

Poison gas, proposed as a weapon of war in the nineteenth century, had attracted enough horrified attention to inspire a resolution at the Hague Convention of 1899, everyone voting to outlaw it except the delegates of Great Britain and the United States. No army possessed poison gas in 1914, and none contemplated its use until stalemate set in. Then, almost inevitably, the German Army turned to it. For one thing, the German command, beleaguered and frustrated, found itself in a situation that tended to induce violent decisions, given sanction by a relative freedom from the constraint of public opinion. For another, Germany had a large, technically advanced chemical industry. Finally, Germany had Fritz Haber, the outstanding chemical genius of his day, and a dedicated patriot. Before the war, Haber had solved the baffling problem of nitrogen fixation, making available the nitrogen of the atmosphere for the manufacture of high-explosive ammunition. In 1915, he led the team of scientists and technicians who provided the German Army with chlorine gas, which—released from canisters when the wind was favorable—drove the enemy choking and coughing from his trenches. Unfortunately, the German command was unprepared to exploit the technical triumph, and the Allies soon recovered, first improvising and then perfecting protective devices and, naturally, producing their own chlorine gas. Fritz Haber developed a more effective choking gas, phosgene ($COCl_2$, a compound of chlorine with carbon monoxide), but again the Allies countered, with improved gas masks and their own phosgene.

But by 1918 the Germans had a much more promising delivery technique, the gas artillery shell, which freed the weapon from its limitation in range and dependence on the wind. When Kerensky, Lenin's democratic predecessor in Russia, tried to stir his failing army into an offensive, the Germans struck back at Riga with an intensive artillery barrage, loaded with gas shells, and followed up with a new-style infantry attack in which the riflemen and machine gunners advanced in files rather than waves, seeking to filter through rather than confront the enemy lines. The result was a swift, complete rout that had no little to do with Kerensky's downfall. A month later, when the Austrian Army in Italy stood on the brink of catastrophe, the same technique was applied to the Italians at Caporetto, again with brilliant results —six hundred Italian dead were found gassed in a single ravine. It was true that the Russians and Italians were both very short of gas masks, with which the British and French were well supplied. The Allies were also quick to copy the new German gas artillery, and by 1918 had so many gas shells of their own that their press protested the International Red Cross's suggestion that poison gas be banned.

Yet by 1918 Fritz Haber had come up with a new chemical formula that promised Ludendorff something extra—mustard gas (dichloroethyl sulfide), a vesicant that attacks any part of the body, especially moist areas, blistering and burning tissue. Mustard promised especially good results in neutralizing enemy artillery. By the time the attacking infantry reached the enemy's rear positions, the gas would be dissipated.

But if the chemically proficient Germans had been ahead in the development of poison gas, they had been distinctly laggard in the development of the other wholly new weapon of 1918.

The tank, like poison gas, had been thought of before. The first self-powered military vehicle dated all the way back to 1769, when Captain Nicolas Cugnot built a three-wheeled iron steam engine in Paris and drove it for twenty minutes at two miles an hour. Though remarkably innovative in 1769, Captain Cugnot's iron monster was a blind alley because of problems of starting, fuel, and power-to-weight ratio. Steam-powered vehicles were studied by the British and French at the time of the Crimean War (1854–56) and used by the British to haul supplies in the Boer War (1899–1902), but meantime the French-German-invented gasoline piston engine introduced a more practical prospect. The American farm tractor, with its off-the-road capability, supplied the missing ingredient, and in the years just before 1914, inventors on both sides of the Atlantic were tinkering with the future tank. French, British, Austrian, and German military authorities were given the opportunity to consider a variety of designs, and turned them all down. The last before 1914 was rejected by the German General Staff in December, 1913.

The generals' skepticism was not entirely grounded in blind conservatism. Even though many of the proposals originated with military men, the concept was basically amateur. Suppose an army possessed a hundred (which seemed an enormous number) of the giant armored cars mounted on tractor treads and carrying guns. They could go no faster than men and horses; they could not, despite their treads, handle steep grades or forested terrain; and they presented a new, difficult supply problem, their appetite for gasoline being practically insatiable. Most important, in 1890, 1900, and even 1910, there was no way to make them nearly as reliable as horses. Horses were not armored, but on the other hand they were cheap to replace.

In the early fighting, the French, Belgians, and British found a use for armored cars, of which they improvised a number, but not till trench warfare settled in did anyone revert to the idea of an armored, tracked, road-free gun carrier. Two Allied officers in particular were struck by the possibilities inherent in the American-made Holt tractor used to haul heavy guns. One, Colonel Sir Ernest Swinton, became father of the British tank program; the other, Colonel Eugene Estienne, of the French. Early in 1915, the British experimentally crossed an armored car with a farm tractor, and at least identified some problems, such as the total deafness, and near-total blindness, of the resulting vehicle. The Royal Navy, which had a division of marines at the front, came up with a machine, essentially a British farm tractor powered by a Daimler motor, that developed 155 horsepower. That combination approached viability, and though the model was adjudged unequal to combat demands and assigned to gun hauling, the Navy group was encouraged by Winston Churchill, First Lord of the Admiralty, to persevere, and a second Daimler-powered machine was credited with combat potential. In February, 1916, the War Office ordered it in two versions, "male" and "female." The male was armed with two six-pounders (57-mm. guns) and four machine guns, the female with six machine guns. These thirty-ton monsters became the first "tanks" to be used in battle. The strange designation reflected a misguided mania for secrecy; in 1915 the German War Office had studied and fussily turned down a very similar vehicle.

In an astonishingly brief time William Foster & Company of Lincoln produced 150 tanks and shipped them to the British Expeditionary Force in France. Forty-nine arrived in September, 1916, when the Somme offensive should already have been abandoned. General Sir Douglas Haig, commander of the British Expeditionary Force, who had previously been tepid toward the new weapon, seized on it as a possible savior for his lost battle. Of the forty-nine, only thirty-two succeeded in lumbering to their jump-off point. Most of these broke down, got stuck, or fell behind; only nine managed to keep up with the attacking infantry. Yet these nine proved distinctly effective, causing a panic among the Germans similar to that produced among the Allies by the first gas.

As with the gas, the opportunity provided by the new weapon was thrown away by failure to provide for adequate exploitation—in a word, failure to appreciate its surprise potential. There were no infantry reserves to follow up, and besides, the number of tanks used was nowhere near large enough.

Further, the surprise was not limited to the Germans. Britain's French allies were not only surprised but chagrined. Thanks mainly to Colonel Estienne, a French program had been launched at the same time as the British, in February, 1916, with nearly equivalent secrecy, less production speed, and a more farsighted strategic aim—use of tanks in a large mass. A stocky, erudite, articulate man gifted with a resonant voice, Colonel Estienne liked to illustrate his expositions to guests at his command post by cramming them under the dinner table to give a sense of the cramped but secure interior of the vehicle he was describing. He formally submitted a proposal to the French General Staff late in 1915, and was presently sent to discuss the production problem with the Schneider arms company in Paris.

Under Colonel Estienne's guidance an order was placed for four hundred pieces of "assault artillery," to be powered by a 70-horsepower four-cylinder Schneider engine. Once aroused, the Department for Artillery was carried away. While Colonel Estienne was back with his regiment at Verdun another order was placed, with the St. Chamond Company, for four hundred vehicles with an ingenious but mechanically troublesome combination of gasoline propulsion and electric transmission, armed, like the Schneiders, with sawed-off 75-mm. guns, and cruising at over four miles per hour.

The British meanwhile did some remodeling of their original tank, designated Mark I, and presently were in production with the improved Mark IV. In April, 1917, both the British and the French used their new tanks in offensive action. Success was at best mixed; the British had terrible luck in the deep mud of Artois, while the French Schneiders and St. Chamonds got badly shot up along with the infantry in the bloody assault on Ludendorff's new defense line in Champagne. In a less ambitious attack a few days later, the Schneiders performed well, but of sixteen gasoline-electric St. Chamonds, only one managed to reach the German trenches.

Both Allies had second thoughts about their basic conception of a heavy, large-crew, big-gun vehicle. The ponderous Marks, Schneiders, and St. Chamonds shared a number of characteristics that endeared them neither to the generals nor to their crews. Ventilation was poor and temperatures inside rose above 40° C. (104° F.); yet in chilly weather they were maddeningly difficult to start. Their cruising range was barely what a Renault automobile would get on a couple of liters of fuel, but the crews went into combat sitting on and amid a vast reservoir of gasoline. Visibility was terrible, but the tanks were highly conspicuous. The Germans had made their new Hindenburg Line trenches more than five yards wide, halting the clumsy monsters and turning them into sitting ducks. At four or five miles per hour they were slow-waddling ducks at best; their bulky silhouettes made inviting targets for direct-fire guns and even howitzers. Turning was a maneuver requiring up to four men, and luck;

on the Mark IV it was accomplished by running one track at low gear and the other at high; the gearmen watched for hand signals from the driver, while the tank commander, sitting next to the driver, operated the brake. Using the powerful clutch was a painful strain on the driver's thigh muscles, while the crews wore leather and chain-mail masks to protect their faces against metal splinters flaked off the interior of the hull by machine-gun fire.

Colonel Estienne had already realized the value of a large number of easily produced light vehicles, able to advance immediately in front of infantry to attack enemy machine-gun nests. The War Ministry at first opposed the idea, but gave in to the Colonel's persuasiveness, and ordered test models from Renault. Field trials were held in the spring of 1917, beginning shortly before the Champagne offensive.

That catastrophe gave a new impetus to the French tank program. General Nivelle, the cheerfully confident artillerist whose interminable barrage merely led the troops to slaughter, was summarily replaced by a sober, skeptical infantryman, General Pétain. Pétain found a large part of his army in a state militarily described as mutiny.

In reality, like the tanks, it was something new to warfare. The French soldiers did not run up red flags and shoot their officers; on the contrary, many of them told the officers, "It's not your fault—we're all in this together." They simply said the war had gone on too long and killed too many men; it was time to stop. In two and a half years the French Army had lost well over a million dead, perhaps as many as had fallen during the more than two decades of the Revolutionary and Napoleonic wars. Hardly a man was unwounded; many had four, five, or six stripes on their faded blue sleeves. They felt they had done too much fighting; it was time to stop while some were still alive.

Yet Pétain led them back to the trenches with astounding ease. He did it by going around in person to visit the affected divisions, in a series of pathetic, drama-laden scenes, carrying a simple message: "I agree with everything you say, but the Germans are still in France."

The bearded, exhausted men had no answer. But it was understood that there were to be no more Champagnes and Sommes, no more senseless slaughters. The men agreed that the front had to be held, and Pétain, who wanted to win the war, agreed that it could not be won by the old methods.

A cool-blooded Norman, with a terse, ironic turn of phrase, Pétain was a military skeptic of long standing. Before the war he had been unfavorably marked in the eyes of his superiors by his negativism toward the popular doctrine of the offensive to the limit. In 1914 he had seen his doubts about the wisdom of massed "shoulder-to-shoulder" attacks vindicated, and had been one of the first commanders to instruct his troops to lie down, take cover, and dig holes. In the holocaust of Verdun his Second Army had held the line against a large German superiority in artillery and had made the enemy, for the first time in the war, take casualties nearly equal to the French. His handling of the 1917 war resisters received far less publicity, but did him even more credit than the defense of Verdun, and perhaps taught him more.

Of all the top generals, Pétain best appreciated the potential of tanks. In mid-1917 he summed up his plan for victory in 1918 in a succinct phrase: "*J'attends les américains et les chars*" ("I'm waiting for the Americans and the tanks"). His view ran sharply counter to that of many staff officers, who thought French production facilities should concentrate on artillery. He took the gamble and caused the War Ministry to give the Renault firm an order for 3,500 *chars* (recoiling from the barbarism *tanque,* Colonel Estienne had adopted the French word for the war chariot of the ancients). The little Renault model introduced a feature suggested by some designers before the war, a turret capable of a 360-degree traverse, multiplying the value of its single weapon, alternatively a heavy machine gun or a 37-mm. cannon.

Meantime, the Allies tried their heavy tanks again. In October, in a limited French offensive at Malmaison, the Schneiders performed well, though the St. Chamonds again failed. Then in late November the British sprang one of the best surprise attacks of the war, at Cambrai. A force of 475 Mark IV's was assembled, the assault tanks equipped with huge bundles of brush (*fascines*) to dump into the wide Hindenburg Line trenches. Advancing with no preliminary bombardment at all, the Mark IV's scored an astonishing success, clanking some eight miles in twelve hours, clear through all three lines of enemy trenches. Once more it seemed as if the generals' dream of the "breakthrough" had been achieved, but in the next few days the Germans not only plugged the gap but shot up the Mark IV's with direct-fire artillery, counterattacked, and turned the battle into a resounding British defeat. Recrimination followed (for several years) about poor tactics and lack of foresight, but the battle seemed to illustrate the limitations as well as the potential of the new weapon. The Germans repaired some of their captured trophies to use against their former owners, but when Ludendorff had a look at an exercise by them (February, 1918), he refused to be impressed.

His assessment may have been colored by a decision he had already taken. The Daimler Company had been given an order for a number of heavy tanks—thirty-three tons, with two powerful Mercedes-Daimler engines, armed with a 57-mm. gun and six machine guns—but only twenty had been produced when Ludendorff was confronted with a choice between tanks and trucks; Daimler could not meet the army's demands for both. Ludendorff opted for the trucks. He felt that the Riga-Caporetto assault technique, named the "Hutier tactic" after the general commanding the Riga operation, could achieve breakthroughs without tanks, but the offensive could not be sustained without a steady stream of ammunition and rations.

Ludendorff's predecessors in the Supreme Command had been equally negative on tanks, partly because an earlier option had been the choice between tanks and farm tractors for food production. The German defensive posture on the Western Front had undoubtedly also contributed, tanks being admittedly mediocre defensive weapons. This factor operated in a reverse sense as Ludendorff completed plans for *Frieden-*

sturm: the French and British tanks could be disregarded as long as the Allies were kept on the defensive.

Tanks were thus an added reason for making sure the initiative remained in German hands.

Ludendorff had in his arsenal one more weapon, of a particularly intriguing nature, the massacre of civilians by bombardment. Dropping bombs on cities with the aim of terrorizing the population was nothing new in 1918, and in fact had been done even before 1914, the Bulgarian air force, of all unlikely outfits, having registered the historic first over Adrianople in 1912. By 1918 the bombs had grown to 660-pound packages of explosives, carried by the four-motored bomber—an aircraft type improbably pioneered by the Russians. The Germans, whose lighter-than-air Zeppelins had been used for raids early in the war but had proved vulnerable to antiaircraft fire and fighter planes, had by 1918 developed the four-motored R-plane (for *Riesenflugzeug,* "giant aircraft"), capable of carrying four thousand pounds of bombs. The R-plane supplemented earlier two-motored planes that had long raided Paris and London.

In the earlier part of the war, the Germans had enjoyed an advantage in the air, thanks partly to Britain's slowness in getting aircraft production started (until 1917 all British planes had French engines). By 1918 the 3,000 planes of the German air force were ranged against 2,800 French and 1,300 British aircraft, and bombing Paris and London was becoming something of a luxury, but the Germans still retained the important geographical advantage of having airfields close to the Allied capitals. This German advantage was reflected in the fact that the outraged voices raised against anticivilian warfare were mostly on the Allied side. Yet a shade of ideological difference seemed present also. Aristide Briand, French premier earlier in the war, expressed the feelings of most of the world, neutral as well as Allied, when he wrote in his diary, "The bombardment of open cities is the stupidest, most odious and most useless thing conceivable." Ludendorff did not agree. To professional soldiers it appeared obvious that civilians could not stand up to death and wounds because they were not subject to military discipline. The failure of air power up to the present to break civilian morale was attributed to insufficiency of the quantitative factor. Further improvement of the air weapon would doubtless accomplish the result, and German technology was at work on the problem. Apart from the obvious solution—larger bomb loads—another tack was being taken: the development of incendiary bombs, by which Paris and London might be set on fire.

The new incendiary bombs would not be ready till late summer. Meantime, a radically different approach to the assault on civilian morale, advanced by a genius at the Krupp plant, was maturing. Dr. von Eberhard had begun with the idea of a cannon that could fire sixty miles, the distance of the front from Paris in 1916–17. Such a range, he thought, could be attained with available propellants in a specially designed gun, made by an operation on one of the German Navy's giant 380-mm. (15-inch) rifles that would result in an enormously long, thick barrel with a bore of only 210 millimeters (8.24 inches). The weight of the barrel would create a problem of droop, but this could be mastered by a specially rigged support, provided the gun was emplaced in a fixed position and fired at a single elevation. A muzzle velocity of 5,500 feet per second could be attained, sufficient to lift the projectile to an apogee of twenty-four miles, farther into space than anything man-made had ever soared, and making it possible for the shell to travel fifty miles in a virtual vacuum. Krupp director Dr. Fritz Rausenberger checked with Ordnance, which gave a prompt go-ahead. Work was progressing well in the autumn of 1916 when a sudden order came to Essen: the supergun's range had to be extended from sixty to seventy-five miles because Ludendorff, though enchanted with the idea of bombarding Paris, had decided on the withdrawal to the Hindenburg Line. Like good soldiers, Rausenberger and Eberhard went back to their drawing boards, and by the summer of 1917 had a gun ready for testing at the required range. The first firing was a failure; so were the next several. Finally, a projectile was designed that met all the requirements of the unique gun. The propellant charge was divided among a metal cartridge and two silk bags, so that it could be varied to compensate for the terrific wear on the gun barrel. Test-firing success was achieved in January, 1918.

By this time, three mammoth guns had been cast at Krupp, with three more under construction at Krupp and three at the Skoda plant, in Bohemia. Work on the permanent concrete emplacements at the site was well advanced. Since the guns required transport by standard-gauge railway, and since visual concealment was indispensable, the choice of site was limited, and in fact virtually dictated: the Laon corner, where the front changed direction from north–south to east–west, and where a rail line ran through the St-Gobain wood at a point just seventy-five miles from Paris. Three positions were prepared, and the disassembled guns began moving forward.

His secondary surprise against the French ready, Ludendorff turned his full attention to his main surprise, against the British.

6

LUDENDORFF PLANS THE PEACE OFFENSIVE

Ludendorff had originally conceived his strategy for the 1918 offensive in the autumn of 1917. On November 11, four days after Lenin's overthrow of the Kerensky government in Petrograd, he had convened the chiefs of staff of the army groups in Mons, Belgium. The two most important of the chiefs came armed with plans of their own.

Von Kuhl, representing the army group of Crown Prince Rupprecht of Bavaria, northernmost in the line, argued for an offensive in Flanders. Von der Schulenburg, of the army group of Crown Prince Wilhelm of Germany, proposed an offensive at the opposite end of the line, against Verdun. Colonel Wetzell, Ludendorff's own chief of operations, an officer for whom he had exceptional regard, seconded Schulenburg's proposal, which Wetzell envisioned as a pincers encircling the powerful fortress from either side.

Ludendorff listened with his customary careful attention, then brought out his own plan. Instead of a single offensive, Ludendorff's design involved a succession of offensives, because, as he pointed out, no single operation could by itself be decisive. The question was, where should the basic thrust of the spring's operations be directed?

At the British sector, said Ludendorff.

A first blow, in Picardy, would be followed by a second, north of it, in Flanders, also against the British. The order of these two operations was dictated by the weather, which ruled out muddy Flanders till April. Only the third blow would be aimed at the French; its purpose would be to pin the French reserves and prevent them from succoring their Allies. A fourth blow could then safely be struck, once more at the British, and this would be the *coup de grâce*.

The target for Ludendorff was thus the British Army. There were a number of more or less technical arguments to be advanced, such as the fact that the British were considered less skilled adversaries than the French ("too rigid," said the Germans). Though the Tommies were given credit for defensive obstinacy, Ludendorff thought them "less apt than the French to support a defensive battle on a large scale." On the other hand, it was assumed that the French would go to British aid quicker than the British would go to French.

None of these considerations influenced Ludendorff's decision. Neither did the fact that Britain was considered in the long-range sense to be Germany's principal enemy, the Carthage to Germany's Rome. The basis for the *Friedensturm* strategy he summarized very briefly: only against the British could major strategic objectives be attained. The reason was twofold: the British Expeditionary Force was only a little over half the size of the French Army, and it lay crowded close to its Channel bases of Dunkerque, Calais, and Boulogne. Offensive operations, by inflicting serious losses and bringing the British bases under artillery fire, could force an evacuation of the British Army from France.

In contrast, Colonel Wetzell's Verdun operation could not hope to knock the French Army out of the war. Why then did Colonel Wetzell push the idea? Because pinching off Verdun would foreclose the Alsace-Lorraine question. With their army pressed well back from the frontier, the French would be in no position at the peace table to put in a claim for the lost provinces, and in fact would be forced to hand over more territory themselves, minimally the Longwy-Briey basin, hopefully much more.

In short, Colonel Wetzell's plan would provide an excellent basis for a negotiated peace, a peace with plenty of honor—on one condition.

That condition was that Germany relinquish Belgium. This sacrifice was necessary in order to neutralize Britain and isolate France at the peace table. In a word, Colonel Wetzell thought of using diplomacy against one adversary (Britain) in order to reduce the military task to merely dealing with the other (France), something definitely within the capabilities of the German Army.

Ludendorff would have none of it. He was playing for total victory over both opponents, with all the booty to the winner—Belgium, Luxembourg, northern France, the Channel coast, eventually the Netherlands, a commanding position on the Atlantic and North Sea for the Master Race—a true "Victory-Peace," a *Sieg-Fried.*

At the time of the Mons conference, the number of troops available for an offensive in the West was still indeterminate, but within a few days Ludendorff was able to calculate safely on a 5-to-4 advantage (200-plus German divisions versus 160-plus Allied divisions). By maximizing the difference at the point of attack, he could achieve an advantage on the order of 2 or 3 to 1 wherever combat was taking place. Even if the overall superiority was reduced by the arrival of Americans, he could still retain the battlefield advantage provided that the initiative remained in his hands—that is, provided it was always the Germans who were doing the attacking. It would be lost only if the Allies passed to the offensive. That was something Ludendorff was determined to prevent.

The Riga-Caporetto battlefield technique on which he pinned his hopes—the Hutier tactic—substituted for the prolonged artillery barrages lasting days and nights on end, and the stumbling follow-ups by massed throngs of infantrymen that had created the shambles of Verdun, the Somme, Champagne, and other offensives, a secret concentration of infantry and artillery and a sudden surprise assault. First came a short, only hours-long but extremely intensive bombardment, with a high proportion of gas shells. Next the artillery switched to a rolling barrage, and the infantry advanced in large numbers of small, heavily armed groups, following so close behind the barrage that they were in the enemy trenches before the defenders could emerge from their deep shelters and set up their machine guns. Resistance was dealt with by grenades, and dugouts were cleared with flamethrowers. A problem that had not occurred in Russia or Italy, but conceivably could develop in France, was brought up: suppose the infantry's advance was delayed for any reason—how could the moving artillery barrage be kept synchronized with it? Radio communication was entirely too undependable, and intensive study yielded no solution to the problem. Islands of serious resistance, it was decided, must be bypassed, and the attacking units generously supplied with machine guns and automatic rifles to provide their own firepower against counterattacking enemy reserves.

An important advantage of gas shells was that they left the ground unravaged, making it easy for attacking troops to advance, provided they were equipped with gas masks. Much depended on precision in timing and attention to detail, especially in regard to the artillery. Even more depended on secrecy. If the concentration of men, guns, supplies, and ammunition could be concealed, and the artillery and infantry closely coordinated, the effect would be to swamp the enemy defenses, which within hours would be drenched in poison gas, blasted by high explosives, and overrun by leapfrogging divisions of infantry in open formation.

General von Hutier's chief of artillery, Colonel Bruchmüller, had proven so skillful at synchronizing this concert of hell that Ludendorff had entrusted him with planning the entire artillery preparation for the first phase of *Friedensturm.*

Infantry trained in the new type of combat was given a

new designation, "storm troops" or "shock troops." The stimulating names, as Ludendorff was aware, masked a certain deterioration in the quality of the soldiers themselves. The letters home, read by Army censors, reflected a change in attitude, even on the part of the officers:

"On account of our continual losses the Company Commander has the difficult, unceasing task of fitting reinforcements in the Company. There are no old, experienced men left—nothing but Deputy-Reservists and recruits. . . . And what soldier nowadays has any self-reliance? All impetus must come from the officer."

"How different this departure is from . . . the first, in December, 1914! . . . That impatient longing to fight, the wild joy at the idea of being on the spot when the enemy got his death blow, that cannot be expected from anybody who knows what life in the trenches is like."

The spirit of 1918 was resignation. Even the peace with Russia, which had momentarily kindled hopes among the front-line soldiers, "no longer excites any enthusiasm," noted Rudolf Binding, adding, "Now come the Americans."

Ludendorff's approach to problems was always positive; if there was a question, it must have an answer. For the Army's morale he prescribed a cure. The men leaving the trenches for the small comforts of a reserve area were treated to a new routine: lectures on patriotism by selected officers and noncoms. The theme of the course was that the enemy, world democracy, was striving to encircle Germany from the outside while undermining it from the inside through the franchise reform. Victory on the Western Front in the coming battles would save Germany from both dangers. It would also guarantee the postwar economic well-being of Germany, so important to returning veterans, by extracting from France an indemnity of from 100 to 200 billion marks. Lest this line of reasoning invite questions, Ludendorff specified in his order that "when patriotic instruction is given, discussion must not be permitted."

The transfer of troops from the East continued, but with exasperating delays. The chaos behind the former Russian front acted as a sort of magnet, drawing German troops deeper into the country. When the separatist Ukrainian government was overthrown by the Bolsheviks, the Germans moved, over the vehement protests of Lenin and Trotsky, to occupy the entire Ukraine. This and other operations provoked by the stubborn Bolsheviks meant that the 200-plus divisions Ludendorff wanted in the West would not all arrive even by the end of March. About 190 divisions would have to suffice on D-day, with the others to follow as soon as possible.

Even making peace with wholly occupied Rumania, whose orphan army in Russia no longer had a home, created difficulties that delayed the release of German troops. Count Czernin and Emperor Karl vainly objected to the grossness of the German demands, which included cession to German companies of the Rumanian oil fields, railways, and harbors, and German control of Rumanian finances. (Hearing of Karl's protests, Kaiser Wilhelm demanded, "Who does that young man think he is?")

Milder terms for Russia and Rumania would have freed more German troops, and might even have tied up some strength of the Allies, who were lending support to various White Russian groups in an effort to get Russia back into the war. An irony that would have been lost on nobody but Ludendorff was his failure to get the idle Turkish XV Corps sent to the Western Front as he had hoped. Enver Pasha, the general running the Ottoman Empire, instead sent it to the Caucasus to secure a piece of Russian territory for Turkey.

D-day for "Michael" (sometimes "St. Michael") as the first phase of the offensive was called in code, was at last fixed for March 21, at which time Ludendorff would have 192 divisions on hand, with about fifteen more due shortly. Careful calculations had been made in respect to the arrival of the Americans. On the basis of the British experience in raising a mass army, Ludendorff's staff figured on ten months for recruiting, training, and equipping "large formations," and concluded that an American Army of 450,000 could appear in France by midsummer of 1918. To forestall the Americans, therefore, victory would have to be won by the end of July, in a little less than twenty weeks of campaigning time.

In February, Colonel Wetzell played a war game at headquarters with another staff officer. The object was to find out the maximum speed with which the French could come to the aid of their British ally. The location of French reserves was well established. Colonel Wetzell arrived at the conclusion that using the available roads and rail lines, the enemy could bring twenty to twenty-two French divisions into the British sector within eight to ten days of the battle's start. That seemed a rate too slow to save the situation.

As the first weeks of March passed, presenting splendid though by no means unusual weather for northern France, the Paris papers expressed surprise that the offensive had not yet begun. Three weeks in which guns could be rolled and infantrymen could walk on firm ground, and in which Americans were all but invisible, were lost.

Tardily, the long German columns moved west: ammunition wagons, motor transport, artillery, labor companies, air-force ground crews, searchlight trains, infantry, engineers, field dressing stations, and the wagons carrying the large canisters, marked with a yellow cross, that held the poison gas. In Germany, the people watched with mixed feelings as the endless parade passed by.

Nearing the front, the troops marched by night and bivouacked by day. Trucks and trains rolled only at night and at daybreak were covered or camouflaged by their crews. Huge ammunition dumps grew up close behind the front; occasionally an enemy long-range shell happened to hit one and blow up the neighborhood, but because this had occurred irregularly throughout the war, there was little danger of the enemy drawing conclusions. Aggressive patrolling was carried out up and down the entire front.

In favor of the surprise element was the fact that on this front large-scale surprise had long since been abandoned. The preparations required for a large offensive, and the length of the indispensable artillery barrage, had caused both sides to relinquish it. Yet as Ludendorff and Bruchmüller were now proving, even preparations on the Verdun or Somme scale were feasible in complete secrecy. Because the great density of batteries (thirty to fifty for each mile of front) had to be concealed until the last moment, registry fire was not possible. To meet this problem, Colonel Bruchmüller worked out a system by which "errors of the day"—that is, wind and atmospheric pressure—and "errors of the gun," from wear, could be estimated and allowed for in advance. The Artillery Meteorological Service and the air force cooperated in producing the necessary data, and over the complaints of artillery officers, especially the older ones, painstaking map work, aerial photography, and photogrammetry were carried out that permitted determination of battery zero points without ever firing the guns. In the final nights, ammunition was carried forward and stacked around the batteries in giant heaps.

The army groups had been reorganized to accommodate the new troops from Russia. From northwest to southeast there were four groups, of unequal size and importance. Those destined for *Friedensturm* were the two northernmost, commanded by Crown Prince Rupprecht of Bavaria and Crown Prince Wilhelm of Germany. The two southeastern army groups, commanded by General von Gallwitz and the Duke of Württemberg, were given no role; their function was to provide rest havens for battered outfits coming out of the combat cauldron, for which they would trade their own fresh units.

In the opening blow—"Michael"—against the British in Picardy, both the princely army groups would be involved, an arrangement Ludendorff had deliberately set up so that he could keep the operational reins in his own hands. Two new armies, von Below's Seventeenth (formerly called the Fourteenth), from Italy, and von Hutier's Eighteenth, from Russia, were sandwiched around von der Marwitz's Second, the Seventeenth joining the "Army Group Crown Prince Rupprecht," and the Eighteenth, the "Army Group Crown Prince Wilhelm." The troops of the Seventeenth and the Eighteenth were not necessarily those who had fought at Caporetto and

Riga, because much shuffling of units had taken place, but the headquarters of these two armies were essentially unchanged, and having had experience in the new battle tactic, they were now put in command of training and operations.

Opposite the three German armies lay two British armies, the Third and Fifth. "Michael" was intended to drive these sharply back, causing them to draw away from French support; they might be separated from each other in the valley of the Somme River. The second blow, "George," would fall on the other two British armies, to the north, in Flanders. Even these two offensives, as Ludendorff explained in his briefing to the Kaiser, would not suffice; the gigantic battle would have to be recommenced over and over at different points. It was, in fact, open-ended as far as tactical planning went: the British might succumb either sooner or later; the French might come to their ally's aid sooner or later, with much or little. The important thing was to retain the initiative, keep the enemy's reserves occupied by diversions as necessary, and persevere in the great basic aim of forcing the British to quit French soil.

That would start the dominoes falling. The French could not hold out against the resulting 2-to-1 odds, and the few Americans in France would be caught up in the disaster. Italy would have to make peace, and Ludendorff-Siegfried would be master of the Eurasian continent.

As D-day drew nearer, Ludendorff was the object of several renewed peace appeals. On February 11 a Reichstag group, grounding its fears in the "good, objective reasons" of the war's financial burdens as well as the impending bloodshed, urged "a political offensive" against Britain. An "unequivocal declaration regarding the future restoration of the sovereignty and integrity of Belgium . . . the postulate of the British and American peace parties" would force British Prime Minister Lloyd George to declare "that he wishes to continue the war for the sake of Alsace-Lorraine," and the British people would "be made to feel that their Government is responsible for all defeats and all bloodshed, as an honorable peace could have been attained by diplomatic means." In

Britain either a peace ministry would be formed or war resistance would grow to the point where Britain's military effort would be compromised.

Ludendorff replied that there was no need to give up Belgium; the new battlefield advantage would suffice to bring total victory. A group of Austrian political and military leaders received the same response.

On February 19, Prince Max of Baden, another prominent conservative who favored a negotiated peace, visited Kreuznach and lunched with Ludendorff, whom he found affable and intractable. Prince Max discreetly avoided the phrase "peace of understanding"; with Ludendorff he restricted himself to the need to "smash the enemy's home front." Under Prince Max's gentle pressure on the matter of Belgium, Ludendorff disclosed that he had already forwarded to Berlin with his "urgent recommendation" a report by Colonel von Haeften, the head of the military section of the Foreign Office, outlining a propaganda offensive against Lloyd George's alleged policy of "unconditional surrender." However, before forwarding the proposal, Ludendorff had cut out its heart, the recommendation of a pledge of Belgian restoration. Prince Max's pleas had no more effect than Colonel von Haeften's logic; Ludendorff would not be budged.

A few days later, when Chancellor Hertling made a speech in the Reichstag seconding a new British Opposition call for exploratory peace talks, he stated that Germany had to prevent Belgium from becoming a "base for enemy machinations," and invited suggestions from the Belgian government at Le Havre. Subtle though the approach was, in deference to Ludendorff, it drew a response. Lord Lansdowne wrote a new letter to the *Daily Telegraph,* pointing to the outward similarity of Wilson's and Hertling's positions, and asking Hertling whether the Pope's formula, that Belgium should be guaranteed full political and economic independence, would satisfy him.

Once more the question of peace was reduced to its essence. Neither Alsace-Lorraine nor the Polish Corridor, the African colonies, Mesopotamia, Trieste and the Trentino stood as a serious obstacle to ending the bloodbath and reconciling Europe. Had Hertling possessed the strength and courage, the backing in the Reichstag, the acquiescence of the leaders of German business and industry, he could have stopped the war.

But when he spoke in the Reichstag on March 18, with the world tensely braced for the impending clash, he said not a word about Belgium. On the eve of battle, the Reconciliation Chancellor did not dare deviate from the line laid down by Ludendorff.

Supreme Headquarters had left Kreuznach in early March to establish itself in the Hotel Britannique in Spa, Belgium, and on March 19, Hindenburg and Ludendorff quit these comfortable accommodations for a new forward headquarters at Avesnes, just inside France, where they found themselves rather austerely situated in a large red-brick house with yellow trim, surrounded by a park of elms and oaks.

Hindenburg was setting foot on French soil for the first time since 1871, not having found it worthwhile in the intervening forty-seven years to visit this enemy country. Judging from Avesnes, it was little changed. A sleepy backwater town with an undamaged seventeenth-century fortress by Vauban, Avesnes had not suffered from the war except for the loss of its young men. The old men and the women sat before their doors, the old men lost in thought and the women chattering, while the children played and sang in the playground, just as in '71. "Lucky children," mused the old Field Marshal. Accommodations in Avesnes were limited, and when the Imperial entourage arrived to join headquarters for the battle, the Kaiser elected to live on board his train, drawing approval from Hindenburg for "the simple ways of our Warlord."

Besides the Kaiser, Supreme Headquarters regaled the children and old people of Avesnes with another picturesque attraction—a circus elephant. Jenny had a function, to labor at the railway station loading logs for field fortifications, but her field-gray color also made her an ideal mascot for the German Army.

In the last week before D-day, newspaper editors and correspondents from Germany and abroad were invited to special briefings in Cologne, at which staff officers outlined the broad strategy of the coming offensive (without giving away its details). Ludendorff wanted maximum publicity and maximum psychological impact.

A break in the fine weather brought violent rainstorms that aided in concealment. Enemy airmen dropped flares on the roads at night and turned their machine guns on anything that moved, but the absence of any special enemy artillery fire on the fronts of the German Eighteenth, Second, and Seventeenth Armies showed that the concealment was successful. The shock troops crowded into the forward shelters, and the last field guns were brought up, some dragged all the way to the barbed wire in front of the first-line trenches and hidden in shell holes.

On March 20, the day before the jump-off, it rained nearly all morning; at 11 A.M., with the chiefs of the attacking armies gathered at Avesnes, Ludendorff had to make the final decision. The meteorological officer, Lieutenant Dr. Schmaus, was asked if the wind would be favorable for gas. Dr. Schmaus equivocated, but thought the attack possible, and at 12 noon the generals were summoned by Hindenburg and told that the assault would take place. The Field Marshal gave his invariable impression of rocklike firmness. "I am convinced that we will win," he said. "Where the will is, the way is also found. So forward with God!"

7

THE ALLIES PREPARE FOR BATTLE

While opinion in Paris was at first divided over whether a German offensive was coming, opinion at Allied headquarters was never in doubt. No professional soldier, the professional soldiers thought, could resist playing at Ludendorff's 5-to-4 manpower odds.

At the headquarters of the British Expeditionary Force at Montreuil, the likelihood of the blow falling on the British sector was acknowledged. Yet there was no undue concern. Field Marshal Sir Douglas Haig, the commander in chief, was outwardly at least a trim-moustached rock of Gibraltar. Inwardly he was something of a subject for Freud, and his lack of imagination masked a mercurial temperament ready to swing from placid optimism to the height of alarm. A youngest son, favorite of his mother, he had lived most of his adult life with an older sister, and had only married at forty-four. An expert polo player, a poor speaker, devoid of a sense of humor, in love with the Army, he had risen on the strength of his devotion to military detail and the influence of his whiskey-distilling family to become director of military training at the War Office. In this capacity he had prepared the plans for the landing in France of the British Expeditionary Force, which had crossed the Channel in 1914 with model efficiency but with only two machine guns per battalion and destitute of howitzers and high-explosive ammunition. As a dedicated cavalryman, Haig had experienced even more difficulty than the average 1914–18 general in grasping the new technology of war. Nevertheless, he had climbed steadily from corps to field army to Expeditionary Force command. He had conducted the battles of the Somme (1916) and Passchendaele (1917), which between them had brought war home to the British people as had no others in their history. Large casualty lists were not part of the British military tradition. Lloyd George, the energetic, intelligent Welshman who had become prime minister in the middle of the war, profoundly mistrusted the competence of both Haig and Sir William Robertson, the chief of the Imperial General Staff, an attitude complemented by the reciprocal view of the two soldiers, who agreed that Lloyd George was too clever by far.

Haig considered Passchendaele a victory, and had a field marshal's baton from old family friend King George V to prove it. Before the Bolshevik Revolution, Haig's program for 1918 was to fill the gaps in his ranks and resume the offensive, a project Lloyd George regarded as criminal folly. Sending men to Haig seemed to him like sending calves to the butcher, and Lloyd George therefore clung tenaciously to a major limitation on the British conscription system that kept a large number of able-bodied soldiers in the British Isles, labeled "B-men," qualified for home service only (a "sailor's notion," scoffed Clemenceau, who nevertheless realized that Lloyd George's political life depended on keeping the B-men at home). Lloyd George also remained extremely wary of applying conscription at all to Ireland, though Haig considered that trench life would do the Irish a world of good.

Still another source of contention between the Prime Minister and the Field Marshal was the "Eastern"-versus-"Western" strategy debate. Early in the war, Winston Churchill and others had pushed for a defensive posture on the Western Front and an economical offensive against Germany's small ally

Turkey. This concept had had some justification when a munitions-starved Russia was blockaded by Turkey, but with Russia out of the war it hardly seemed to make sense. Yet to Lloyd George anything appeared preferable to the resumption of Haig's brutish frontal assaults, and in 1918 the Prime Minister remained immovably "Eastern."

For his own "Western" strategy, Haig had the backing of Robertson, and powerful support in the press and Parliament, but skillful Lloyd George beat the two generals at the political infighting and succeeded early in 1918 in getting Robertson replaced as chief of the Imperial General Staff by Sir Henry Maitland Wilson. Haig himself escaped replacement, apparently in part because Smuts told Lloyd George that the other British generals in France were no better. The British and British Empire divisions assigned to the Turkish front were left in place, and no B-men were sent to Haig, who found himself forced to follow a French and German lead by reducing the size of his divisions from twelve to nine battalions.

That, however, was not the end of the debate over British manpower. On January 31, at the Supreme War Council meeting at Versailles, French Premier Clemenceau brought it up.

In 1914 France had fought almost single-handed against a Germany whose population outnumbered hers by 67 million to 39 million, and whose military manpower, thanks to a high German birthrate in the 1880's and 1890's, outnumbered hers by more than 2 to 1. The French solution in 1914 had been the most rigorous application of conscription that any nation had ever undertaken. Approximately 80 percent of all military-age Frenchmen were drafted into the army, as compared with a more normal 50 percent for Germany. The expedient had provided equal numbers on the Marne battlefield, but in the relentless attrition since, the Germans had profited from their much larger untapped reservoir of manpower. Though losses had been about equal, in 1918 France could with difficulty sustain a hundred plus divisions, including several colonial divisions largely filled with black Africans, while Germany was able to field well over two hundred. Despite holding 160,000 men over forty-two in combat units, and despite calling up the nineteen-year-olds and eighteen-year-olds, the French Army foresaw a net deficit of over 300,000 men in 1918.

Not surprisingly, the French turned to the British. Britain, after all, was a nation of 46 million, with a vast empire to draw on, yet the British Expeditionary Force in France had grown in four years from an initial six infantry divisions to only fifty-eight.

The Supreme War Council, consisting of the premiers, war ministers, and military representatives of at first the three, and a little later the four, major Allied nations, had been called into being as a result of Caporetto. That disaster had itself had an important effect on the manpower situation on the Western Front. Seven German divisions, Ludendorff's entire general reserve, had created such havoc and alarm by the Caporetto breakthrough that several French and British divisions sent to help the Italians were still needed there in early 1918, while the German divisions had been transferred to France. Thus Caporetto had made a substantial difference in the balance on the Western Front. The French military representative on the Supreme War Council, General Foch, urged that provision be made against a future Caporetto by formation of a general reserve made up of contributions from all the Allied armies.

At the January 31 meeting, when Clemenceau brought up the question of a larger British manpower contribution, Lloyd George made a dexterous reply, stressing the needs of the British Navy, merchant marine, and critical industries (coal, shipbuilding), and politely closing the door.

Clemenceau was not the man to take a No, and he had the united backing of his generals, press, and public, who were united on little else. French military circles had their own controversy, one group advocating a "preventive offensive" before the German offensive could be launched. Among the politicians in France, as in Britain and Germany, there was a peace-by-negotiation group, headed by Clemenceau's predecessor Briand, and French munitions workers had carried out several Spartacist-like strikes in January. But everyone in France was agreed that the British should take over more of the front.

Pétain, who like Haig had no use for the Supreme War Council, made a proposal to his British opposite number that had Clemenceau's backing: instead of putting reserves under the control of a committee like the Supreme War Council, would it not make more soldierly sense to divide up the whole front, from the Atlantic to the Adriatic, between the two Western generals? Haig could have the front from the coast to the Aisne River, in the middle of France; Pétain would take over from there to the Adriatic. The scheme was doomed by Italian opposition, yet Pétain was convinced that the Italian danger was over; the coming German offensive would be against either the French or the British.

Pétain was perhaps the only Allied general who had given serious attention to the Riga and Caporetto battles. From them he had concluded that a dangerous source of defensive weakness lay in the now traditional pattern by which the most advanced portion of the elaborate trench networks was made the main line of resistance and heavily manned with infantry. Such massing of troops in the front line guaranteed maximum effect for the intensive enemy artillery and mortar barrage employed in the Hutier tactic, and left the rear positions inadequately manned in case of a breakthrough. On January 8, Pétain issued a new order, Directive No. 4, on defensive alignment, prescribing the Second Position, out of enemy mortar range, as the main line of resistance. The order caused an immediate furor; Pétain's subordinate generals objected to the implied surrender of terrain that had been won at great cost to what might be only a minor enemy attack. Pétain visited all his field armies to attempt to impose the new tactic. At headquarters after headquarters the opposition was so unanimous and open that he was forced to temporize. A typical experience was that at the headquarters of the French Fourth Army, in the Reims sector. General Gouraud, commander of the Fourth Army, was a handsome, bearded, one-armed warrior whose intellectual capacity was as limited as his physical courage was renowned. Gouraud strenuously protested that a weakening of his front line, with the incumbent danger of losing a portion of it to a minor attack, would fatally impugn his honor as a soldier. Dour, impassive Pétain saw that it was useless to argue, but catching the eye of Gouraud's youthful chief of staff, Colonel Prételat, he read a more reasonable reaction, and seized the opportunity of a moment alone to urge Prételat, "Make your chief see reason!" Prételat promised to do his best.

On February 3, Pétain assembled his army-group commanders at Versailles. He summarized the state of the French Army's preparedness: in the air, excellent; in artillery, very good; in tanks, some delays at Schneider and St. Chamond, but Renault promised eight hundred of the new light vehicles "in the summer." The one serious problem was infantry. The French Army counted only ninety-nine divisions, five having been disbanded during the winter to supply replacements, and the divisions were down from twelve to nine battalions, nearly all below strength.

Despite his alarming shortage of infantry, Pétain could get no support for Directive No. 4 either from Premier Clemenceau or from Foch, who was chief of the General Staff as well as French representative on the Supreme War Council. Foch regarded Pétain as a pessimist, and Clemenceau thought that if French generals were permitted to give up French territory, their British allies might abandon it altogether. Pétain had to forgo implementation of Directive No. 4, but he did not withdraw it and remained convinced of its wisdom.

Pétain could, however, get the support of Clemenceau and Foch in pressing Haig to take over more of the front. The British held only 25 percent of the Allied line, a ratio that seemed disproportionate despite British arguments that their closeness to the coast made a more dense front necessary. In the end, Haig gave in to the extent of stretching his right wing south to the Oise River, permitting Pétain to withdraw two army corps and turn them into a general reserve.

The two generals also made a mutual-assistance pact. In

case of an offensive directed against either, the general not attacked would send effective help within four days. The size of the forces earmarked for the purpose indicates their estimate of the threat: six divisions. They did not anticipate a Caporetto on the Western Front.

Haig did not distribute the added twenty-five miles of front equally among his four field armies. Instead he gave it all to the southernmost, General Gough's Fifth Army, whose fourteen divisions were consequently strewn over forty-two miles, compared with only twenty-three miles of front for the northernmost British army, the Second, which had the same number of divisions. The two middle British armies, with sixteen divisions each, held only sixty-one miles between them. Haig's rationale for the odd distribution was that the northern armies were near the coast, and so had little room to retreat. That was true, but it was a narrow, technical explanation of a deeper-lying phenomenon.

The positioning of the British Expeditionary Force was no military accident. Its center of gravity, the coastal littoral of Flanders and the Pas de Calais, represented the political sense of the war to Britain. Haig's headquarters was at Montreuil, close to the coast south of Boulogne; and the three ports of Boulogne, Calais, and Dunkerque were not only supply bases but ports of embarkation. This doorstep to Britain was the part of the continent that the British wanted to defend (Ludendorff credited them with the intention of keeping Calais permanently), but more than that, it was the exit they needed to go home by.

Haig's thought was that if Gough was hard pressed, he could swing back toward the other British armies and toward the ports, leaving Pétain's promised six divisions to come and fill in. In a word, an attack on Gough would bring a simple return to the January division of the Allied line, with the British prepared to bail out toward the coast and leave the burden of the juncture to the French.

Haig did not anticipate a large-scale breakthrough, merely a shallow dent in the line of the kind that all the previous offensives had produced. Gough was not so sure. He did not much like this new extension of his front, unaccompanied by any increment of troops to hold it, and was not reassured by General Humbert, commander of the French Third Army, who cheerily warned him that he might get a *vilain coup* ("rough knock") in his new position. Humbert gave Gough a copy of a new French Army pamphlet issued by Pétain. It turned out to be an analysis of the Hutier tactic, and was the first Gough had ever heard of the thing.

Signs multiplied of the impending German offensive. Up and down the front, raiding intensified. Colonel Cartier, code expert of French headquarters, noted that the Germans changed their cipher on March 11, a sure sign of an offensive within ten days.

On March 14, the Supreme War Council met in London to take a last look at preparations to meet the coming storm. Clemenceau and Lloyd George were satisfied with the arrangement made between Haig and Pétain. Only one voice was raised against it, that of Foch. Foch's demand that a general Allied reserve be formed, regarded by everyone as unrealistic if not self-serving, was turned down, and the Haig-Pétain accord was ratified. Defeated, Foch fired a telling last shot: "The governments may well approve the accord reached by the chiefs of the two Allied armies . . . but who will make the decisions . . . in the name of the general interest?"

On March 19, Winston Churchill, minister of munitions in Lloyd George's cabinet, lunched at Montreuil during a visit to the front. He told Haig with satisfaction that he had inaugurated a program to produce four thousand tanks, mostly the new lightweight Whippets, but drew little thanks from Haig, who wondered with some justice where the tank crews were to come from. Chancellor Hertling had made his Reichstag speech the day before, and Haig was asked his views on peace terms. He thought that if the Germans would get out of Belgium they might be allowed to keep some of Alsace-Lorraine, thus confirming the views of Kühlmann, Prince Max, and Colonel Wetzell. Haig expressed another popular theme of British conservatives, that if the war continued too long, "America will get stronger, and finally will dictate *her* peace, which may not suit Great Britain."

Haig had intended to take home leave the following weekend, but wrote his wife on the twentieth to defer the trip because of the threatened German offensive. The postponement he proposed, however, was for only a week. It would take no longer, he thought, to contain the offensive. Haig's one fear, in fact, was that "the enemy may find our front so powerfully defended that he will hesitate to launch his attack."

II

THE OFFENSIVE BEGINS

8

"MICHAEL"

On the morning of March 21, Churchill awoke early, before dawn, in a house in the village of Nurlu, a divisional headquarters of the British Fifth Army, and thereby became an eye-and-ear witness to the overture to Armageddon:

> Suddenly . . . exactly as a pianist runs his hands across the keyboard from treble to bass, there rose in less than one minute the most tremendous cannonade I shall ever hear. . . . Far away, both to the north and to the south, the intense roar . . . rolled upwards to us, while through the chinks of the carefully papered window the flame of the bombardment lit like flickering firelight my tiny cabin. . . . The enormous explosions of the shells upon our trenches seemed almost to touch each other . . . there rose at intervals, but almost continually, the much larger flame of exploding magazines.

From a quarter to five until just before seven, the 6,200 guns the Germans had secretly massed along a sixty-mile stretch from the Scarpe in the north to the Oise in the south concentrated their fury on the British rear positions. The exploding gas shells shrouded the British artillery in clouds of poison, and the British return fire ceased almost as it began. Then the hurricane retreated to the trenches of the British infantry. At 9 A.M. the gray shock troops clambered out of their own trenches and plunged forward. No-Man's-Land was curtained with fog; the survivors in the British front line were overwhelmed almost before they glimpsed their adversaries, materializing out of the mist in helmets and gas masks like beings from another world.

> It was flamethrowers forward [reported Shock Trooper Nikolaus Schulenburg in a letter home]. The English dugouts were smoked out and we took our first prisoners. They were trembling all over. Now we went forward without resistance. The next dugouts were passed, and we came to the railway. There the English had dug a field post in a declivity, and before it were corrugated iron huts. Here they had their kitchen, canteen, etc. The kitchen was naturally stormed immediately. I was astonished at what the English still had. The stove was still lit, bacon was sizzling, a side of beef lay on the table. . . . We stuffed our knapsacks. Each man took an English iron ration. In the next hut, a canteen, we found English cigarettes in great supply. Each man lit up. . . .
>
> The prisoners now came running toward us with their hands in the air. We had in the heat of the attack already advanced too far, our artillery fire had not been able to follow up, and we had almost come under our own barrage. Now we wheeled right and stormed the village of Grugies. On the entrance to the village we found a machine-gun nest. We made an effort to take it, but there was much barbed wire in front, and it would have cost many lives. It was

> very hazy still, and our artillery could not help us. We let it go and went on.
>
> Then came the English third line. This was our last objective for the day. We settled it quickly, and waited for further orders. . . . Time was again taken up with eating. Sugar was eaten with a spoon, then white bread, corned beef, etc.
>
> Our Third Battalion . . . overtook the First Battalion and went into the first line. We were given the command to hurry to the aid of the Third Battalion, they were meeting with tough resistance, the English were counterattacking. We had to advance through the English barrage, with planes close overhead attacking us with bombs and machine-gun fire.
>
> In the afternoon the sun came out. We came through very well, and wanted to cut off the English. When the English saw us they directed a murderous fire on us and many were hit. Then I got my wound and had to head for the rear. As I afterward heard, we completed our assignment fully and completely.

The fog, which heightened the effect of surprise, also helped create a general breakdown of communications. The barrage had wiped out British wire communications, and the rapid advance of the shock troops took them out of electronic communication with the German rear. As a result, on both sides, the higher headquarters were left in a state of ignorance. In the red-brick house in Avesnes, an imperturbable Hindenburg and a tense Ludendorff all day long read a succession of frustrating, piecemeal, contradictory reports; not till evening was it evident that while the right-hand German army, the Seventeenth, had been stopped at the enemy's second line, the Eighteenth, on the left, had gone farther than anyone had thought possible, taking the town of St-Quentin and reaching the banks of the Crozat Canal. Even at the day's end only scattered and ineffectual enemy resistance was reported. As the battlefield picture grew clearer, tension turned to jubilation in German headquarters; the Kaiser, always an optimist, and eager to have some role to play, assumed that of cheerleader.

At Haig's château at Montreuil, the day passed in equal uncertainty. General Byng asked and obtained permission to withdraw his Third Army from the Flesquières salient, an awkward bulge that the Germans were obviously trying to pinch off. General Gough, of the Fifth Army, wanted to withdraw to the St-Quentin Canal, and Haig approved this maneuver also. From the communications, he had no idea that while Byng's formations were intact and holding, Gough's were in rout. To both armies he sent his congratulations on the day's fighting.

Pétain received the news of the "Michael" offensive in his headquarters in Compiègne, where he was housed in the ponderous eighteenth-century château built by Louis XV. His initial reaction to the information that the enemy blow had fallen on the British front was relief, but as the day passed, the absence of precise information began to be ominous. At 11:30 P.M., Pétain alerted three divisions of his reserve Third Army, half of the pledged six, to be ready to move next day. General Humbert, the Third Army commander, drove to Gough's headquarters, where he found himself at once importuned—how much help had he brought? "At the moment," he explained, "I have only my *fanion* (staff pennant)."

Not till the following evening (March 22) did a request for aid reach Compiègne from Haig. When it came, it made up in scope for its tardiness; Haig wanted Pétain to take over the entire front between the Somme and the Oise. The German air force underlined the message with a heavy air raid on Compiègne.

Haig had tried all day to look on the bright side, noting in his diary that the Flying Corps had reported that it had wonderful targets in the long columns of enemy infantry, guns, and supplies. But at 8 P.M., Gough telephoned that "parties of all arms of the enemy are through our Reserve Line"—that is, the rearmost trenches—and asked permission to fall back behind the Somme.

Even at that, Haig did not feel it necessary to visit Gough's front till next morning, Saturday, March 23, and there he made a disconcerting discovery. Hutier's shock troops had produced a real shock; they had reached the Somme before the bridges could be demolished, and had seized them intact. The Somme line behind which Gough wanted to retreat had already been breached.

There were no more reserve divisions near enough to be thrown in. Some 370 tanks were scattered behind the British line in small groups, but they could not be put into action quickly and where needed; many could not even retreat fast enough to avoid capture.

For the first time in the war, the British Army needed help badly. At the crises of the Marne and Verdun it had been rather in the position of being coaxed to help the French who were in trouble. Its basic instructions, written by Field Marshal Kitchener, ornament of the Edwardian Empire, emphasized the importance of always keeping in a situation from which it could bail out for home.

To this fundamental British posture were added certain factors on the command level. Jealousy of the French was a chronic condition. The tank breakthrough at Cambrai had turned into a defeat because of the lack of infantry to follow it up. Yet an offer of infantry from Pétain had been turned down as a cheeky French attempt to get in on a good thing. Rather illogically, Haig and the British command also viewed the French as militarily too lax and democratic. In Haig's eyes, Pétain had been far too lenient with the war resisters of 1917. Pétain had shot only thirty or forty; Haig thought a proper number would have been two thousand. As a result, Haig had told his government a few weeks earlier that the French Army had only doubtful capacity to resist a German offensive, whereas the British, provided Haig was given ample support and not interfered with, could win the war single-handed.

Two days of "Michael" had sufficed to turn Haig completely around. Now he wanted all the French troops he could get, never mind the January agreement.

The French Third Army was pouring onto the battlefield as fast as the excellent French motor-transport system could carry it. The four files of trucks, two going up and two going back, crowding the highway between Estrée-St-Denis and Roye, reminded drivers of the *Voie Sacrée* that had supplied Verdun two years earlier. But the soldiers dismounting from the trucks had to plunge into combat without waiting to form complete regiments, let alone divisions, and without even knowing where the enemy was. Nevertheless, they succeeded in improvising a line.

More help was on the way. Corporal Georges Gaudy, of the French 57th Infantry, later recalled how his outfit, in reserve east of Paris, was alerted:

> Our regiment had assembled on the road to Épernay. The men were smoking, sitting in the ditch next to their stacked arms. . . .
>
> From the far end of the road a steady roar grew, and soon we felt a tremor in the ground. The trucks were coming.
>
> "Here they are!"
>
> From behind the first house of Chouilly, a beam flashed its glaring light on us, and in a few moments the first trucks had reached us. Their swaying line stretched along the road and filled the night with a formidable roar. . . . Gone were our hopes of a few weeks of peaceful rest in the village of Chouilly. . . .
>
> "Where are you driving us?" some of the men asked the drivers, who had stepped down from their seats.
>
> "We don't know! Nobody knows!"

At Compiègne the scale of the German smash suggested a design to sever the Allied juncture. To the French Third Army already committed, Pétain had therefore decided to add the First, withdrawing it from Lorraine despite the expostulations of General de Castelnau, the group commander there.

General Bullard's American First Division was in the line with the French First Army, but was not taken along, being judged not yet ready for this kind of thing. Bullard watched the long horizon-blue columns heading north and was struck by how little the men reminded him of the excitable Frenchmen he had always heard about. "They were very quiet, very serious, with the air of veterans who face everything. . . . It looked to me as if they knew that they were going to sacrifice, but that they were going."

The addition of the First to the Third French Army meant twelve divisions committed, double the January agreement. Yet Pétain no more than Haig was confident that these would suffice. He met Haig at Gough's headquarters at Dury on Saturday afternoon. It was a chilly conference. Pétain declined to commit himself to more than the twelve divisions he had en route or in combat, while Haig pleaded for at least twenty. Pétain did not conceal the fact that he thought the British should have held better, that it was Haig's fault that the Allied juncture was in peril, and that Gough's retreat ought to be stopped. The meeting broke up in an atmosphere of frost, panic, and uncertainty.

In the red-brick house in Avesnes, on the contrary, there was a spirit of lively optimism. Hundreds of enemy guns had been taken, and long columns of British prisoners were marching east. The Kaiser had Hindenburg stop the car during a trip to the front so that he could offer his personal condolences to a group of British officers. Hindenburg, more sixteenth-century than the Kaiser, noted with satisfaction that "his words seemed to produce a great effect, especially on a very tall young officer who, in intense emotion, had been hanging his head as if from shame. The thin form now straightened itself like a young fir tree freed from the weight of snow, and its grateful glance met the eyes—of my Emperor!"

That same Saturday (March 23), the Germans seconded

their blow against the British Army by unveiling Krupp's secret weapon against the French civilians.

At seven twenty in the morning, on the Quai de Seine, in the heart of Paris, an explosion smashed the ancient pavement and hurled fragments against the nearby houses. The street was nearly empty, but a crowd soon gathered. Parisians were accustomed to air bombardment, but this was the first time in nearly three years that a bomb had fallen in the daytime. What was odder was that nobody had seen or heard an aircraft. Twenty minutes later a second explosion, near the entrance to a Metro station on the Boulevard de Strasbourg, strewed the busy thoroughfare with victims. Again the crowd looked skyward, but there was no sign of aircraft and no antiaircraft fire. People picked up fragments of still hot metal; some were grooved and threaded, a detail the gendarmes telephoned in with their reports.

On the outskirts, the alerted AA batteries turned sound detectors on the clear and empty sky, while the little Spads and Nieuports climbed aloft. They found nothing, but as one after another, at intervals ranging from a few minutes to half an hour, more explosions came in widely scattered parts of the city, the air-raid sirens sounded. Shop and office workers crowded into the bomb shelters, while the subway trains halted.

Telephones were busy in the offices of the Paris Defense Service, police headquarters, and the War Ministry. The direct line to Compiègne confirmed that no enemy aircraft had passed over. By the time that report came back, the officers at Paris Artillery Headquarters had reached the astounding conclusion that the projectiles were being fired from a gun: the thick steel casing, the reinforcing copper bands, the rifling grooves and threads, made the thing unmistakable. Yet despite the German offensive in the north, the line was still about seventy miles away at its nearest point, three times the range of the heaviest guns known.

An examination of the map led the Paris artillery officers to the conclusion that the German gun or battery was located near Laon, at the corner where the front turned from north–south to east–west. Someone recalled that two weeks earlier, aerial photography had revealed what looked like a piece of fresh railroad construction, a pair of curving lines at the village of Crépy-en-Laonnais. The sound-ranging division was rung up and ordered to put units to work detecting and triangulating in the Crépy region. Air reconnaissance was also ordered, and the air observers soon reported heavy smoke camouflage in the suspect area. The sound rangers at first got only a confusion of noises, but in the afternoon picked up sounds that seemed to synchronize with the shells that, following a midday interval, recommenced falling at one o'clock sharp. The last of twenty-five explosions burst in a northern Paris suburb at a quarter to three. Altogether, sixteen persons were dead and twenty-nine wounded.

By late evening a battery of the heaviest French artillery, giant 305-mm. (12-inch) rifles, was started on railway cars for Vailly, on the Soissons–Reims railway line, with orders to commence firing at map coordinate 47:23.

The noon pause in the bombardment had been occasioned by a visit to the Crépy gun emplacement by the Kaiser, who was having the time of his life on this day of German victory. His special train pulled into the siding in the woods amid the three monster guns, their carriages planted in great pits and their long muzzles held up by cranes. As Dr. Rausenberger and Dr. Eberhard, who had come from Essen to witness the initial firing, explained to the admiring Kaiser, many esoteric calculations had to be made for these unusual guns, including even a correction for the rotation of the earth during the projectile's flight. The Supreme Warlord inspected the guns, the underground ammunition stores, the generator that supplied electricity to operate the guns, and the overhead camouflage made of grass-covered wire netting. Wood cleats nailed to trees permitted men to climb quickly and fasten the netting into place or take it down for firing. The whole site was fenced in with barbed wire to keep the gun crews in and the curious out.

The Kaiser watched the first after-lunch firing at 12:57 and several more before taking his train back to headquarters. En route he received the latest encouraging bulletins. At headquarters he shouted to the station guard like a boy home from a football game, "The battle is won! The English have been utterly defeated!" Champagne was served at dinner.

That evening Clemenceau dined at Compiègne, whither Pétain had returned after his meeting with Haig. The air raid of the night before had caused Pétain's chief of staff to requisition several houses outside town for some of his shot-up staff units, and the general received the Premier in one of these rather than at the château. In the middle of dinner a new message arrived from the British front: the Germans were across the Somme in force, south of Péronne.

The sense of the news was alarmingly clear to everyone at the table. Not only was the Allied juncture imperiled, but the left flank of the whole French Army was in jeopardy. Hutier was already west of the French Third Army, committed in a northerly direction. Suppose the shock troops wheeled south?

Pétain dictated an order to the French First Army, en route from Lorraine, to cover the line, "Beauvais-Clermont," due west of where they were sitting, to block the road to Paris. A few minutes later he abruptly called out to General Duval, his chief of aviation, who put down his fork in astonishment and rose. Pétain told him to get on the phone, and Duval, grasping his meaning, hastened out to send bombardment squadrons over the area south of Péronne, where the victorious Germans were now bivouacking.

Pétain made no secret of his concern at the way the battle was going. Driving back to Paris, Clemenceau commented to General Mordacq, his military aide, "Maybe Pétain with his frankness sees the bad side of the situation a little too much, but he acts, and that's what counts."

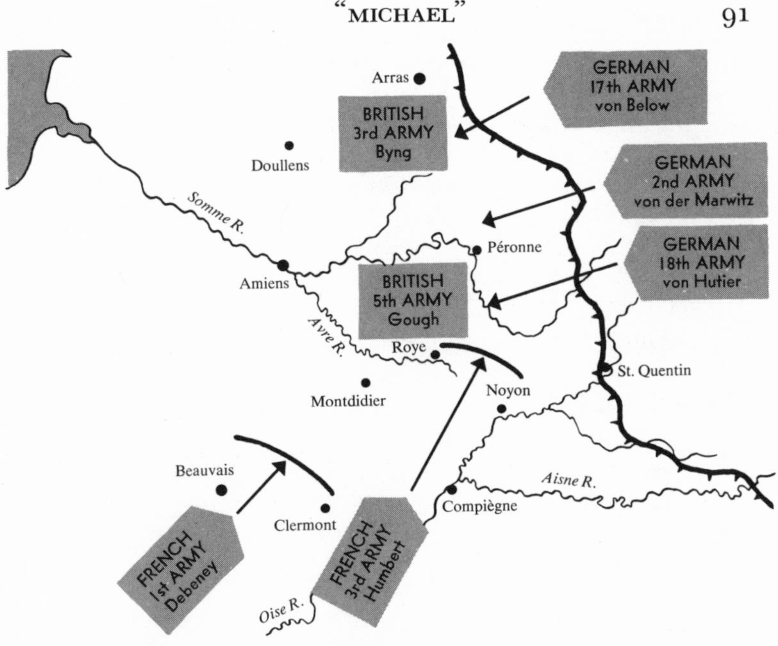

"Michael" offensive.

On Sunday evening, March 24, Corporal Georges Gaudy of the relieving French Third Army awoke during a halt to learn that there were British soldiers outside:

> . . . a long line of artillerymen on horseback was moving past us in the opposite direction. From their pace, one could see that their horses were tired. Wagon followed upon wagon in a steady rattle, but the guns were missing. I tried to talk to the men, but there was no answer: they were asleep on their horses!

Presently one waking Briton approached the Frenchmen in the trucks and Gaudy interrogated him:

> "Has the going been rough? D'you think they'll break the front?"

> "It's already broken," he replied casually.
>
> And out of the darkness, amidst the clatter of hooves and wheels, another Briton shouted:
>
> "It's all over! They're going to Paris!"
>
> The men around me were stunned when I translated the remark to them, and in the far corner of the truck the last sleepers woke up. . . .
>
> We halted in a village filled with extraordinary animation. Lights flickered in every house, people were throwing mattresses, linen and clothes through the windows. Horses whinnied, cattle lowed. Wagons were being harnessed before the doors, people were piling furniture and food into them, and placing bewildered children on top of them. . . . British officers and French gendarmes were banging against still-closed shutters [to warn the occupants to leave]. . . .
>
> [Early on the morning of the twenty-fifth] ambulances drove by; in the rising sun, we saw exhausted British soldiers lying by their wagons and sleeping horses. On the road the flood of refugees was tramping along in the midst of a cloud of powdery dust. . . .
>
> We arrived at Ribecourt. . . . We got off our trucks [after thirty-six hours], and arranged our equipment before assembling. The street was full of British soldiers eating lunch by their stacked arms. . . .

The French were about to do the same when the order came to fall in and march:

> The captain came running along, and the sergeants got busy. "No time to eat! Throw your soup away! Everybody take arms!" . . . "Column by four, forward—march!"

Ludendorff, pleased, though within reason, at Hutier's success, studied his map. The battle was not going according to plan, and yet it seemed to be going even better than the plan called for. More a tactician than a psychologist, Ludendorff had scarcely taken account of the likelihood of the British Army swinging back toward the Channel coast and so separating itself from the French. He had intended rather to punch a hole in the British line and separate Gough's Fifth Army from Byng's Third. Now, with the Fifth fleeing headlong in a westerly direction, he preceived the enticing prospect of driving a wedge between the two Allies. He could let the Eighteenth and Second Armies press on toward Amiens, while Below's Seventeenth turned in a northwesterly direction. By so doing, it would help pin down the northern British armies, keeping them from sending help south, and would also protect the flank of the next phase, the "George" attack up north.

That Sunday (March 24), as Dr. Eberhard's guns renewed their bombardment of Paris, the shock troops pressed ahead all along the line. Morale was high; looting was the best it had been since 1914. "We smoke none but English cigarettes," wrote Rudolf Binding in his diary, "and plaster our boots with lovely English boot-polish."

The possibility of wedging the two Allies apart now beckoned unmistakably. As the tidings poured in from the front, the Kaiser pinned on Hindenburg's tunic an almost unique medal: the Iron Cross with Golden Rays, given previously only to Blücher for Waterloo. To Ludendorff he gave the Iron Cross with Swords and Palms.

Hindenburg in turn bestowed on the Kaiser permission to drive close to the front, along the Cambrai–Bapaume road, in his gray Daimler. The sights along the route proved a little strong for the Supreme Warlord's appetite, and he made a defensive exclamation to his party: "What have I not done to preserve the world from these horrors!" Reported by Karl Rosner, his faithful personal correspondent, the words drew editorial jeers from Paris to San Francisco, the Kaiser's image in the Allied world being such that his remark was believed to reflect not naïveté but cynicism. A fatuous headquarters communiqué had attributed to Wilhelm "personal leadership" of the offensive, causing the *Kölnische Zeitung* to name it the *Kaiserschlacht* ("Kaiser's battle").

To the Allied generals even more than to Ludendorff it appeared that a severance of their juncture was imminent. Each immediately thought of his own army's danger. To Haig it appeared that he must husband his three intact armies, pull back the remnants of the shattered Fifth, and at all costs keep the three Channel ports covered. Not only did Haig leave the problem of maintaining the Allied juncture entirely to Pétain, but he felt the French should protect his open southern flank. Pétain naturally had a completely different view. What had happened, in his eyes, was that the British had allowed a deep enemy penetration that endangered the French Army. Pétain felt himself in the position of a middleweight boxer who in partnership with a lightweight had taken on a heavyweight; now the lightweight had been knocked out of the ring by one swing, and while he climbed back through the ropes, the middleweight had to look out for himself.

What Pétain feared was that his initial commitment to the battle, the French Third Army, put in piecemeal as it arrived, might be carried away by the torrent of the enemy advance. He sent orders to General Fayolle, commander of the Reserve Group (the French First and Third Armies) warning that the imperiled Third "must not be cut off from the remainder of our forces." Only if this were assured was Fayolle to maintain contact with the British. The mission of the cavalry corps deploying north of Noyon on the extreme left was defined categorically: first, to cover the flank of the French Army (*mission principale*) and only second, to try to maintain liaison with the British (*mission subsidiaire*).

Thus the two Allied commanders who in January had prepared for the coming storm by arranging to lend each other up to six divisions found the hurricane so much more violent than they had anticipated that they mutually parted company.

That morning, Pétain sent his liaison officer to Paris to request Clemenceau to intervene with the British government to get Haig to halt his retreat toward the coast. Pétain considered that if the British gave up Amiens, the main rail and road center in the area, it would be impossible to reestablish the juncture.

The same Sunday, as the German advance continued, Haig's early optimism completed its metamorphosis. At 11 P.M. he again met Pétain at Dury. Now Haig wanted Pétain to take over the front on both sides of the Somme, in front of Amiens—in other words, to relieve the entire British Fifth Army. Pétain was bluntly negative: in view of the direction of the British retreat, the French Army must sever its connection with its ally in order to cover Paris.

As soon as Pétain left, Haig telegraphed London and asked that someone be sent over at once to set up a supreme command—in other words, to put the British Army under a French general. The general had to be French, but at least he did not have to be Pétain, whose attitude of frigid reproof infuriated Haig. He thought instead of Foch.

9

FOCH

Haig was not alone. Foch had been thinking the same thing himself since the battle began. He spent Sunday morning in his office on the Boulevard des Invalides writing a memorandum, to the accompaniment of the intermittent explosions from the mystery shells, and after lunch drove to the Quai d'Orsay to hand his written views to Premier Clemenceau: in the light of the direction the battle was taking, there was an urgent necessity to create "an organ to direct the war—one capable of giving orders and seeing that they are executed."

Clemenceau promptly telegraphed London; the result of the two messages, Clemenceau's and Haig's, was that the machinery was set in motion for providing the Allies with a long-overdue unified command.

There was actually little doubt in anyone's mind about the identity of the Allied commander in chief. Foch's seniority, experience, prewar reputation, reasonably favorable relations with the British, and reasonably successful command performance made him the logical choice, entirely aside from Haig's antipathy to Pétain.

Short in stature, baroque in mustache, pithy in speech, picturesque in gesture, Ferdinand Foch was the image of the old-fashioned French general, outwardly corresponding more to Hindenburg than to Ludendorff. An unfailing communicant at daily mass, he illustrated Anatole France's observation that the Savior had found his last refuge in the hearts of the generals of the Third Republic. Like d'Artagnan, he was a Gascon, though born a little farther south, in Tarbes, where in 1851 his father was a civil servant of the Second Empire. When the war of 1870 broke out, he was attending an engineering prep school in Metz; as he and his classmates took their finals, through the open windows they heard the guns of the battle of Gravelotte. Foch and his fellow students escaped from Metz and enlisted in Paris, but the war was over before they saw action. Back at school in Metz, they shared quarters with the occupying Germans, "who were determined to make us feel the weight of their victory . . . by violence and brutality, on or even without the slightest pretext." The novice engineer made a sudden decision. He dropped civil engineering and entered the French Army, soon demonstrating exceptional capacities. He was singled out for special attention by one of his instructors at the War College, Major Millet, who believed that the 1870 war had revealed the dominant role of firepower on the modern battlefield, and that this dominance was certain to increase. Foch became Millet's chief of staff, first of a corps and later of an army, yet he never quite accepted the implications of Millet's views, and at heart preferred the later doctrine of Colonel Grandmaison of the War College, who believed infantry attacking in mass could overcome firepower. Foch's own lectures at the War College in the 1890's, published as *Principles of War* and *On the Conduct of War,* and widely cited, emphasized the offensive and counteroffensive rather than reliance on firepower.

Like Ludendorff's, Foch's career received a setback at one point. In the aftermath of the Dreyfus Affair, overzealous republicans moved Catholic officers out of General Staff and War College positions to line assignments. But in 1908 Clemenceau became war minister. Though as fanatic a Jacobin as ever appeared in French politics, Clemenceau was also a superpatriot, and manfully swallowing the fact that Foch had a brother who was a Jesuit priest, appointed him director of the War College.

In 1914 Foch commanded a corps, and in the Marne crisis, when Joffre wanted an aggressive general for the new Ninth Army, which had been formed to plug a gap in the middle of the line, he picked Foch. Foch's repeated counterattacks with dwindling formations helped win the battle, at no slight cost in casualties, and Joffre chose him to act as "assistant commander in chief" of the French Army. He was assigned to coordinate the developing British-French-Belgian front in the north, a function that evolved into command of the French Northern Army Group, which fought alongside the British in the Somme offensive of 1916. The new French commander of 1917, Nivelle, jealous of a possible rival, used the failure of the Somme to relegate Foch to an office job, drawing up plans to meet a hypothetical German invasion of Switzerland. But when Nivelle's own Champagne offensive proved a bloodier fiasco than the Somme, Nivelle was replaced by Pétain, and Foch, after a mission to Italy, was appointed chief of the general staff, a role that in republican France meant, not commander in chief, but merely top military adviser to the government.

In the summer of 1917, when Pétain summarized his program as awaiting Yanks and tanks, Foch summarized his own in a memorandum containing four points: stick to defense on the Western Front; hurry up the creation and transport of the American Army; bring all surplus troops back from secondary fronts; and—Foch's own pet—establish an "inter-Allied military organ." The British would not hear of such a thing, but in October, Caporetto gave Foch's proposal some new meaning. Western troops had to be sent to Italy, and a conference at Rapallo set up the Supreme War Council.

In January, 1918, Foch pointed to the threatening German offensive as a fresh reason for creating a "higher organ of command." He won the immediate backing of the Americans, newly seated on the Council, and Lloyd George went so far as to express himself as personally in favor, but British public opinion, convinced by its press that Britain was carrying the main burden of the war, remained immovably opposed. Clemenceau undertook to sell the idea to Haig, but received a frigid rebuff: "My soldiers and I have but one chief, our well-beloved sovereign the King." Clemenceau concluded that it would take "the help of the German cannon to . . . convert the English."

Foch and Clemenceau settled for the best they could get, an executive committee composed of the four Allied military representatives, with Foch as chairman, an advance made possible by the support of the American representative, General Tasker Bliss. But Foch's efforts to form a general reserve under the committee's control, thereby giving it (and himself) a major voice in the strategic direction of the war, failed. Pétain ultimately agreed to furnish twelve divisions (four of which were in Italy) but Haig, having extended his line south, declared that he could spare no troops at all, torpedoing the scheme and with it Foch's aspirations for supreme command.

That was March 2. Three weeks later Haig turned completely around, and called for the immediate formation of a supreme command. On Monday (March 25) Foch was preparing to leave for a conference with Haig at Abbeville when Clemenceau telephoned to tell him to send Weygand, his chief of staff, to Abbeville and come himself to Compiègne to confer with Pétain. At the Gare du Nord he had a word with Javary, the director of the French rail network. "Save Amiens," Javary told him, "or everything's lost. It's the center of all our communications [in the battle zone]." Foch agreed. At Compiègne he listened as Pétain outlined his latest actions and plans for giving help to Haig: he had increased the twelve divisions to fifteen, with six already heavily engaged against Hutier. To send more, said Pétain, would dangerously thin his own front, exposing Paris.

Clemenceau asked Foch what he thought, and Foch at once argued the overriding necessity of closing the gap which was opening between the two Allied armies east of Amiens.

The clear implication was that the Allies needed a generalissimo who could constantly weigh Amiens in the scales with Paris. Foch scarcely guessed that at practically this same moment, at Abbeville, Haig was astonishing General Sir Henry Maitland Wilson, chief of the Imperial General Staff, by proposing flatly that Foch be given full power. Wilson thought British opinion, even though shocked by "Michael," needed some sort of compromise arrangement. He thought of assigning strategic direction of the war to Clemenceau, with Foch as his military adviser.

Weygand returned to Paris and reported Wilson's proposal to Foch, who heard it from Wilson himself that evening when the British general called at Foch's apartment in the Avenue de Saxe. Wilson, who spoke French fluently, offered the idea in a half-joking vein. "My dear Wilson,"answered Foch, "for an intelligent man you say some unreasonable things."

Wilson drove to Versailles, where he conferred with Lord Milner, a senior Cabinet minister sent by Lloyd George to help weigh the question. Early next morning, March 26, Wilson called on Clemenceau to propose that Foch be assigned the task of "insuring a closer cooperation between the armies." Foch was not satisfied; he wanted full authority to command the two Allied armies, and especially a clear-cut control over the reserves. Clemenceau was determined to give Foch what he wanted. Haig was holding a conference with his generals at Doullens, a small town behind the British front. Clemenceau proposed an impromptu inter-Allied conference there, and everyone was notified.

When Foch's car drove into the town-hall square of Doullens at 11:30 A.M., Clemenceau was already there, with Poincaré, the president of the Republic, and Loucheur, the minister of munitions, the three frock-coated politicians pacing up and down to keep warm. Along one side of the square a column of khaki-clad British troops, interspersed with horses, guns, and wagons, was moving in good order. They looked reassuringly far from beaten, but they were moving west; every step they took carried them away from the counterattacking French to the southeast. From east and southeast of Doullens came the thunder of artillery fire. There, twenty or twenty-five miles away, a scraped-together collection of British rear-echelon details—labor battalions, railwaymen, cooks, orderlies, and even three hundred Americans who had been training with a Royal Engineers outfit—were battling to save the appearance of a front line until the French could get there.

Foch took advantage of the delay in the start of the conference (Haig was still talking to his generals) to revisit the schoolhouse he had used as headquarters in 1914, and on his return told everyone where he had been and affirmed that he felt more confident of victory now than in '14. Pétain arrived, wearing his usual expression, described as perpetual anxiety by some and as habitual gravity by others. Behind him he had left a headquarters frantically evacuating the château and town of Compiègne, now threatened by Hutier's advance. New French Army headquarters was set up in a dragoon barracks in the old walled town of Provins, some forty miles southeast of Paris. His headquarters commandant had thought to send along to Doullens a mess detail with sandwiches, and the generals and politicians munched while waiting. Outside the iron railing surrounding the town-hall park, local townspeople had collected, curious and worried.

Finally the British cavalcade carrying Lord Milner and General Wilson pulled into the square, Haig's meeting broke up, the party mounted to the council chamber on the second floor, and the conference began. Clemenceau opened by asking Haig to clarify a statement he was reputed to have made that Amiens must be given up; Haig explained it as a misunderstanding, but added that though he was committing every division at his disposal to reinforce his right, he could do nothing south of the Somme, where he had now placed the British Fifth Army under Pétain's orders. Pétain commented dryly that there was very little of the Fifth Army left, and in fact that "in strict truth we may say that the Fifth Army no longer exists." To this gloomy pronouncement Haig added that he might have to "rectify his line" before Arras, northeast of Amiens—that is, give up Arras.

Poincaré asked Pétain what he was doing to meet the crisis. Pétain had in fact made a momentous decision. In the first days of the offensive he had expected Ludendorff to break off his attack against the British and switch to an offensive in Champagne, northeast of Paris, and for this reason had hardly dared strip his front of reserves to assist Haig. Now he was convinced by the scale and endurance of the German effort in Picardy that an immediate offensive against his own front was for the moment impossible.

In reply to Poincaré's question, he therefore now stated that he had studied his resources once more and found that by stripping his entire front of reserves and leaving it weak everywhere he could scrape together a total of twenty-four divisions, nine more than he had thought possible the previous day. Several of the twenty-four, he noted, had now been exposed to severe combat. As for the pace at which fresh divisions would arrive on the British front, Pétain was again pessimistic. He suggested that Haig strip his front of reserves, to which the British Field Marshal replied that he had already done so, adding that there were no men left in England capable of going immediately into the line. This claim, which Lloyd George had reiterated to Haig, most of those present did not really believe, but this was not felt to be the moment to argue it.

Clemenceau summarized: the problem was not so much the number of French troops available to succor the British, but the speed with which they could be deployed. That was indeed the point, but Pétain refused to be drawn into further promises.

A pall descended on the meeting, broken finally by Foch, who had been sitting bolt upright with a look of barely restrained impatience: "We must fight and win at Amiens, where we are."

Haig turned. "If General Foch will give me counsel, I will accept it gladly."

Clemenceau rose and signaled to Milner, who followed him to a corner of the room. "We must make an end of this," said the old Premier. "What do you suggest?"

Clemenceau wanted the proposal to come from the British, and Milner obliged: Foch should be entrusted with coordination of the British and French armies to meet the present German offensive. Clemenceau called Pétain over and informed him, while Milner took Haig aside. Both generals accepted at once, Haig even taking care to make certain that Foch should have the power to coordinate the action of all the Allied armies on the Western Front and not just those around Amiens.

Years later Clemenceau explained his own reason for choosing Foch over Pétain for the supreme command. "Pétain said we were beaten while Foch behaved like a madman and wanted to fight. I said to myself, 'Let's try Foch. At least we'll die with the rifle in our hand.' I dropped the sensible man, full of reason, Pétain, and adopted the madman, Foch. The madman saved us." It was a pleasantry with a grain of truth, but Clemenceau had actually favored Foch for the supreme command all along. As for the "madman" saving the situation, at the moment of the Doullens conference, all the strategic moves to parry "Michael" had already been made, and as the event proved, made successfully, by Pétain. Nevertheless, as Pétain himself foresaw, Foch would have a future role, and it could hardly fail to be crucial.

The conference adjourned to the Hôtel des Quatre Fils Aymon for a tardy lunch, at which Clemenceau addressed Foch jovially: "Well, you've got the job you wanted so much." Foch rejoined rather tartly that to assume direction of a battle that had been a losing one for a week was "no treat, but an act of duty." He did not, however, pretend to be disappointed.

If Foch did not conceal his satisfaction, Haig did not conceal his relief. When Lord Milner stopped at Haig's château en route to Boulogne he found the Field Marshal about to go for a canter, in high spirits, a weight lifted. Haig expressed his confidence in the new arrangement in a face-saving phrase to the effect that he "would have to do with a man, and not a committee."

In the Doullens conference with his generals, Haig had heard complaints from Gough that Foch had spoken "impertinently" to him about his leadership of the British Fifth Army. Gough, who back in February had vainly protested the weakness of his front, now had to put up with a call from Foch in his new role. Foch "instructed" the British general to stop his retreat at once and hold at all points. Foch's "instructions" were the same as the "orders" Gough had been unable to comply with for five days. Foch then visited the generals commanding the French First and Third Armies, striving to block the German advance to the south, and the Reserve Group commander, General Fayolle, who happened to be an old schoolmate of Foch's from nearly sixty years earlier. Next day (March 27) he called on Gough again and delivered a stricture on the British XVIII Corps, a battered remnant that Foch nevertheless insisted should stop and fight, with or without artillery. Gough's hours as a commander were numbered. The defeat demanded a scapegoat, and in any case, his army, as Pétain had said, hardly existed any more.

Foch then dropped in on General Byng, whose Third Army either had acquitted itself better than the Fifth, or (Ludendorff's view) had been less skillfully attacked. Byng was in good fettle, and readily subscribed to Foch's view that an early counterattack was desirable. That evening Foch returned to his temporary headquarters at Clermont to learn the disconcerting news that the Germans had pressed between the two deploying French armies and seized the important town of Montdidier.

Ludendorff, seeking to exploit the weakness of the Allied juncture, had reinforced Hutier's Eighteenth Army, now given the mission of advancing toward Compiègne—that is, forcing back the French left—while Below's Seventeenth attacked northwest toward Arras, and Marwitz's Second pushed straight ahead on Amiens.

Next day (March 28) there was fierce but even fighting all along the battlefront, with the Germans making some gains toward Amiens and the French counterattacking toward Montdidier. Then the third French field army that Pétain had committed, the Fifth, from Champagne, began arriving. As it made its weight felt, the Oise–Scarpe front slowly jelled, and the exhausted survivors on both sides dug deeper holes. Simultaneously, Ludendorff's attempt to push Byng's British Third Army back in a northwesterly direction ran into trouble; freed from responsibility for the Oise–Scarpe sector, Haig could feed Byng reserves drawn from the two northernmost British armies.

On the evening of March 28, in the midst of a conference with Pétain and Clemenceau at Clermont, Foch received unexpected visitors. General Pershing, commander of the American Expeditionary Force, and General Bliss, American military representative on the Supreme War Council, requested an audience. Pershing handed Foch a letter written in his own hand:

> *To General Foch:*
>
> I have come to say to you that the American people would hold it a great honor for our troops were they engaged in the present battle. I ask it of you in my name and in that of the American people.
>
> There is at this moment no other question than that of fighting. Infantry, artillery, aviation—all that we have—are yours to dispose of as you will. Others are coming who will be as numerous as may be necessary. I have come to say to you that the American people would be proud to be engaged in the greatest battle of history.
>
> *Pershing*

To this Bliss added a few words in French: "We have come over here to get ourselves killed; if you want to use us, what are you waiting for?"

Only Clemenceau, who had spent a bit of his youth in New York, was able to thank the Americans in their own language, but hands were pressed warmly and sincerely.

Yet, to Pershing's slight vexation, neither Foch nor Pétain thought of using the American divisions against Hutier's veterans. They were much too green. But the battle was just beginning; before it was over, everybody would be needed.

As March turned to April, "Michael" angrily subsided amid a nightmare litter of twice-ruined villages, torn-up fields, and wrecked military equipment. Dead men were usually buried promptly, but not so dead horses, which strewed the roads and fields in thousands. (They were, however, often salvaged —the Germans skinned them for their leather, and both the French and the Germans butchered fresh dead horses for meat.)

Corporal Georges Gaudy and the survivors of his company, relieved from the line after helping stop the Germans in the Noyon sector, found themselves billeted in a deserted village a little to the rear:

> The population had left the village, but the houses were intact. What an activity when we woke up! All around, one could see *poilus* carrying rabbits by their ears, potatoes in linen bags, lumps of grease or chunks of meat on canteen covers. My buddies and I took possession of a well-kept house, in which we found a great quantity of chinaware, glasses, and drinks.
>
> While we skinned the rabbits and peeled the potatoes, somebody built a blazing fire in the fireplace. . . . One *poilu* had found a stray cow [which] was now mooing in a stable next to our room. Some busied themselves setting table, others filled canvas buckets with apple cider. . . . The sight of all these busy bearded fellows, sleeves rolled up and brandishing knives, made one think of the preparations for a barbarian feast. . . .
>
> Exploring the house, I discovered British soldiers sleeping in their clothes on sofas and beds. I woke them up and invited them to join us. They gladly accepted, and for more than three hours we shared a monstrous meal. Everybody was ravenous, and our Frenchmen displayed an unquenchable thirst. . . .

> Our volunteer cooks prepared tea for our British guests. Pipes were lit all around, amidst laughter and talk. It was one of those rare moments when everyone most deeply enjoyed the luxuries of life.

But if the Allies enjoyed their relief, it was the Germans who felt the victory. While the shock troops settled down to enjoy their looted cigarettes and rations, the Kaiser allowed his optimism to bubble ahead of that of his generals.

At breakfast with Marwitz, commanding the German Second Army, Wilhelm impetuously pulled open Hindenburg's coat to show the "Blücher star," and happily pointed out that Blücher had received it for triumphing with the English, while Hindenburg had earned it by triumphing against them. "Father Hindenburg," dryly recorded Marwitz in a letter home, "stood as dumb as a wall." Marwitz ventured to observe that the battle was not over, but the Kaiser rebuked him by emphatically asserting that the first great portion of it had ended victoriously.

That was true. Yet Hindenburg and Ludendorff regretted that it had not ended victoriously enough. Despite the headline-making advance, and the handsome bag of prisoners, they were disappointed by the failure to capture Amiens or at least the heights commanding the town. The attack, several times renewed, "was in vain," recorded Hindenburg; "our strength was exhausted. . . . The French . . . with their massed attacks and skillful artillery saved the situation for their Allies and themselves."

Colonel Wetzell, remembering his February war game, added another element: ". . . the fact that the French, by skillful utilization of their railways and, even more, owing to the unsuspected capacities of their motor transport and their motorized artillery units, succeeded at the last moment in closing the breaches."

In fact, the principal fruit of "Michael" was the gift to the Allies of a unified command. That could not have happened if the first blow of *Friedensturm* had been directed, not against the British, but against the French, as Colonel Wetzell had wanted.

Nevertheless, Ludendorff judged the prospects ahead as excellent, and Hindenburg wrote that "the kind of victory we need for Germany's political and economic future can no longer be wrested from us."

10

"GEORGETTE"

The shock waves of "Michael" reached Vienna and Washington. In Vienna it suddenly looked as if the redoubtable German ally, whatever his faults, was going to bring the thing off just as he had said he would. Count Czernin hastened to put himself and his Imperial master securely aboard the *Siegfried* train.

The Reichsrat, the recently minted parliamentary body of the Habsburg monarchy, would have been the natural forum for the declaration Czernin had in mind, but the Reichsrat was pointedly not in session. After being prorogued for three years, it had been summoned in 1917 and had responded by making a strong, embarrassing declaration in favor of the oppressed nationalities. Czernin therefore had to improvise an occasion for his speech reassuring the German ally of Austria's fidelity. He found one in the somewhat anomalous occasion of Easter Sunday (April 2), when he delivered a speech to the Vienna City Council on peace. The obstacle to peace, it appeared, was the French government. In a garbled reference to the Armand–Revertera talks, he called "God to witness, that we did everything that was possible to avoid a new offensive on the Western Front. The Entente did not want [peace]. . . . Monsieur Clemenceau asked me some time before the beginning of the Western offensive whether I was ready for negotiations and upon what basis. In agreement with Berlin I replied at once that I was ready for negotiations, and that I saw no hindrance to peace with France except France's desire for Alsace-Lorraine. The reply came from Paris that negotiations were impossible on this basis. Our armies will prove to the Entente that French and Italian aspirations on our territories are utopian dreams, calling for a terrible vengeance."

The heady effect of "Michael" was evident in Czernin's mood. In his earlier speech replying to Wilson's Fourteen Points he had been careful to say nothing at all about Alsace-Lorraine. Now, with German victory looming, he not only denied that Austria had ever sought a separate peace, but pictured Clemenceau as a paper Tiger, surreptitiously suing for peace and receiving a lordly rebuff from a loyal member of the German brotherhood.

He mistook his man. As premier, Clemenceau seemed to have collected all the energy of half a century of political combat in a superhuman effort to win the war—jailing former friends, shutting down newspapers, sacking generals, hectoring allies. So far from having pressed the Armand–Revertera talks in Switzerland, as Czernin implied, he had found them in progress when he had assumed office, and had at once instructed Armand to "listen and say nothing."

Clemenceau was lunching with Foch at Beauvais when General Mordacq brought a telephone message from Paris: Count Czernin had stated that Austria had never made a proposal for a separate peace. By chance, Clemenceau had in the past few days been shown the Prince Sixtus letter. It did not occur to him that Czernin had never seen it. "This count is a liar!" he exclaimed, and instructed Mordacq to have it announced in the press that "Count Czernin lied." Jumping up from the table, he followed Mordacq to the phone to adjure, "Say it everywhere that he lied. When I get back to Paris he'll hear from me!"

Somewhat startled at the violence of the published reaction of the French government, Czernin reiterated his claim that the peace move had come from Paris, not Vienna.

Clemenceau at once disclosed that the Habsburg monarchy had made more important overtures than the Armand–Revertera talks, through a person of "far higher rank," documentation of which existed in the form of "authentic, and very remarkable proofs."

In Vienna, Czernin felt himself getting into deep waters. He sought to end the bizarre debate by reiterating that France was to blame for continuing the war because of Alsace-Lorraine. That claim sufficed in Clemenceau's eyes to justify tearing the veil of secrecy. He regaled the Chamber of Deputies with the sarcastic oratory for which he was famous: "Who would believe that it would need a Revertera to enlighten Czernin about a question in which the Emperor of Austria had already pronounced the final word? The Emperor Karl himself . . . in a letter of March, 1917, written with his own hand, confirmed his consent 'to the just claim of France to Alsace-Lorraine.'"

That bomb exploded in Vienna with shattering effect. Angry and baffled, Czernin hurried to the Baden palace, where he found poor Karl lying on a divan holding compresses to his aching head. At Czernin's insistence, Karl signed a telegram to Kaiser Wilhelm denying everything and concluding, "My answer to the calumny will be given by my cannon in the West," an allusion to some batteries of artillery sent to the Western Front. Ludendorff had found the Austrian batteries deficient in ammunition, and Karl's telegram to Wilhelm proved deficient as well. Clemenceau, an old duelist, delivered the *coup de grâce* on April 14 by publishing Karl's letter for all the world to read. In addition to the concession of Alsace-Lorraine, the letter contained a noteworthy declaration in favor of the reestablishment of Belgium, and included the damning statement that Czernin "concurred."

Czernin's first thought was to procure Karl's abdication; failing that, he had no recourse but to resign himself, while unhappy Karl, guilty only of wanting peace as badly as did his people, was reduced to journeying to his Canossa at German rear headquarters at Spa, where he signed a twelve-year "offensive and defensive" alliance that placed Austria's foreign policy in German hands. The day before Karl left Vienna, Clemenceau told the Chamber of Deputies that the time had come to give all aid to the oppressed nationalities, with the aim of breaking up the Habsburg Empire.

The possibility of a lifesaving move by Vienna for a separate peace was thus erased. Clemenceau's political adversary, Briand, thought the disclosure of Karl's letter a shocking blunder (Romain Rolland on the contrary thought Poincaré's long silence on the letter a crime), and blamed Clemenceau's impetuosity for robbing the Allies of a potential diplomatic maneuver. But Czernin's speech made it sufficiently clear that separate peace with Austria was only possible following a German military defeat on the Western Front—when it would no longer be needed.

A historic turning point had been reached. The six-hundred-year-old Habsburg Empire now had no hope of survival save by the arms of its Prussian ally. In the overwhelming frustration of his country's situation, moderate pacifist intellectual Stefan Zweig found himself turning to thoughts of violent revolution: "Can one want to live, if this crime goes on endlessly and if its authors escape without punishment?"

Coincidentally with the Clemenceau–Czernin duel, the Allies cemented their Supreme Command structure, and before the affair's denouement, Ludendorff unleashed his second offensive.

Foch having argued persuasively that his Doullens title of "coordinator" gave him a function only on defense, since there was nothing to coordinate when the enemy was not attacking, Clemenceau agreed to call a new conference. On the Easter Monday (April 3) following Czernin's speech, the Allied leaders met in the town hall of Beauvais, ancient bishopric 45 miles north of Paris. Thither Lloyd George motored, changing automobiles to alternate his company between Haig and Haig's chief of staff. He had what he imagined would be good news to impart to his generals. The "Michael" crisis had provided him with a weapon against the stubborn, business-as-usual British shippers, who now found it possible to divert enough cargo vessels to ferry American troops across the Atlantic at a greatly accelerated pace. Left mainly to their own slow-starting shipping program, the Yanks had been sending doughboys over at the rate of a thousand a day; British shippers, stirred into action, promised at least to double that.

Lloyd George presumed that the country boys from across the sea could fill the depleted ranks of the shattered British outfits and permit him to keep the B-men safely at home. He envisioned the fulfillment of a scheme he had proposed to Colonel House back in December, that Americans in company-size units be put into British battalions. Haig had at that time approved, and proposed going a step farther and training American battalions in British brigades. But now, to the Prime Minister's surprise, the Field Marshal and his chief of staff were "cool and sniffy." They gave him to understand that the incorporation of American troops into British units would be a nuisance, creating extra staff work, and in some ways providing a source of weakness rather than strength.

Apart from a revulsion against any idea emanating from Lloyd George and a natural inclination to asperse other nation's soldiers (which did not stop short of Irish, Australians, and Canadians), Haig could afford to be negative on the still remote manpower from America. His ruined Fifth Army had now been relieved by the French in the Oise–Somme area, and Lloyd George's "Eastern" offensive ideas had been squelched in favor of the transfer of British Empire troops from Egypt and Mesopotamia to France. As a result, even though the B-men were still withheld, Haig could reconstitute his Fifth Army, or rather replace it with a new organization, the Fourth Army, and securely hold a compact front. The improvement left him feeling so comfortable that he had done a complete about-face in his attitude toward Foch. He no longer saw any great necessity for an Allied coordinator; and as for transforming the coordinator into a commander, he found the idea obnoxious.

Haig's opposition strengthened Lloyd George's determination to give Foch what he wanted. Pershing and Bliss, who supported the unified command as the best way to guarantee American equity, had been especially invited to Beauvais by Clemenceau, and their presence made it difficult for Haig to do more at the town-hall meeting than sulk. Pétain, whatever his feelings, as usual concealed them. The motion to which Lloyd George gave Britain's formal support stated that the three Allied governments "entrust to General Foch the strategic direction of military operations." At the suggestion of General Wilson a reservation was attached giving each Allied commander the right of appeal to his own government "if, in his opinion, the safety of his army is compromised by any order received from General Foch."

After the meeting, the Prime Minister went so far as to promise Foch he would speak to the Cabinet about conferring the title "Allied commander in chief."

He indicated the role he now felt that Foch played by a jocular question: "Which must I bet on, Ludendorff or Foch?"

"Back me and you will win," Foch promised without hesitation.

In the prospect of a growing inter-Allied reserve Foch already saw the dim shape of a major Allied counteroffensive. That, he realized, was still some distance off; for the immediate future he wanted an attack against the new, not yet solidified, German front northeast of Amiens. But even that limited project was premature. Ludendorff still held a strong advantage on the board. As the Allies met in Beauvais, Crown Prince Rupprecht's army group in Flanders was hauling up guns and supplies for *Friedensturm*'s second phase, originally coded "George," but because of the unexpected success and duration of "Michael" now scaled down and with a sort of irony rechristened "Georgette." After a pair of minor distracting attacks on the old "Michael" front to the south, suddenly on the morning of April 9 the Hutier formula was repeated: a short, intensive barrage by secretly massed artillery, clouds of phosgene and mustard, and advances by shock troops infiltrating in small parties. The blow fell against the

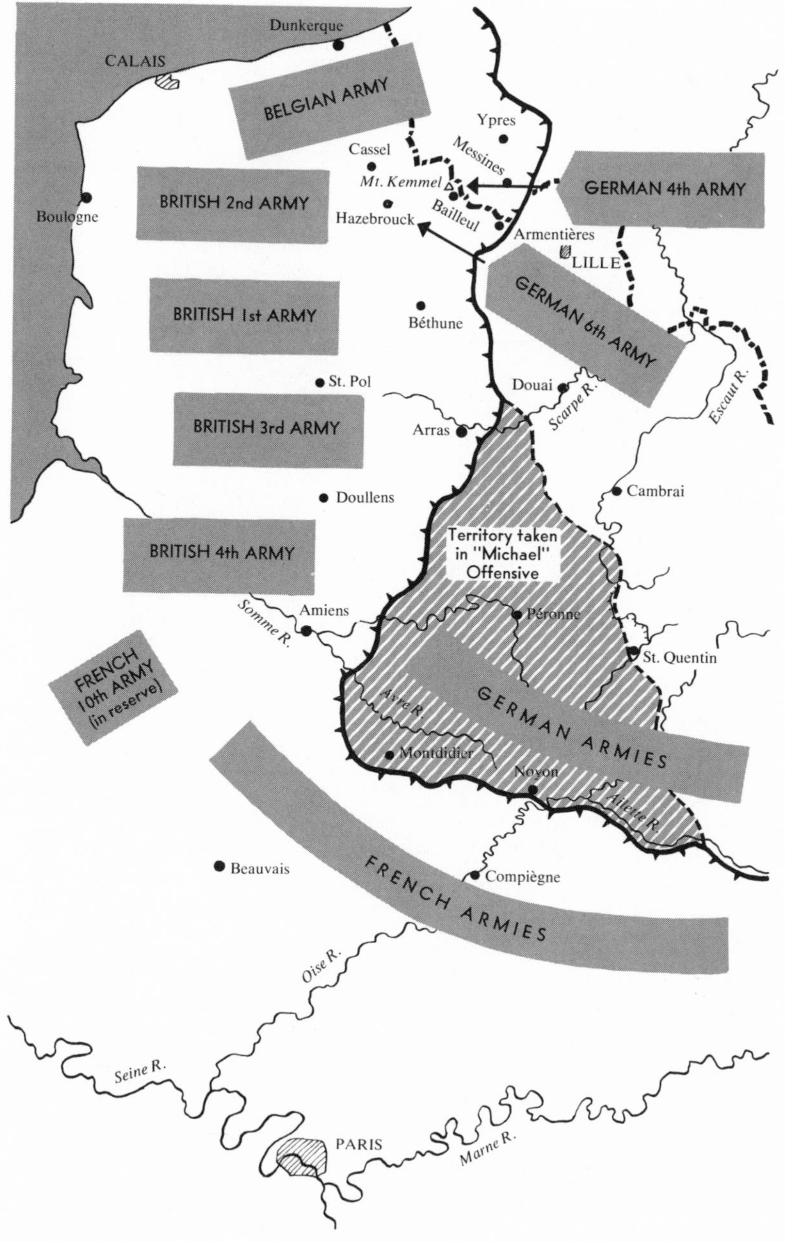

"Georgette" offensive.

British First Army, in the lugubrious Flemish "sea of mud" west of Lille.

On the first day, nine shock divisions were committed against four defending divisions. One of these was part of the Portuguese Expeditionary Corps, recruited by Britain through political and economic leverage. The Portuguese soldiers had given a good account of themselves up to now, despite the lack of any visible reason for their being there, but a new government had come into power in Lisbon, pledged to getting its men out of a war nobody in Portugal could see any sense in. The British were in the process of replacing the Portuguese in the line at the moment of the attack. As a result, only one division was holding a section which two had formerly held, and it gave way. The British overblamed the Portuguese for a five-and-a-half-mile German advance through the Flemish morass, pocked with water-filled shell craters. Next day the Germans committed five more divisions, extending the fighting front north to include the right of the British Second Army. Here they overran two British divisions that had been through "Michael" and had been brought north to rest. Armentières and Messines fell to the shock troops, who threatened to pinch off the entire northern end of the line.

Mercurial Haig swung from optimism to despair. "One moment," noted Lloyd George, "the attack was only a feint, then GHQ rushed to the other extreme . . . and came to the conclusion that the Channel ports were in imminent jeopardy." Such was the alarm that the Cabinet in London pressed Clemenceau to have the entire British sector treated as part of the French front, and all but swallowed its objections to the designation of Foch as commander in chief.

Once more desperate for French help, Haig now had to importune Foch rather than Pétain. Foch responded promptly enough by driving north from his new headquarters in the village of Sarcus, near Amiens, but to Haig's intense disappointment, proved even more difficult than Pétain. Foch found the battlefield situation much less alarming than did Haig, though (again like Pétain), he viewed the British collapse as a reflection on British defensive skill. Foch was busy constituting a reserve of his own around the headquarters staff of the French Tenth Army, recalled from Italy. He had only four divisions, hardly enough for a serious counteroffensive, but it was a nucleus he wanted to conserve. On the evening of the first day of "Georgette" (April 9), he moved the Tenth Army a little closer to the scene of action, but refused to commit any of it. The next night, in response to a fresh written protestation from Haig, he directed Pétain to scrape one division from his front and send it by rail to Dunkerque. Next evening, the German offensive having widened farther, Haig's operations chief called at Foch's new headquarters, to deliver a letter from Haig emphasizing the exhaustion of the British forces in Flanders and strongly requesting the immediate concentration of at least four French divisions between St-Omer and Dunkerque, in the immediate rear of the threatened front.

Foch remained resolutely cautious, sending only a French cavalry corps (equivalent in firepower to an infantry division) to join the division at Dunkerque, but moving the little Tenth Army into the British zone to free British reserves in the Somme area; Haig was thus able to send some help north. Foch lectured the exasperated British on tactics, ordered the governor of Dunkerque to open dikes, making muddy Flanders even muddier, and asked the Belgians, in the extreme north, to stretch their line southward. Compliance with this last request was not forthcoming, because King Albert feared that he would be giving the Germans a pretext for canceling his dynastic rights if he took any of his army out of Belgium.

Late in the evening of April 11, Haig issued a message to his troops: "There is no other course open to us but to fight it out. Every position must be held to the last man. . . . With our backs to the wall and believing in the justice of our cause each one must fight to the end. . . ."

The message became famous, but it did not accurately describe the real situation. Haig actually had no thought of committing the British Army to a fight to the last man on French soil; on the contrary, he discussed with Wilson, the chief of the General Staff, the question of retreat to the ports and preparation for evacuation. His general commanding the threatened front, Plumer, was also not planning to hold every position to the last man. Plumer, the portly, sensible, unruffled type of British general, had little room in which to maneuver, but what room he had, he meant to use. Despite Haig's message, Plumer ordered withdrawals.

The fourth day of the battle, April 12, found the British pressed back in a great bulge between Ypres in the north and Béthune in the south, with the arc of the bulge pointing at Hazebrouck, a key road–rail junction barely six miles to the west, and less than twenty-five miles south of the nearest point of the coast, Dunkerque. Yet the mud-covered Tommies, their regiments reduced to battalions and their battalions to companies, fighting till they dropped from exhaustion in the ditches, under the hedges, in the open fields, sleeping till they were kicked awake to fight again, were giving ground only slowly, and making the German attackers pay for it.

Still the German pressure continued, and Plumer, notwithstanding Haig's "backs to the wall," ordered a withdrawal from the entire Passchendaele salient, won at immense cost in 1917. Thus, as Lloyd George said, "The worthless territory which it had taken four months' terrible fighting and 400,000 casualties to capture was abandoned in a single night. The conquest was a nightmare, the relinquishment of it was a relief and an inspiration."

Late on the evening of April 16, Foch motored north to a rendezvous with Plumer, whom he met with Robillot, commander of the French Second Cavalry Corps, on the road in pitch darkness, with the bombardment resounding all around them. Foch at last agreed to commit more French reserves, and accompanying Plumer back to his headquarters, telephoned Weygand to move a division by truck to Steenworde, west of Ypres.

The visible British dependence on French reserves brought the London Cabinet's approval of Foch's title as Allied generalissimo, but the fillip had no effect on Foch's parsimony. Haig and Wilson switched tactics and proposed to Foch that

Plumer's initiative be carried to its logical conclusion and the whole northern end of the line pulled back, giving up Dunkerque. A move long advocated by Pétain, it would shorten the line and give Haig some reserves. But Foch refused categorically.

From the moment of his appointment, Foch had been pressed by the British to say which he would defend if the choice had to be made, Paris or the ports. Foch's natural penchant for combativeness in doctrine and expression helped him find the formula for an answer: "*Ne lâchez pas pied*" ("Don't give way; stand where you are"). The application of the formula to Dunkerque at first glance seemed rash, especially since giving up Dunkerque would make it more difficult for the British to leave France. Yet there was some sense in Foch's attitude. He himself put it that one had to be very firm with the British, who didn't give in readily. In his account of the Ypres battle of 1914, he liked to tell how Sir John French had announced his decision to retreat, but when Foch answered, "Good, but as for me, I'm staying!" Sir John had at once rejoined, "Then I'm staying too!"

If he let the British surrender Dunkerque, Foch thought, he might lose some of his authority over them, and if they decided to pull out for home he would have more difficulty ordering them to stay. Clemenceau agreed. A not insignificant factor was the refusal of the Belgian Army to leave Belgian soil, which meant its elimination from the battlefield if Dunkerque were abandoned.

Over the next few days, as the Germans forced Plumer's men back step by step, Foch continued to move French formations north, one after the other, until there were five French infantry and three cavalry divisions in this distant part of the line. All were borrowed from Pétain, whose line steadily thinned; the Tenth Army, Foch's own reserve, though again moved nearer the scene of action, was still kept in hand.

On their side, the Germans were performing a labor of Hercules in keeping ammunition and rations wagons moving. The German infantry was as exhausted as the British. "The men could hardly fire their rifles," wrote Rudolf Binding. "They were like used-up horses which stand fast in the shafts and dumbly take the blows of the whip without a movement."

Yet Ludendorff determined to make one more effort. If the chain of low hills now just in front of the German Sixth Army could be captured, heavy guns could reach Boulogne and Calais. It was worth a gamble.

Ludendorff had noted Foch's appointment with no little interest, and he now sought first to halt the flow of Allied reserves north by a diversion on the old "Michael" battlefield. The resulting combat at Villers-Bretonneux, east of Amiens, was notable for a first: the Germans used fourteen of their Daimler tanks, and three of them ran head on into three British Mark IV's. Two British and one German tank were knocked out in this *Monitor*-versus-*Merrimac* of tank history. But the attack, improvised with local forces, bogged down amid counterattacks ordered by Foch and executed by Australians and French Moroccans, and failed in its desired effect.

The renewal of the offensive in the north, however, by General von Arnim's Sixth Army, chalked up another opening-day success, similar to those of March 21 and April 9. Four French divisions had relieved the exhausted British of Plumer's army around Mount Kemmel, a low height (100–150 meters) that would have provided a strong anchor had it had enough space in front for a field of fire. The German line, however, was already well within a mile. Foch was aware of the danger, and prescribed a Foch-like solution: the French Twenty-eighth Division, atop Kemmel, should attack and gain enough ground in front to make the height secure. In the early hours of April 25, parts of two regiments were moving out to try to apply the prescribed remedy when Colonel Bruchmüller's newest barrage cut loose.

It was the first time the French had come under the Burchmüller firestorm, and what they got on their narrow front was an exceptionally intense version. Captain Hans von Pranckh of the Bavarian Alpine Corps described its sound and fury:

> The sky in the north and east reddens like a distant storm. . . . Thick layers of gas shells whisper over us. Softly and almost carefully they hiss over behind Kemmel. . . . The Kemmel slope disappears in a whitish wall of gas mist, which slowly spreads toward us. Soon our eyes begin to water, and it is time to put on the gas masks. . . . The ceaseless flight of the German gas shells lasts for three hours; by 6 A.M. everything is gray and dim. Then the gas fire changes to explosive . . . a roaring and whining and howling of projectiles. Close forward now a thundering crashing, fountain of earth rising in the air, flames burning fiercely, lumps of earth and whirring splinters. . . . The walls of the earthworks crumple and explode, clods are loosened by the shock, the noise is frightful. . . . Roaring, stamping, raging, the annihilation fire dances over the slope and down again; it crumbles, tears, destroys, it seems almighty. . . .

Then the assault:

> Gray-blue figures out of the half-buried entrances of the dugouts spring up and try to pull machine guns after them; once they bring one into position, but the hand grenades of our first wave destroy weapon and crew before it can be used. Most of the defenders think no more about resistance; when the firestorm has passed over them, the German shock troops are already before them, and it is better to raise one's hands. Ever more frequently come the blue figures creeping out of the ground, smeared with mud, with fixed, bewildered eyes. . . .

The Alpine Corps swarmed over Kemmel, capturing the height and six thousand prisoners.

Receiving the news at Avesnes, Hindenburg and Ludendorff once more had visions of a major prize, this time the town of Cassel, on a hill commanding Dunkerque. Inter-Allied relations suffered as the British blamed the French for losing "impregnable" Kemmel; and a joint counterattack to recover it broke down through failure in communications.

But the French soon got themselves organized on their new front as the *Détachement de l'Armée Nord* ("Army Detachment North"), or D.A.N., and over the next days, repeated bloody attacks and counterattacks left both sides decimated and exhausted, with no change in their positions.

As the fighting degenerated into a contest for a few blood-soaked square miles, a repetition of the early Western Front battles, Ludendorff broke off "Georgette." Of the 208 divisions he had now been able to assemble, he had been forced to engage 126 in his two offensives, including nearly all the shock divisions. Casualties had been heavy. But Allied casualties had been heavy too, and there was the large bag of prisoners besides. Most significantly, the heaviest losses and nearly all the prisoners were British. The target British Army was now seriously reduced in strength, and pressed close to the sea.

One more Hutier surprise, Ludendorff calculated, would confront Lloyd George and Haig with a choice between abandoning the Channel ports in order to preserve contact with the French, and evacuating the British Expeditionary Force. Ludendorff had no more doubt than Foch and Clemenceau as to which course the British would choose.

Hindenburg thought of an attractive by-product of reaching the Channel shore—not only could the British southern coast be bombarded by heavy artillery, but a modest improvement in the Paris gun—"that mysterious marvel of technical science"—would bring London under fire.

11

THE AMERICANS

On the Allied side of the battle line the end of "Georgette" brought uneasy relief. Fresh clumps of crosses dotted shell holes, ditches, fields, and hillsides across Picardy and Flanders. Churches and schoolhouses were jammed with wounded men, the decks of Channel steamers carpeted with litters. In the cold arithmetic of army headquarters, ten British divisions had been reduced to cadre—commanding generals and staffs, with no troops—while some fifty others, British and French, were categorized as "tired"—that is, reduced to far below normal strength.

Lloyd George, who previously had been under pressure from the British Left to hold down British casualties, suddenly found himself under pressure from the Right to provide the British Army with replacements. Instead of limiting the British commitment in the slaughterhouse of France, he now had to increase it. He canceled exemptions for men in forty-four occupations formerly held essential, persuaded mine-union leaders to accept a draft of fifty thousand young coal miners, and in Parliament carried a new, broader conscription bill, but still did not escape acerb Opposition strictures over his failure to give Haig enough men. The adroit Welshman parried the parliamentary attack with his usual forensic skill, abetted by trickery; he gave the House manpower figures for the Western Front that included noncombatant laborers and British troops en route from Italy.

Foch and Pétain were equally preoccupied with the manpower problem. Never before had a warring nation found itself in the situation in which both France and Germany now stood—that is, with so many soldiers buried and incapacitated that, putting every other consideration aside, it was impossible to replenish the depleted formations.

Had Foch even been certain that Ludendorff was in the same case as himself, he would have been somewhat reassured. But Foch shared with many other Allied leaders an apprehension that Russia might furnish a manpower reservoir of either combat troops or labor battalions for Germany. This fear led Foch to give support, even at the price of committing a little of the precious Allied manpower reserve, to schemes designed to overthrow the Bolsheviks, mistakenly regarded as friends of the enemy. The Bolshevik leaders in Petrograd were well aware of, and even exaggerated, the sentiments of Russia's former allies. "The discord among the great bandits of imperialism saves us for the moment," wrote Kalinin to Romain Rolland.

Whatever resources Ludendorff might find, Foch knew he had to discover fresh ones on the Allied side. He called for the return of the French and British troops from Italy, but the Italians still balked. A compromise was reached by which some of the French and British divisions would be returned to France, and would be supplemented a little later by troops from the Italian headquarters reserve. A few troops could be taken from the Allied force camped at Salonika, Greece, and Foch welcomed the transfer of British Empire divisions from Egypt and Mesopotamia. But even these reinforcements left the Allied battle line stretched tight. As a general reserve, he still had only the four divisions of the little French Tenth Army. His nervy gamble in withholding them from "Georgette" was richly vindicated, but they did not constitute a strong enough force either to plug a new breakthrough on the "Michael" scale or to undertake a limited counteroffensive to push the Germans back from the sensitive Amiens rail center.

Pétain's problem was that the commitment in Flanders of the D.A.N.—ultimately ten divisions plus heavy artillery—added to that of the thirty-plus divisions of French First, Third, and Fifth Armies west of the Oise, left him with only fifty-five divisions, many far below strength, to hold the long front from the Oise to Switzerland.

There was obviously only one place to turn. General Pershing's gesture of March 28 had been on the American side more sentimental than substantial, since only six (four complete) American divisions were in France. One division, the First, was now ready for serious battle. The First was moved to a reserve position north of Paris. Otherwise, about all that could be done was to move American divisions a little more hastily into their programmed quiet-sector status in Lorraine and the Vosges to relieve French divisions for battle. Pershing readily acquiesced in these moves, but there agreement ended between Pershing and Foch. Agreement on the other hand among Foch, Pétain, Haig, Clemenceau, and Lloyd George began at this very point. All the Allied generals and statesmen were now united on the desirability of shipping American infantry across the sea as rapidly as possible to fill the holes Ludendorff had torn in their armies. The project that Lloyd George had broached to Haig in the frosty drive to the Beauvais town hall now had the endorsement of everyone—the British government, the French government, the Supreme War Council, the Allied generals, even the Washington government—everyone except Pershing.

A Missouri boy with a strong streak of the reputed Missouri stubbornness, Pershing had the advantages and disadvantages of an invincible American military innocence. He had fought the Indians on the plains and the Moros in the Philippine jungles, and had even been an observer of the Russo-Japanese War of 1905, but he grasped the new military technology scarcely at all. He considered that the development of trench warfare was the result not of the devastating character of the new weapons, in which he took slight interest, but simply of laziness and want of spirit by the generals and their troops. His views were an echo of those entertained by Foch and the rest before the war, and even some distance into it, but it was astonishing that an American general, afforded the opportunity to study objectively the appalling lessons of 1914, 1915, 1916, and 1917, should in 1918 arrive on the battlefield armed with the doctrine of 1898. He had a Haig-like view of the troops of his allies, except that he included the British in his strictures, and even singled them out, since the common language facilitated the infection of his Yanks by the demoralized Tommies. He was reputed to have made an adverse comment on the appearance of British troops that had provoked an astringent British rejoinder: "Wait till your fellows have torn their guts out on the barbed wire for a couple of years and see how they look."

The Allies would have found it easy to overlook Pershing's tactlessness and obtuseness had it not been for his unshakable opposition to what had come to be called "amalgamation." The word had originally been applied to the very effective training program by which arriving American divisions had been temporarily broken up into small groups for coach-and-pupil indoctrination with French and British outfits. Such training on an individual basis and under actual combat conditions was much superior to conventional drills and exercises, and its follow-up, the assignment of the division to a quiet sector, was infinitely better than maneuvers against a simulated enemy. Quiet sectors were quiet only in the sense of having no offensive going on. Their principal feature was the "raid," a single experience of which turned rookies into veterans. A combination of reconnaissance and combat patrol, the raid was most distinctively characterized by its preceding bombardment, a "box barrage" that first pounded a section of front-line trench and then cut it off by laying down a curtain of fire in its rear and on either side, while the raiding party, numbering up to several hundred, crossed No-Man's-Land to grenade and bayonet the survivors. The Iowa boys of the 168th Infantry, Rainbow Division, lost twenty-one killed and twenty-two wounded in their first enemy raid, and nine killed and thirty-three wounded in their own first raid, carried out under French tutelage.

To the amalgamation of the training program, Pershing had no objections. He admitted freely that the American Expeditionary Force had much to learn from the older Allies, especially the French. To American officers the designations G-1, G-2, G-3, and G-4 (for the personnel, intelligence, operations, and supply sections of a staff) were intriguing mysteries. Pershing and Bullard were astonished to learn that orders for a divisional attack required more than one staff officer to prepare. Younger American officers were charmingly ignorant. A wealthy air-force officer, unable to figure out how to prepare his payroll, simply drew his own check and paid his men himself.

The doughboys too had many lessons to learn. They could shoot their rifles; the country boys were all hunters, and even the city boys could quickly master the excellent clip-loading, bolt-action Springfields and Enfields. But they knew nothing of grenades, mortars, gas alarms, rockets, night signaling, wire cutting, telephone maintenance, and other technical niceties of the new warfare. Up to now the American Army had known only five kinds of soldier—infantry, cavalry, artillery, signal corps, and engineers—and a whole array of new specialists had to be created, down to dog and pigeon handlers.

French officers, indoctrinated by Pétain, were supertactful with their large, innocent, and confident protégés. They organized training camps for the enlisted men and schools for the officers, who went under protest, but profited. The program was operating with commendable smoothness when Ludendorff suddenly upset the orderly timetable with "Michael."

The thought in all Allied minds was that since the Americans had no artillery anyway, it would be sensible to bring them over in small infantry units and fit them into Allied formations. Lloyd George, Haig, Foch, and Pétain had all discussed the idea at one time or another since January. Now the Supreme War Council passed a resolution proposing that during the present emergency only American infantry and machine gunners should be sent over. General Bliss, the American representative, acquiesced. Bliss notwithstanding, the Supreme War Council proposed and Pershing disposed. Amalgamation was for training, not combat, emergency or no emergency. As soon as enough divisions were trained, the American Army would go into the line under Pershing's command. Its sector was all picked out—Lorraine-Vosges—and in his headquarters at Chaumont, behind the future American front, Pershing was already busy mapping operations against the St.-Mihiel salient and Metz. The American Army must be kept as an entity, with its own complete large units, which meant, more than anything else, its own artillery. This struck Clemenceau as preposterous. "You want to bring artillery and France is overflowing with it!" he told Pershing, who, tight-lipped, unyielding, evasively courteous, caused partings in which, according to Clemenceau, "smiles on both sides concealed gnashings of teeth."

Inevitably, the Allies decided to go over the head of this stubborn American general who knew so little about war anyway. The British made the first attempt. Through their ambassador in Washington, a smooth, titled professional named Lord Reading, they sounded out the American government, and found it something of a pushover. The "Michael" crisis had brought a rude awakening among the League-of-Nations builders in Washington. President Wilson, having long struggled with his conscience over the question of should-we-go-to-war-or-shouldn't-we, suddenly faced the embarrassing possibility that his conscience might as well not have bothered to struggle; the thing might be settled without America. The very abatement of "Michael" and the switch to "Georgette" seemed an ominous portent of the depths of German resources. Wilson and Secretary of State Lansing, both distinctly anglophile, were perhaps especially affected by the fact that the blows were falling on the British, but in any case the reality of the danger was enough to scare them into looking for ways to help. They quickly agreed to Lord Reading's proposal that the American drafts be increased and that

Foch (left) and Pershing at Pershing's headquarters, Chaumont, June 17, 1918. CREDIT: U.S. SIGNAL CORPS

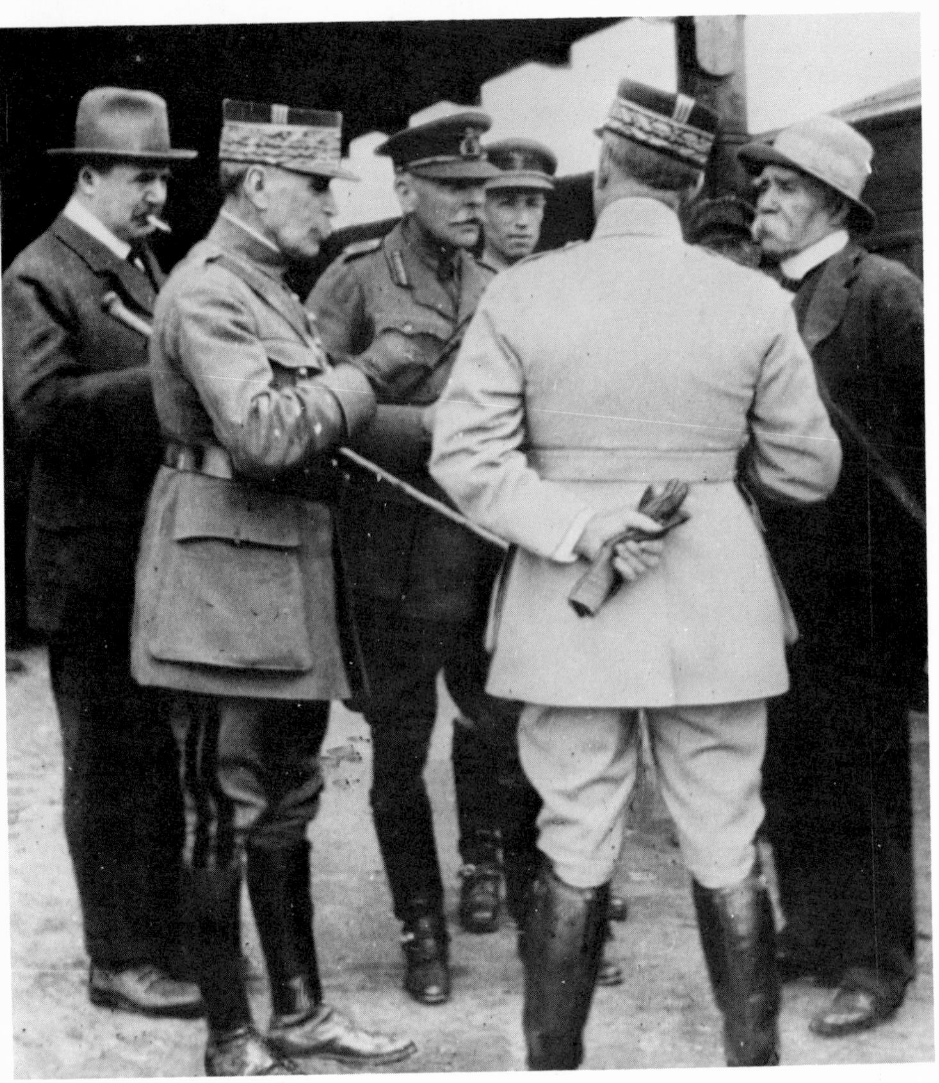

Haig (facing camera) meets Foch (left) and Clemenceau at the railroad station at Amiens, target of the "Michael" offensive. CREDIT: ROGER VIOLLET

Left to right: Hindenburg, Kaiser Wilhelm II, and Ludendorff at Supreme Headquarters, 1917. CREDIT: WEHRGESCHICHTLICHES MUSEUM

General Petain (second from left, with cane) and General Mangin (second from right) in the town of Villers-Cotterets, July 22. The guns are captured trophies. CREDIT: ÉTABLISSEMENT CINÉMATOGRAPHIQUE ET PHOTOGRAPHIQUE DES ARMÉES

Ludendorff. CREDIT: SÜDDEUTSCHER VERLAG

Foch. CREDIT: IMPERIAL WAR MUSEUM

Pigeons, an important part of communications for all armies, being carried to the front line by Royal Engineer motorcyclist, June 2, 1918. CREDIT: IMPERIAL WAR MUSEUM

German engineers laying gas projectors. CREDIT: IMPERIAL WAR MUSEUM

British women ambulance drivers attending to their cars at St. Omer, February 28, 1918. CREDIT: IMPERIAL WAR MUSEUM

Wounded horses and mules in a French veterinary hospital at St. Omer, April 16, 1918. CREDIT: IMPERIAL WAR MUSEUM

German flame throwers. CREDIT: IMPERIAL WAR MUSEUM

120,000 men, in whatever state of training, be shipped across at once to fill the depleted British ranks.

Wilson, however, had the prudence to attach the condition that the matter be cleared with Pershing. As a result, Pershing received an invitation to come to London, where he was put up at the Savoy and given dinner at St. James's Palace by the King's brother, the Duke of Connaught, after which, softened up by the preliminary bombardment, he was assaulted with the British plan: ship over all the American riflemen and machine gunners that were ready, or half ready, and put them straight into British outfits in Flanders and Picardy. What, Lord Milner asked, did Pershing say to that?

Pershing said No. The American units, as they arrived, would be brigaded with larger Allied units for training, and if an emergency arose, would fight, but otherwise they would complete their training and be withdrawn to form large American units to build the American Army.

Lord Milner cited a fresh cablegram from Lord Reading stating that the President had agreed in writing to the British plan. That cut no ice with Pershing. He still said No, relying on Wilson's repeatedly expressed distaste for dealing with military problems to make his decision stick.

Yet there was an aspect of the British plan that was too attractive for Pershing to resist—the large step-up in the shipping rate. The British now said they had the ships to bring him his army much more quickly than he had hoped, and who knew—if he delayed too long the war might be over.

There lay the basis for the compromise that was worked out. In May, the infantry, engineers, signal corps, and headquarters units of six divisions would be brought over, for training with the British Army; any surplus shipping space would be allocated to artillery, which would train with the French as already planned, and to rear-echelon troops.

The London agreement elated Pershing, who now envisioned an American Army of several corps by fall, growing by the spring of 1919 to 1,500,000 men. It satisfied the British, who saw in the infantry of six large American divisions, divided among their four field armies, replacements for the ten British divisions destroyed by Ludendorff. But it did not go over at all with the French, who felt bamboozled by the Anglo-Saxons. Clemenceau was having none of that; if the Americans coming in May were to go to the British, then the Americans coming in June should go to the French. To Foch, who whatever his legal status might be, was in Clemenceau's eyes simply another French general, he assigned the task of putting this across to Pershing. Foch, at one with Haig and Pétain in concern over the infantry shortage, was more than willing.

Inviting Pershing to his headquarters, he began with a disarming query about the implementation of the agreement to put the first four American divisions into the line, and then abruptly switched, like an amateur seducer, to the real point, proposing bluntly that only infantry and machine gunners be brought over for the next three months. Pershing protested that unless division and corps troops were brought over, he would not have an American Army until 1919, whereas the London agreement seemed to promise him one by the autumn of 1918. Foch, now a frustrated seducer, and never the calmest of men anyway, grew heated: "If we do not take steps to prevent the disaster which is threatened at present, the American Army may arrive in France to find the British pushed into the sea and the French driven back behind the Loire, while it tries in vain to organize on lost battlefields over the graves of Allied soldiers."

Foch's eloquence had no more effect than the Duke of Connaught's hospitality. Clemenceau, receiving news of the negative results, had recourse to another conference of the prime ministers, a device that automatically put Pershing at a disadvantage. The Supreme War Council was convened at Abbeville, on the Channel coast, near the embattled Flanders front, on May 1.

"Extreme pessimism prevailed regarding present crisis," Pershing noted in his diary. "Everybody at high tension. Allies persistent in urging unlimited shipment of our infantry and machine gun units."

The pessimism and tension were real, but they were not over the present crisis, "Georgette," which the French and British now knew they had mastered. Their problem was how to meet Ludendorff's next blow, as inevitable as it was unpredictable. Even if during the present month Americans arrived in numbers sufficient to restore the British Army, what about the stretched-thin French Army, and what about Foch's reserve? Clemenceau reminded his hearers of an earlier inter-Allied agreement, and asserted that to keep it, all Americans brought over in June must go to the French. Pershing's original instructions of May 26, 1917, had in fact stated that until the American Expeditionary Force was strong enough to form an independent command, "you will cooperate as a component of whatever army you may be assigned by the French Government"—very different instructions from those given by Kitchener to the British Expeditionary Force of 1914.

Turning to Pershing's insistence on a proper proportioning of his troops between front-line and rear-echelon men, Clemenceau acidly observed that of 400,000 Americans now in France, only 125,000 were combat troops.

Lord Milner rose in defense of the London agreement, and the air grew warm as the old Tiger reiterated his objections even more categorically.

Lloyd George, something of a British lion to Clemenceau's tiger, then made one of the lucid, extemporaneous speeches for which he was renowned. Supporting Clemenceau in principle, he said that Allied interests were identical and that unity must be maintained. He then referred to the British divisions that had been too shot up to be reconstituted with available manpower, interrupting himself to ask Foch the exact number (ten), and pointed out, "As we cannot again put them in line, they must be replaced by new units. The Germans are now fighting with the object of using up our effectives. If they can do this without exhausting their own reserves they will, sometime, deal us a blow which we shall not be able to parry. . . . In May, in fact, either of our two armies may be hard pressed. That is the one which should be reinforced. It is not desirable now to decide how troops arriving in June should be allotted." And as Pershing showed no signs of surrender, the Prime Minister reiterated Foch's warning in another image: "If we lose this battle, we shall need tonnage to take home what is left of the British and American armies."

Clemenceau adjourned the meeting to give Foch and Lord Milner a chance to bully Pershing in private, but the Missourian turned their arguments against them by saying that if the Allies were on the point of collapse and the American Army might have to bear the brunt of the war, it would be wiser not to fritter it away.

In the end, Pershing was bribed with another shipping promise; Lloyd George would scrape up still more ships and the May and June totals would be raised to minimums of 130,000 and 150,000 men respectively. The May arrangement with the British would stand, and the June troops would be turned over to Pershing for allocation, with the implied understanding, strong enough for Clemenceau to accept, that they would be available to Foch.

As it happened, the American Expeditionary Force was infantry-heavy anyway, Pershing having opted for a large, "square" division consisting of four regiments of infantry and one of artillery, with four battalions in each. Each infantry battalion had four rifle companies of 250 men. The American Army, piecemeal or in a lump, was certain to have exceptionally high rifle strength—in other words, to be extra valuable in the attack.

The Abbeville agreement had an interesting follow-up the next day. Clemenceau did not find it necessary to invite the Americans to an intimate gathering at the local prefect's house, and yet it was probably the assurance that the Yanks were coming that made the conference a success. The purpose of the meeting was to define "the strategic objectives of the Allied armies in France." Two points were set forth: first, the junction between the French and British armies must be maintained; and second, the Channel ports must be covered. But, and here was the crux, if circumstances required the Commander in Chief to decide between the two objectives, the choice would be in favor of the former, and the British Army would be withdrawn toward the Somme; in other words, there would be no evacuation.

Pershing returned to Chaumont in high spirits. Almost at once he received two surprising requests from the British. The first was a petition from Haig for the loan of ten thousand American artillerymen, despite all the strenuous arguing about shipping only infantrymen over. Pershing dryly replied that all his artillerymen were busy except some howitzer crews whose British-promised weapons had not materialized. The second request was even more unexpected. It reached Pershing at second hand, having originally been made by the British military attaché in Washington. It was to the effect that the American Ninety-second Division, among those scheduled for shipment, should not be assigned to the British sector for training. The British wished to make a present of this division to the French. The gesture, so little in keeping with the tenor of the month-long inter-Allied argument, was prompted by the fact that the Ninety-second was a "colored" division. Pershing protested, but Washington acceded, and in the end the Ninety-second was sent for training to the French, who had already gratefully accepted the Ninety-third Division, whose four black infantry regiments not only trained but served with the French to the end of the war.

Pershing had other problems: venereal disease among the troops, at which the French and British shrugged, but which the general found an outrage and took vigorous steps to hold down; disciplinary troubles with the doughboys, ranging from chicken stealing, drunkenness, and window breaking on British railways to serious crime—arrests at a base camp in England ran to 1 per cent of the command strength per night; the aircraft dilemma, whether to let the French and British build planes for the American air force with the excellent Liberty engine shipped from home, or to hold out for an American full-plane production program; shortages of all kinds of equipment, which he tried to make good by a salvage program for shoes, boots, uniforms, and haversacks; a shortage of indispensable animal power, which the French promised but failed to provide and for which the answer was finally found in Spain; and a shortage of rear-echelon troops. This last, Pershing's G-4, General Johnson Hagood, met in part with imported Chinese "coolies" and volunteer French war widows; in a competition, five hundred Breton peasant women unloaded cargoes faster than five hundred of the professional Chinese.

Not all the friction was inter-Allied. General Edwards, a military fussbudget who commanded the Twenty-sixth (Yankee) Division, in relieving General Bullard's U.S. First Division in Lorraine, wrote a lengthy nit-picking report on the condition of the position as left by the First. Pershing had no trouble putting that one in perspective; he told Bullard to forget it.

On the credit side of Pershing's ledger, the First Division moved from its reserve position into the line in the active Somme–Oise sector, the first American outfit to do so, though it was put into a French army corps. Bullard reported to the corps commander, General Vandenburg, who proved to be a battered veteran who "had been shot in the leg and could hardly walk, and shot in the mouth and could hardly talk." Bullard complained to Vandenburg that a French colonial division had drunk up all the wine in the sector; Vandenburg beamed through his ruined face and said this proved that though colonials, they were good Frenchmen.

The Yanks were coming along, but they still had things to learn. Despite gas-mask drills, the First was slow to react to a gas alarm when it entered the line in its new sector, and took eight hundred casualties, while the Twenty-sixth, commanded by carping General Edwards, was given a rude welcome to Seicheprey, in Lorraine, in the form of a heavy German raid that inflicted a thousand casualties and carried off 180 prisoners. German propaganda trumpeted Seicheprey at home and in the neutral countries, but to sober observers the main news was that American troops were really in the battle line.

Insiders knew something more than that. By the end of May, the massive ferrying program that Lloyd George had gotten started was producing truly impressive results. The

German Navy command had decided to forgo U-boat attacks on the plodding troop convoys with their strong destroyer escorts and to concentrate on less heavily guarded shipping. That decision may have been a mistake. In May, convoy after convoy of former liners, fruit steamers and tramps, their decks and cargo holds bulging with seasick young Americans, made it safely across without the loss of a ship or man. The Supreme War Council's May quota was far exceeded; Pershing's American Army virtually doubled before his eyes.

Edward A. Filene, the Boston department-store magnate who presided over the Tonnage Committee of the U.S. Chamber of Commerce, was actually shocked by the achievement, pointing out that "at the request of the Allies we are now sending men to France in absolutely senseless numbers . . . without having tonnage enough to keep them supplied." Filene concluded that America was risking her sons' lives on the assumption that the government's shipbuilding program would close the supply-shipping gap in time. It was a typical American assumption: if it had to be done, and it involved production, it could be done.

12

LUDENDORFF'S CHESS GAME

I stood this morning at 10 A.M., a dim, cool Sunday morning, at the grave of four of my young regimental comrades [August Oberer wrote home to Germany]. Beside us, six sunburned men shoveled a mass grave for fifteen men already stretched out stiff beside it. Forward thundered endlessly thousands of guns, to bring new fodder to the freshly erected military cemetery. They tolled like funeral bells. Here are only such dead as have died at the aid station from serious wounds. The many comrades who die up front usually remain where they are. If they lie in a place under only occasional fire, they are quickly buried on the spot. A little cross hastily made of two sticks shows the resting place. If you look more closely at the grave, you find an upturned bottle stuck in the loose earth, in which a company leader has put a note with the name and personal details of the dead man. When the battle has quieted down or pushed farther on, the grave is given a cross with the name, or the body is exhumed and buried in a heroes' cemetery with his comrades.

Ludendorff took little interest in the details of burial parties, but he could not overlook the scale of their operations in March and April. The figures from the Adjutant General showed that the new drafts did not cover the losses, and to keep up battalion strength, he had to order two infantry divisions and some unattached cavalry outfits broken up and distributed through the under-strength divisions. To compensate for the loss of rifle strength, he assigned a fifth light machine gun to each rifle company, though with reluctance, because although the added weapon increased firepower, it preempted the service of two riflemen—that is, two trench-assault men—and he still thought exclusively in terms of attack.

New recruits joined the German front-line outfits, their places in the training camps taken by still younger boys and by men combed out of the factories. Officers complained that the new men brought dissension to the depots; they had more money than the veterans, and they voiced their feelings about the war more freely.

There were no more troops to be had from Russia, where the Germany army of occupation, made up of men in the older age categories, was forced to execute still another offensive operation in April to seize Kharkov, in order to extract from the chaotic Ukraine grain shipments for ravenous Central Europe. Next, sufficient coal could not be spared from Germany to fuel the Russian railways, so the Donetz Basin had to be occupied.

Not all the German troops in the East were engaged in the antifamine offensive. Some were committed to the job of heading off the possible reopening of the Russian front by the western Allies: the Crimea was occupied, and a division sent to Finland. In these moves there was an element of Siegfried-ism; in the very midst of the life-and-death struggle in the West, political projects were afoot to link much of the formerly Russian border territory to Germany through personal union under the Kaiser. To implement these schemes, local German or pro-German minorities had to be given military backing. Ludendorff's mania for a super-empire continued to ensure that Russia, far from relieving the German manpower shortage as the Allies feared, added a further drain.

Ludendorff was not blind to the solution the Allies were claiming for their own manpower crisis. The prominence given by the French and British press to the new program of transporting American troops could not be overlooked, but reading the staff officers' reports, he refused to be panicked. He thought no enemy should be despised, but "neither should he be overestimated." He agreed with the German press, gloating over Seicheprey, that the Yankees had much to learn: "The individual American fought well; but our success has nevertheless been easy."

Ludendorff's main conclusion about the Americans was the same in early May as it had been in early March: the Allies could not count on substantial American reinforcements until midsummer. The U-boat, he thought, had proved "unpleasantly effective after all" in its creation of an Allied (and even world) shipping shortage. He had three months—May, June, July—in which to win his gamble.

That, he still felt, should suffice.

He was aware too of the flow to France of Allied troops from other theaters, especially Italy. To halt or reverse it, he urged an Austrian offensive. The Austrian command accepted the proposal, setting a tentative date of early June. But on May 15, a disconcerting omen appeared in the form of an action by the Italian air force. The Austrian front and rear areas were bombarded with hundreds of thousands of leaflets encouraging Czech, Yugoslav, and Polish soldiers to desert and join the Czech and other legions forming in Italy and France.

That same day, British Foreign Secretary Balfour put out a new peace feeler, stating in the House of Commons that Britain stood ready for serious negotiations at any time or place. Once more, the only word that had to be spoken on the German side was "Belgium." But once more, Reconciliation Chancellor Hertling and his foreign minister, Kühlmann, remained silent. Single-minded Ludendorff, portents and problems notwithstanding, clove to his purpose and carried everyone else along with him. If Germany was bruised and bleeding, so were France and Britain. Two offensives had been victorious; the current was still running for Germany. High tide seemed directly ahead.

Setting aside the distraction of threatening famine, rebellious populaces, slippery allies, and irreplaceable casualties, Ludendorff, with Hindenburg and Wetzell, again studied the map. It was still a chess game. Now the adversary had to be forced to move certain of his pieces in order to open the way for checkmate—that is, the offensive against the British, code-named "Hagen" (for a leading character in Wagner and the Nibelungenlied). The French masses in the north and in the Oise–Somme sector had to be forced to return to their own zone. Above all, the Army Detachment North, or D.A.N., had to be drawn away from Flanders.

Ludendorff therefore mapped an interim offensive "to break up the present united front of the Entente opposite Crown Prince Rupprecht's Army Group, and therewith create a fresh possibility for a successful renewal of the offensive against the English."

His plan was for a one-two punch against the French, to be delivered as soon as possible, the second blow ("Gneisenau-Yorck") following the first ("Blücher") by three days in order to permit transfer of the heavy artillery. The aim was to press the French back on a broad front northeast of Paris while quickly consuming Pétain's few local reserves, forcing Foch to come to his aid with the French reserves from the Oise–Somme and Flanders. The attack would have distinctly limited objectives; once the British front was stripped of French divisions, the main offensive would be launched, also in the form of a one-two punch: "Hagen" in Flanders followed by "New Michael" in Picardy. The result would be decisive. The British would be sent home.

Ludendorff was unaware of the British pledge to stay in France given Clemenceau and Foch at Abbeville. Had he known, he probably would have discounted it. In the realpolitik of battle, few allies could be trusted: witness the Emperor Karl.

The exact locale of "Blücher" was determined by considerations of transport. Transport was not the strongest element in the German Army, and "Michael" and "Georgette" had put considerable strain on it. The attack therefore had to be mounted west of Verdun, which virtually dictated Champagne, on the front of the Army Group Crown Prince Wilhelm. Especially favorably situated for the attack was the German Seventh Army, which faced a long, low plateau called, from an ancient Roman road that ran along the crest from west to east, the Chemin des Dames ("Ladies' Way"), and defended by an enemy force known to be thinly spread. General Schulenburg, chief of staff of the Army Group Crown Prince Wilhelm, argued for a widening of the attack front. For an offensive on the scale that Schulenburg (and the Crown Prince himself) wanted, it would be necessary to rob the Army Group Crown Prince Rupprecht of some of its heavy artillery, soon to be needed for "Hagen." Ludendorff was firm; "Blücher" was an offensive with limited objectives, and had to be subordinated to the grand strategic design.

Yet to guarantee success, time was required.

For three weeks the mountains of ammunition, including wagonloads of the yellow-cross gas canisters, along with the canned rations, gasoline, fodder, medicine, and bandages, crept by night toward the Chemin des Dames crest. As they accumulated, polite debate continued between Avesnes and the Crown Prince's headquarters at nearby Charleville over the exact breadth, location, and timing of the one-two punch. Colonel Bruchmüller, the artillery expert, prevailed with a recommendation that the initial attack front be limited to the middle twenty-five miles of a thirty-seven-mile bombardment front. A concentration of 1,150 batteries would prepare the specter of a threat to Paris.

Once more extraordinary precautions, now profiting from the March–April experience, were used to assure secrecy. Allied observation balloons were left unattacked, and care was taken to conceal troop movements from the civilian population, which was known to be supplied by French aircraft with baskets of carrier pigeons. German aircraft were kept at distant fields until D-day, May 27. Information on the offensive was withheld from the men in the forward trenches, who were told that the accumulation of reserves was in anticipation of an enemy attack. Artillery registration fire was limited to one test round per gun to check theoretical calculations. In order to leave roads clear for the infantry on the night of May 26–27, all batteries had to be brought forward by daybreak of May 26 and hidden in woods, barns, and gardens just behind the front. Where they had to move across fields, the battery tracks were plowed over. Care was taken to keep horses from grazing in the open during the day, and trucks from raising dust.

By night, the signalmen hauled forward reels loaded with 2,500 miles of wire. Submarine cable was included, to be laid across the little Ailette River. Communication with the assault troops, whose advance could not await line laying, was provided by hand-carried radios. Bridging materials were hidden close to preselected crossing sites, for the Ailette, for the marshy ground in the valley bottom, and for the broad Aisne River beyond. Broken stone and other material was collected to repair the roads which would be cratered by the bombardment.

The trees of the thickly wooded region were in full leaf, while the croaking of frogs in the streams and ponds helped mask the sound of vehicles. Nature itself seemed to be on Ludendorff's side.

13

"BLÜCHER"

At all the Allied headquarters, May passed in heightening tension. At Montreuil, in the north, Haig's intelligence was scaring him with a picture of 80 German divisions poised to spring, a figure which in transmission to the London Cabinet through General Wilson somehow became 100. At Sarcus, to the south, Foch fretted over two points on his map which he considered especially sensitive, and from which he longed to launch offensives of his own: in front of Amiens, where the German "Michael" bulge continued to threaten the critical rail center, and in Flanders, where the Germans were dug in twenty-five miles from the coast. But all he had in general reserve were the four divisions of the Tenth Army, not even enough to plug a "Michael"-size hole in the line.

Farther south, at his forward headquarters at Chantilly, Pétain was no less worried than Haig and Foch, and with more visible reason. The northern third of the Allied line was a dense mass of infantry, backed by a thick forest of artillery, while the southern two thirds, Pétain's responsibility, were manned by thinly strewn combat groups, most of whom were exhausted from the March–April fighting and had been sent south to rest and recuperate. Of 103 French divisions now in France, forty-five were still north of the Oise, and of these, only the six divisions of the French Fifth Army were immediately available to Pétain in case of a German offensive anywhere between the Oise and Switzerland. The eastern sector, beyond Verdun, was so lightly manned by worn-out French divisions and a few of the big green American outfits that the group commander there, Castelnau, warned Pétain that in case of even a limited offensive by the enemy he would have no alternative to retreat. Verdun, where Pétain had made his reputation two years earlier, was now practically ungarrisoned. An offensive on either side of the fortress, on the plan of Colonel Wetzell, could only be met by an immediate general withdrawal, with no natural river line to fall back on.

Pétain took comfort from the visible fructifying of his Yanks-and-tanks plan. The new pell-mell shipping program promised that the infantry (and some of the artillery) of seventeen American divisions would be on French soil by June 1, while Renault and Schneider guaranteed enough tanks for a major offensive in July.

The problem was to hang on in the meantime. Pétain reverted to his controversial Directive No. 4, by which the front line, within mortar and field-artillery range of the enemy, was to be lightly held, and the main line of resistance to be established farther back. Now, after the bloody lessons of "Michael" and "Georgette" had revealed the frightful power of the new-style German artillery preparation, and in view of the desperate condition of Pétain's two thirds of the line, he combined an appeal for the return of some of his troops with a renewed argument for defense in depth.

"Michael" and "Georgette" notwithstanding, Pétain ran into the same opposition as in January. For some of the resistance, there existed practical reasons. Turning the present skimpy second-line trenches into a formidable system of field fortifications, with deep dugouts, machine-gun nests, command posts, barbed wire, aid stations, communications trenches, and all the rest would require an immense amount of labor. Though women, children, and old men were commonly pressed into trench-digging service, and though weary combat troops were forced to work during their reserve tours, the change could not be made overnight, especially with constant troop movements compounding the problem. But beyond the practical difficulty still lay the psychological obstacle. Pétain's two western group commanders, Generals Fayolle and Franchet d'Esperey, were half convinced, but their subordinates, the field-army commanders, were as bullheaded as ever. General Gouraud, the one-armed Achilles commanding the Fourth Army, remained immovable despite the arguments of his more enlightened chief of staff, Colonel Prételat. Gouraud pointed out that his next-door neightbor, General Duchêne, commanding the Sixth Army, refused absolutely to obey Directive No. 4, and Duchêne, in Gouraud's eyes, was "a real soldier." Duchêne was in fact a self-willed tyrant who terrorized his subordinates, and who truculently held out against both Franchet d'Esperey and Pétain. Possibly the fact that he was Foch's former chief of staff gave him extra hardihood. In any case, in the light of Foch's "*Ne lâchez pas pied,*" not to mention Clemenceau's attitude, Pétain found it awkward to remove him. Yet an offensive against Duchêne's front in Champagne was entirely possible, though Pétain was unaware that the shortage of German motor transport ruled out a German offensive farther east. At least the reserve Fifth Army was near at hand, and the Aisne-Vesle river line, which would have been the main line of resistance if Directive No. 4 had been followed through, still provided a back-up barrier.

Duchêne's Sixth Army had had to stretch itself eastward in March to take over the trenches of the neighboring Fifth Army, withdrawn to join in the "Michael" battle and now in reserve in place of the Third. On top of this, the Sixth Army's troops had been exchanged, division by division, for battered outfits coming out of combat. It now consisted of ten divisions, six French and four British, all far under strength. Seven of them were strung out along the front line for thirty-seven miles, giving an infantry concentration even below that of Gough's British Fifth Army on March 21.

Pétain's entire front being in similar case, he did not single out Champagne in pressing Foch for help. Foch remained unmoved. The D.A.N. stayed in Flanders, the French Tenth Army remained untouchable as Foch's own reserve, the French First and Third Armies were kept in line in the former British sector, and the French Fifth Army, though available as a reserve, remained north of the Oise.

Among the intelligence reports that collected in the dragoon barracks in Provins that housed Pétain's main headquarters was an estimate made by Captain Hubbard, the young G-2 of the American Expeditionary Force. Hubbard had the nerve to disagree with both his Allied intelligence counterparts; he forecast a German attack in Champagne, partly on the sensible ground that nobody else expected it there.

And despite the German precautions, intensive Allied reconnaissance turned up suspicious signs. German antiaircraft was observed to be especially quick to react to planes flying north of the Aisne. Dust clouds were detected on the roads. Troops who had been through the March battle heard the rumble of wagons and the sound of working parties at night. Escaped French prisoners reported intensive activity behind the German lines.

On the afternoon of May 26, a French patrol captured two prisoners, one a private and one a non-com. The private said that an attack was scheduled for early next morning. This the non-com denied, claiming that there would only be a heavy bombardment, and that the German infantry was too worn out to attack. His interrogators employed a trick, pointing out to him that while he was not obligated to give any information at all, he was, on the other hand, forbidden by international law to give false information, and if it turned out that he had done so he would be shot as a spy. The non-com then confirmed the private's information, and French Sixth Army headquarters was notified.

General Duchêne ordered a battle alert, and even tried to move his artillery back out of range of the coming bombardment. Too late; his corps and division commanders found it impossible to comply and get their guns into new firing positions. It would have been wise simply to save the guns, but nobody realized that.

At eight o'clock that night the Germans began jamming the Allied radio frequencies.

At one in the morning, out of the blackness of a moonless night, a tremendous crash and a horizon-long burst of flame opened the bombardment from German artillery sited at the unparalleled density of one gun every ten yards. The alerted French and British batteries returned the fire but were overwhelmed at once by a concentration of gas followed by high explosives. The effect was more total than that of March 21. The Allied infantry crowded in their front-line positions were massacred, while their artillery support was canceled out and their communications were obliterated.

A German artilleryman, Heinrich Zellner, wrote home in glowing terms of the bombardment's success:

> There was no resisting it. Four of our batteries were matched to one enemy battery, holding it down with fearful gas fire. Punctually to the second began the barrage of the combined batteries, crushing all life under it. At a distance of 200 meters our infantry, picked troops, followed the fire, and when hidden Frenchmen emerged shaking from their holes and declivities as the fire retreated farther back, they found their trenches already in the hands of our infantry. The [barrage] was a splendid performance of the German artillery.

The shock troops overran with scarcely a pause what was left of the two center Allied divisions, the British Fiftieth and the French Second; by 9 A.M., advance parties supported by low-flying strafing aircraft were in sight of the Aisne. The Allied blunder of March was repeated. The French division in reserve guarding the Aisne bridges was committed to the forward battle, and the detachments sent by Duchêne to hold the bridges did not arrive in time; by 10 A.M., the span at Oeilly was in German hands. Meantime all three of Duchêne's reserve divisions were committed to the hopeless battle in the forward zone, north of the Aisne, where they did not supplement, but merely replaced, the front-liners, and were overwhelmed in turn.

Slowly grasping the magnitude of his disaster, Duchêne put in a call for help. Franchet d'Esperey, the army-group commander, sent what he had available: two divisions, just enough to feed the flames.

But despite the destruction of communications and Duchêne's obtuseness, Pétain gauged the calamity by afternoon and ordered the reserve Fifth Army to return south of the Oise. Foch, startled at the unexpected locale and size of the attack, merely gave his approval and notified Haig.

The Fifth Army consisted of seven divisions of infantry, two of cavalry, and a headquarters staff. Pétain divided it up, ordering the more mobile cavalry at once into the gap in the Sixth Army's center, with the infantry to be committed where needed as they arrived. But the headquarters staff he sent all the way around the salient to Reims. In this first stage of the battle, he perceived the ancient cathedral city to be one of the two keys, the other being Soissons. It was between these two major rail centers, some thirty miles apart, that the German spearhead was thrusting.

That night, as the reports from the German front-line units and air reconnaissance confirmed the existence of a nine-mile gap in front of the center of the German Seventh Army, both Seventh Army and Army Group Crown Prince Wilhelm headquarters were aflame with excitement; General von Boehn, commanding the Seventh, ordered the pursuit to be pushed through the night.

The order was approved by the Crown Prince, but it was not approved by the men to whom it was addressed. The men of 1914 might have kept going, and the officers of 1914 might have kept them going. But these were men of 1918, and after marching twelve hours with full packs, clambering over trenches and shell holes, stumbling through woods, and wading streams and swamps, they needed a night's rest, and their officers gave it to them.

Next morning (May 28), however, they crossed the Vesle on a wide front, seizing the high ground to the south and attacking up and down stream to push back the enemy flanks. On the west, German infantry filed over a weir and a partly damaged railroad bridge over the Aisne into Soissons, which proved to be virtually empty of Allied troops. This striking success was not followed up; on the contrary, the division commander was ordered to pull back. The reason given was that the westward-thrusting spearhead might be exposed to a dangerous flank attack. There was another reason. In March, Ludendorff had expressed displeasure over the tendency of the shock troops to stop in captured towns to drink, eat, and loot. Field commanders now tried, not very successfully, to restrain these natural soldierly tendencies, and the Soissons withdrawal was partly for this purpose.

Ludendorff countermanded the pullback as soon as he learned of it, and the shock troops reentered the city next day. Soissons, he saw as clearly as Pétain, was vital to the success of the offensive. So was Reims, on the other corner. Without these two rail centers, supplying the troops in the developing salient would quickly become a problem. Yet at the same time the doctrine underlying the Hutier tactic called for maximum exploitation of breakthroughs, and Boehn reported hardly any resistance across the whole center of his front. Should he be given a full go-ahead?

Behind the tactical dilemma loomed the strategic. The purpose of "Blücher" was to force Foch to play his reserve cards here, on this battlefield, and clear the way for "Hagen" in the north. Already on the second day of the offensive, the phase line fixed for the total advance had been gained. Yet there was no sign that the French were pulling out of Flanders. Suppose the advance were halted now? Would Foch not keep his D.A.N. where it was, and his Tenth Army in hand, while leaving Pétain to patch up his new front whatever way he could?

In a word, "Blücher" was an embarrassment of success.

That evening (May 28), a succession of Daimler command cars rolled into the courtyard of the Crown Prince's château at army-group headquarters at Charleville. Hindenburg and Ludendorff arrived together from Avesnes. The Kaiser, stepping from a limousine flying the yellow Imperial standard, once more contradicted the signs of age in his face and hair

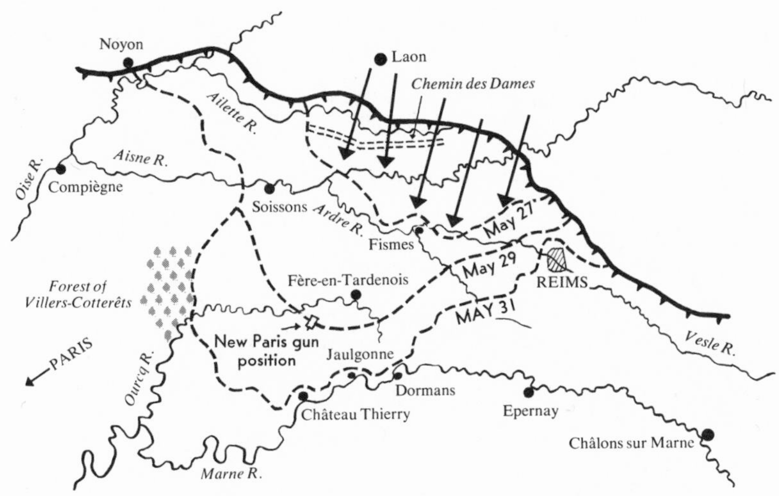

"Blücher" offensive (Chemin des Dames).

by the boyish enthusiasm of his spirit. What he especially relished in the new victory was that it had been won by his son. The son, a chinless but not brainless Hohenzollern, was more restrained. Four years earlier, at the first battle of the Marne, his Fifth Army had been victoriously advancing when the order had been imposed to break off the battle and retreat because of considerations elsewhere. He had always remained convinced that the decision had been a mistake, and feared it might be repeated now.

The thirty-five-year-old heir to the throne naturally had the support of the Kaiser. General Schulenburg, the army-group chief of staff, who had wanted a larger mission assigned to "Blücher" to begin with, multiplied his arguments. Father

Hindenburg cast his vote in favor of continuing the offensive.

Nevertheless, the decision belonged to Ludendorff. He reminded everyone again of the limited role of "Blücher" and the overriding importance of "Hagen," but he argued *pro forma* rather than with his accustomed hardihood. He made no such scene as he had created at Bellevue Castle when he had overruled the Kaiser on the Polish boundary. Some of the reason lay in the realm of tactics and strategy, especially the fear that if he stopped the push now, the French would accept the loss of territory, patch their line together, and leave the D.A.N. in Flanders. The strategic threat, to be credible, had to be maintained.

But beyond even the strategic question lay psychology. Two months and a week had passed since the six thousand guns of "Michael" had opened fire, and "Michael" had been two weeks late starting. On the night of May 28, time was beginning to show on the clock. How much truth and how much exaggeration were in the Allied boasts about the arrival of Americans was impossible to gauge. "Last week 35,000 American troops landed every day," claimed one English newspaper. Before leaving Avesnes for the conference, Ludendorff had received news of a successful assault by four thousand American infantrymen, led by twelve French tanks and supported by French artillery and aircraft, on the village of Cantigny, at the tip of the "Michael" salient. Counterattacks had been ordered at once, but the town itself was of no importance. The question was, How long would it take to multiply Cantigny into something serious?

The other unknown in Ludendorff's equation was the Paris government. The unparalleled casualties suffered by the French Army in the course of the war, bereaving every family in France, certainly made the French civilian population an attractive target for home-front smashing. Would a push to the Marne, plus the effect of the Paris gun, topple pugnacious Clemenceau and bring a peace offer?

Such calculations on Ludendorff's part had a tinge of desperation, and gave the unexpected success of "Blücher" an exceptional allure. Even before the conference, Ludendorff had made up his mind to raise the ante in Champagne. Seven divisions were ordered south from the reserves hoarded in Flanders for "Hagen." It was less a chess master's move than a riverboat gambler's, but it might pay off with all the chips on the table.

14

ADVANCE TO THE MARNE

"Blücher" sent a seismic wave throughout the Allied world. Its inner circumstances were little understood, and it appeared to most as if the French Army, the strong fortress around which the Allies were grouped, had suddenly collapsed. The offensive was accompanied by a renewal of the shelling from the long-range battery, now known as "La Bertha," after Bertha Krupp, or, to Paris children, as "Badaboume." But the new bombardment caused scant concern compared with the thunder rolling from the east, distinctly more audible than that from the north in March. Clemenceau's censorship only heightened the baffled rage in the Chamber of Deputies, where frustration found targets in Foch, Pétain, and Clemenceau himself.

On the same evening (May 28) that the German Supreme Command met at the Crown Prince's headquarters, Clemenceau motored out from Paris to see Foch. The Gascon generalissimo put on a serene face. The German offensive? A diversionary attack to mask the enemy's real intentions. What was Foch doing to stop it? At the moment, nothing.

This was true. Foch had just returned from Pétain's forward headquarters at Chantilly, twenty miles north of Paris. The atmosphere there had been openly hostile, Pétain's staff regarding Foch even more than Duchêne as the author of the calamity for having taken away the reserves. In Pétain's icy demeanor Foch could also read an accusation for the foolish "*Ne lâchez pas pied*" that Duchêne had used to justify his refusal to thin his front line.

Nevertheless, atmosphere and accusations aside, Foch and Pétain had found themselves in a considerable measure of agreement. They were, first, shocked at the size of the German attack, and second, puzzled by its direction. Why was Ludendorff committing so large a force in Champagne of all places? How long would he keep up the pressure?

They were also in agreement on the strategy of defense. The object must be to hold the shoulders of the salient. On the eastern face, this meant Reims and the Mountain of Reims, the high wooded ground to the southwest. On the western face, Soissons itself was gone, but if the plateau to the southwest could be held, the important north–south road and rail lines could be brought under the fire of heavy artillery. On the basis of the enemy's initial commitment, Pétain believed he could hold the shoulders with what he had—in other words, with just the Fifth Army as his reinforcement. But only scattered groups of infantry remained directly in front of the southward-thrusting German spearhead. If Ludendorff put in more reserves, Pétain would find it impossible with his present forces to prevent the pocket from rapidly widening at the bottom and so crumbling the corners. He concluded by again asking for the Tenth Army and for the D.A.N., whose removal from Flanders he proposed to make possible by having the British withdraw from Dunkerque and if necessary Calais.

Foch quickly turned down that radical suggestion, and temporized on the Tenth Army. Thus, as he told Clemenceau in the evening at Sarcus, he was really doing nothing at all to stop the Boche offensive.

The depth of the penetration, in Foch's eyes, was due entirely to the culpable failure of the Sixth Army command to ensure the demolition of the Aisne bridges. He did not mention to Clemenceau that if the two of them had allowed Pétain to organize his defense on the basis of Directive No. 4, the Aisne would have formed the main line of resistance, with the bridges automatically secured. But even with the Aisne breached, the German advance was really much less threatening than it might appear from Paris. Despite the painful sacrifice of territory and the costly loss of rear installations—hospitals, ammunition dumps, quartermaster depots, airfields—the Boche could not threaten Paris by continuing their present advance. Any turn westward toward Paris would place the Tenth Army on their flank. Foch considered the offensive an attempt by Ludendorff to divert his reserves from some "strategically sensitive" point—that is, Flanders.

This assessment was of course accurate, but it did not soothe Clemenceau. Nevertheless, he resolved to give his generals some time. The going would be difficult in the Chamber, but if Foch and Pétain could stop the Boche tomorrow, he would be able to handle the Chamber.

But next day, as the Paris papers played down the Champagne battle and printed glowing reports of the victory of the gallant Americans at Cantigny, the German Supreme Command conference bore fruit in the violent renewal of the offensive between Reims and Soissons. The decimated Allied infantry formations, which had lost their artillery, no longer had trenches to fight from, and had had no sleep for two days and nights, were rapidly routed from the woods, hillsides, and burned-out villages. In the center, the shock troops almost made a spectacular capture. Clemenceau and General Mordacq, driving into Fère-en-Tardenois, discovered that the Germans were entering the town at the other end, and turned their car around just in time to escape. By noon, Pétain was telephoning Foch with another demand for the Tenth Army. He had committed all the troops he could lay hands on, a total of ten new divisions. Twenty Allied divisions had now been engaged, but the actual strength of the bulging line was much less than that, because little was left of Duchêne's original front-line seven.

Foch still held off.

Next day (May 30), behind long processions of women, children, old men, bicycles, wagons, handcarts, and baby carriages, the advance German units pressed to within sight of the Marne on a ten-mile front from Château-Thierry to Dormans.

Captain Fritz Matthaei, a battalion commander of the German 175th Infantry, Thirty-sixth Division, was home on leave when he received a telegram summoning him to the front. Boarding the train in Mainz on May 28, he arrived early next morning in the rear headquarters of Corps Schmettow of the Seventh Army.

> Everywhere was battle joy, battle enthusiasm [he wrote]. Victory called from every corner, prisoners and booty were brought past, and the shining May sun smiled success. The days of 1914 seemed to have returned.

Hitchhiking to the front, first on a supply train, and then in a truck and wagon convoy, the patriotic captain enjoyed a rare experience:

> Suddenly braking, the driver stares with shining eyes ahead—long drawn-out honking, two helmets with high spikes, two gray figures drive past stiffly erect—the Kaiser and Hindenburg! The hand jerks to the cap, the Kaiser makes a gesture of thanks—past, past goes the long train of staff cars. . . . They are coming from the battlefield, from the troops. For the first time in the war, I saw Kaiser and Field Marshal.

After spending the night (May 29–30) in a French dugout with a Badenese ambulance outfit, Captain Matthaei made his way to the front and located his battalion at Fresnes, about four miles from the northward bend of the Marne at Jaulgonne. Orders were to press on to the Marne.

The strength of the troops is exhausted. For two days they have fought without sleep or rest, forward, ever farther. I feel the difference strongly; I am refreshed in body and soul, my battalion is worn out. Nevertheless the higher goal means higher stakes! The Marne, the Marne! Where does it flow? To Paris! The word passes through the murmuring ranks. Their eyes light up. . . .

Lively machine-gun and rifle fire comes from the edge of the wood. They are not numerous, but they must be excellent defenders over there in the forest. I stand up. To the right, forward, lies my First Company; clearly I see the riflemen, the munitions carriers, the light machine gunners lying in the grass. . . . Left, in the field, a cry! Arms thrown back, a signalman falls to the ground, the telephone apparatus drops from his hand. Medic! . . .

I call over to the First Company. Platoon leader Sergeant Michalak reports his observations: "The bastards are sitting tight and shooting damned good. . . ." "We must go forward, Michalak." I did not have to say it twice. Exhausted, he stands up: "Everyone, forward, the Marne is beyond! Today we must have it!" He springs forward, the others after him. As so often, the personal example works wonders. In two leaps we are in the woods. A volley breaks out—too high! It does not stop us. The enemy is confused by the sudden attack. . . . On the paths of the wood we see blue figures running off and disappearing. [Soon] only a distant crackling and rustling testifies to the fleeing enemy.

The battalion concentrates. I see them all, the weary gray comrades, and joy lights their faces. But there is no rest. The wood must be ours. Patrols forward! Rifles under their arms, they slip forward into the depths of the forest. . . . To our left there is still fighting. The rattle of guns is mixed with the burst-

> ing of grenades and light mines. The French too know well what it's about—about the Marne! . . .
>
> It is just dusk. Below, a bright band snakes in many twistings and turnings, disappearing again and again behind hills and woods. . . . the fateful river. . . . In 1914 it stopped us. Will it stop us again? The men also feel what this river means to us, and a murmur runs through the battalion: across, across, and on to Paris! That's all we must do, and there'll be an end of it in the fall.

In the dragoon barracks in once-sleepy Provins, the field telephone and telegraph lines were electronic Job's messengers, bringing new dismay by the hour. But mid the jumble of defeat, G-2 picked out one after another the unit numbers of six new German divisions, not previously on this front. All six, a check showed, were drawn from the Army Group Crown Prince Rupprecht, in Flanders.

The disclosure was of capital importance. It not only explained the unnerving power of this fourth day of the Boche offensive, but destroyed Foch's arguments against the release of the Tenth Army.

Confronted with the evidence, Foch agreed. If, for whatever hard-to-fathom reason, Ludendorff was sending important masses of reserves from Flanders to Champagne, the danger to the British was sensibly diminished.

Foch notified Haig that he was committing the Tenth Army to the battle, and to Haig's intense alarm, added that he might want to borrow British reserve divisions to replace the Tenth Army as his own general reserve. But he still refused to withdraw the D.A.N. from Flanders.

The mission of the Tenth Army was defined as stabilizing the west side of the salient, where the Germans were still advancing south of Soissons. On the opposite (Reims) corner, the French Fifth Army was fiercely engaged and yielding no ground.

That left the tip of the salient, at the Marne, defended only by the remnants of French divisions that had been fighting continuously for four days and had reached the limit of exhaustion.

Once again, and more urgently than ever, Foch needed the Americans. The past month had brought troopship convoys in amazing numbers, but these freshly landed doughboys, who did not yet know a Stokes mortar from a Chauchat machine gun, or a gas alarm from a box barrage, could not be herded straight into the trenches. Only the American divisions that had landed earlier and had been through training could be considered. There were six. The First Division, the American bellwether, given the attack mission at Cantigny to wipe out the Twenty-sixth's defeat at Seicheprey, now had its hands full absorbing local German counterattacks. The Twenty-sixth, Thirty-second, and Forty-second were in the line in the quiet Lorraine-Vosges sector. Only the two remaining American divisions, the Second and the Third, were in reserve positions. The Second, complete, fully trained, and with quiet-sector exposure, lay near Beauvais, in the vicinity of the British-French juncture (and Foch's headquarters), earmarked as general reserve. The Third Division, on the other hand, had only arrived in March, had had no quiet-sector combat exposure, and thanks to the April–May decisions on shipping infantry only, still lacked its artillery. Yet in the present pinch, it was needed too. The Third was in training near Pershing's headquarters at Chaumont, in the east. Would Pershing release it?

Once more, when the crunch came, Pershing proved cooperative, giving Foch full freedom to use the American outfits in whatever way he needed them. The complete Second and incomplete Third were at once ordered to converge from their opposite directions on the Marne front.

That day (May 30) nine shells from Badaboume landed in Paris, the ninth hitting the Madeleine, blowing a hole in the pavement between the pillars in the rear of the church and breaking off the head of St. Luke in a niche in the wall. A fragment of the shell bore the number "41." This, together with the plotting of the bursts, gave the artillerists something to think about. The numbering of the shells implied individuation, the only reason for which must be to allow for the wear on the gun. The battery had obviously shifted location, from the position near Laon to a wood southeast of Amiens, on ground won by the Germans in the "Michael" offensive. The reduction in range, from seventy-five to sixty-eight miles, seemed insignificant until one took into account the possible effect on the guns themselves of firing at extreme ranges, with corresponding pressures. Even a slight reduction in range might greatly benefit the life of a gun. Paris might therefore look forward to a considerable increase in the volume of shellfire. The new site also got out from under the counterbattery fire of the French 305's, which, ironically enough, had just been overrun and captured by the Germans. The latest Boche advance would also provide airfields within minutes' flight of Paris to complement Badaboume.

Yet the threat of long-range guns and air raids seemed academic. Ordinary artillery might soon be ranged in on Paris. Was the city to undergo another siege? After the endless suffering of three and a half years, with the Americans pouring into France, was the war, at this eleventh mortal hour, lost?

15

CLEMENCEAU

Doggedly, stumping around on his gaitered old legs and a cane, Clemenceau visited the front, listening to complaints that the troops had to reply to the massed Boche artillery with rifles and machine guns "like at the beginning of the war." Yet there was plenty of French artillery; France was even lending it to America—why was it not here in the battle?

On May 31, he met Foch and Pétain at Trilport, the new headquarters of the French Sixth Army, about twenty miles east of Paris. Pétain that day had alerted Castelnau's Eastern Army Group for a possible general withdrawal. Pétain explained to Clemenceau the reasons for the continuing disparity of numbers in the salient. Pétain's staff, incensed at the accusations against their chief in the Chamber of Deputies, had urged him to blame Foch, but Pétain selflessly refused, saying that Foch was essential to ultimate victory. He told Clemenceau that the Germans could be stopped, and that he was as convinced as he had always been that if the Allies could hold out through June, victory was certain.

The old Premier turned to Foch. The generalissimo had

changed his tune slightly; he now had to admit that the five-day-old Boche offensive seemed to be more than a diversionary attack. Like Pétain, he believed it could be contained, but he expressed concern about the depleted Allied infantry ranks. As for Paris, the Tenth Army in its new position between the Marne and Soissons would be on the flank of any German thrust westward.

When he left Foch, Clemenceau was not wholly satisfied, yet wanted to believe in him. Despite a natural antipathy on practically every other ground, the two shared respect for each other's fanatic patriotism, and Clemenceau respected Foch's military ability. But had the man made a bad blunder? How could he have mistaken an offensive on this scale for a feint? Motoring back to Paris, he put the question to General Mordacq, his military aide. Mordacq supported Foch. The German strategic objective in Champagne was still unclear; a threat to Paris could only be posed by an entirely new offensive, for example on both sides of Soissons. Even this, Mordacq added, would not end the war.

Clemenceau listened attentively to Mordacq's exposition, as he had to Foch's. Whatever he thought of its technical merits, he agreed warmly with its conclusion: "Yes, the Germans may take Paris, but that would not stop me from fighting. We will fight on the Loire, on the Garonne, if we must even in the Pyrenees . . . but as to making peace, never."

That day (May 31) Captain Matthaei led his battalion in an assault crossing of the Marne:

> 1:30 A.M. The men were awakened. The kitchen served coffee, warming and stimulating. Matches flared, cigars glowed, whispering began.
>
> The leader of the engineers reported. Let's go! Silently the battalion slipped through the village streets. . . . Other companies crossed ours, heavily loaded wagons with half-pontoons moved toward the bank amid shot and shell bursts. . . .
>
> I gave the command to my battalion. . . .
>
> Then suddenly a raging lightning, fire, crackling,

whipping and striking on the bank, sending mud into the air. Cries of "Medic!"—then silence. A burst of enemy machine-gun fire out of the castle had hit the engineers [working at the river bank]. . . . We lay pressed to the ground. Men sprang up to help the wounded and lay the dead on one side. Quickly the first boat was filled and started across, carrying a guide rope to the other bank. . . .

"Third company, up!" Lieutenant Iwanowski sprang into the boat, followed by thirty men. . . . The front-line soldiers are children; the crossing delighted them, and they whispered jokes, leaning over the edge of the boat, kidding the engineers. The boat struck the bank. The gray figures clambered out, crept up the bank, and looked curiously over the walls of a park in the dawn light, across broad, open land. Lieutenant Iwanowski . . . took possession of the bridge abutment, and reported back that the bank was clear of the enemy and all quiet.

The crossing was rapidly completed. By 4:45 everyone was over. . . . Behind the park wall stood hidden my four companies. . . .

The bright morning sun of the 31st May broke over the eastern hills. . . . The attack begins, Third Company on the right, Fourth on the left, First on the road, Second in reserve. . . . The riflemen plunge into the high waves of the wheatfields. The railroad, the castle must be ours. Then from every floor burst fire thick as hail toward the shock troops. Many fell in the wheat, yet the attackers did not stop. . . .

A dull rolling becomes audible behind the hills, and howling and exploding the first enemy shells fall among us, on the shore and in the water, smashing up the barges.

. . . We have the Marne, and our bridgehead is secure; but an advance is now no longer possible. We are cut off from the other bank. Nothing moves;

> we are alone and hold the conquered south bank with clenched teeth.

The exploit of Captain Matthaei's battalion heightened the alarm in Paris. Clemenceau and other civilians could scarcely be as sure as Foch and Pétain that the corners of the salient and not the menacing tip, now across the Marne, were the important thing. Even Foch and Pétain were less certain of the military truth than was Ludendorff, with his exact picture of his logistics. While Clemenceau was promising to fight on the Loire, Ludendorff was bending his efforts toward another battle on the Vesle, the river the Germans had already crossed on a broad front on May 27–28.

The trouble was that the renewed offensive following the conference at the Crown Prince's headquarters had gained ground in the wrong direction. German engineers were frantically laying light track into the salient, but unless both the main north–south lines, through Soissons and Reims respectively, could be used, it would be practically impossible to maintain the huge German Seventh Army, now fighting on a deep, narrow arc, very different from the broad, shallow curve that Ludendorff had envisioned. However exciting to newspaper readers in Berlin, the bridgehead won by Captain Matthaei and his brave comrades at Jaulgonne was of purely speculative value until Reims could be taken. As long as the small French Fifth Army maintained its grip on the ancient Merovingian bishopric, the powerful German Seventh Army felt the pressure on its windpipe.

Ludendorff ordered an attack prepared at once by the German First Army, just east of Reims, to jump off next morning (June 1) and pinch off the corner. There was no time for a Bruchmüller-type artillery concentration; casting about for something to substitute, Ludendorff ordered all available German tanks into action. Unfortunately, it was too late to take back his antitank decision of the winter. Now, when he needed it, the entire operational German tank force consisted of just fifteen vehicles.

On the western face of the salient, he ordered another offensive action by Boehn's Seventh Army to force the French farther away from Soissons by outflanking them to the south, thereby freeing the rail line from the harassing heavy-artillery fire.

Both attacks got started punctually, and early reports of both were good. The First Army managed a penetration of the first enemy line east of Reims, while the Seventh Army found resistance still soft between the Forest of Villers-Cotterêts and the Marne. That was the direction of Paris, and though Ludendorff's intention was merely to force a deeper French withdrawal from Soissons, the psychological effect would be a plus.

It was. Foch, studying the reports of the new westward advance by Boehn, saw the threat of a German pincer around his French Tenth Army if the present attack were complemented by one launched from west of Soissons, southward, aimed in the direction of Compiègne. There were ways to counter that danger, but just in case, he notified Clemenceau that the government might be wise to plan its departure from Paris.

On the other shoulder, the group commander, Franchet d'Esperey, reading the pressure on his French Fourth Army east of Reims, ordered preparation of an evacuation plan for the city, while farther east, Castelnau's staff was mapping a contingency pullback of the Eastern Army Group.

Thus, by noon of June 1, Ludendorff's gamble had brought French preparations to abandon Verdun and Reims and to evacuate the government from Paris. (At Haig's Montreuil château, staff officers hastily dusted off plans for evacuation of the British Expeditionary Force.)

Yet none of the effects actually materialized. Clemenceau thought it would be a good idea for Poincaré to leave Paris while he himself stayed. Paris, he argued, should be treated simply as a fort; if it was captured, nothing was lost but a fort. But Poincaré suspected Clemenceau of harboring a desire to monopolize the glory in case of a siege. Poincaré was having none of that, so they both stayed.

In Reims, General Micheler, the commander of the Fifth Army, disobeyed Franchet d'Esperey's order, and received prompt support from Pétain, who dispatched this message: "I have no reinforcements to send immediately to the Fifth Army. Stay where you are. Make it clear to your general officers that their military honor is engaged. Don't hesitate to use violence if necessary"—in other words, he was to fire any general who failed.

Micheler hung on, and was vindicated next day. The improvised offensive of the German First Army east of Reims had none of the wipe-out power of the thoroughly prepared Bruchmüller-Hutier combination, and the handful of heavy tanks had little value. Consequently, though General Gouraud had his French Fourth Army crowded into front-line trenches, its formations suffered only moderate casualties, and by noon the attack was stopped, with all the German tanks knocked out. In the afternoon, Gouraud gave the order to counterattack and regain the lost ground, the same order that Gough and Duchêne had routinely given their armies. This time it was actually executed; the fighting was tough and bloody, but the ground was retaken. At nightfall the French Fourth Army slept exhausted in the trenches from which it had started the day.

The other German attack, by the Seventh Army to the south and southwest, had better success. Straight south, its advance penetrated Château-Thierry. The streets of the ancient town crackled with gunfire as weary horizon blues fell back before more numerous, but equally weary field grays.

But south of the town a convoy of trucks halted, and soldiers in khaki clambered out. They were men of the Seventh Machine Gun Battalion, U.S. Third Division, and though they had ridden the trucks for 112 miles and twenty-four hours, they force-marched into Château-Thierry and set up their weapons, never before fired in combat, to command the bridge. The confrontation was more symbolic than substantial. The southward thrust had little force left, and the Germans contented themselves with occupying the heights north of the river and waiting for artillery and support units. Boehn's real pressure was against the western face of the salient, between the Marne and the Ourcq. In that direction the Germans gained several miles during the day. But Foch had help on the way thither in the form of an oddly matched pair of divisions: the war-worn, battle-wise French Tenth Colonial Division, mostly black Africans, and the new, untried American Second Division. The Tenth Colonial was positioned between the two American outfits, the Second and the Third, digging in along the Marne. The third was placed under the orders of the Tenth Colonial's commander, General Marchand, whose encounter with Kitchener at Fashoda had made headlines in '98.

As Marchand's mixed corps took hold of the southwest salient corner, both Foch and Pétain could breathe easier. The French Fourth and Fifth Armies were holding firm around the Reims shoulder. The Tenth Army had given some ground, but was close to stabilizing the front west of Soissons, and the Sixth Army, routed from the Chemin des Dames, but now reinforced (and given a new commander), seemed capable of holding its new line astride and behind the Marne. The two generals had only one concern: the total lack of reserves, general or local, behind the fighting front. Once again the French Army had been committed to the last man, and with it all the available Americans.

Pétain reiterated his call for the return of the D.A.N., and added another request. Five new American divisions were training with the British. Pétain asked that they be used to relieve French divisions in Lorraine.

Foch agreed, and proposed an additional measure: to continue the American infantry-priority shipping program through July.

Both Haig and Pershing made immediate waves. Haig was feeling quite chipper now that it was the French who were in the soup. No slave to consistency, he confided to his diary that any French divisions freed by the transfer of Americans would probably "melt away," while protesting vehemently against the transfer of any of the divisions of the D.A.N. from his own front. Pershing was also feeling cockier as a result of the French defeat (even the Italians took some pleasure in what the Rome papers called a "French Caporetto"), noting that his own green G-2 section had come up with the right guess on the locale of the German offensive.

On the question at issue, however, Haig and Pershing were divided. Haig had plans for those five Yank divisions training in his area. He meant to parcel them out among the British skeleton divisions left over from "Michael" and "Georgette," while waiting for the B-men Lloyd George had not yet delivered.

Pershing, unaware of Haig's design, was entirely willing to take his divisions out of the British sector. He wanted them in neither a French nor a British sector, but in an American sector. If someone could have guaranteed to Pershing that the war would still be going on in 1919, he might have been more amenable, but Ludendorff's violent offensives threatened to end the thing one way or the other before he could get to be a commanding general. What Pershing wanted in the worst way was the rear-echelon groups which would complete his corps and armies; Foch's infantry-only-in-July formula consequently infuriated him.

The stage was set for a rousing debate at the Supreme War Council, which met at Versailles on June 1–2, while the French, Germans, and a few of Pershing's Americans shot it out in and around the Marne salient. Clemenceau and Lloyd George discreetly absented themselves to let the four generals —Foch, Pershing, Haig, and Pétain—argue. Foch dominated the debate: "The battle, the battle, nothing else counts!" was the phrase Pershing remembered afterward. But stubborn Pershing gave Foch a fine example of *Ne lâchez pas pied,* and in the end the politicians had to be called in. Another compromise was worked out: 170,000 American infantry to be ferried over in June, and 140,000 in July, everything above those totals to go for Pershing's non-infantry needs.

An agreement was drawn up, the concluding sentence of

which was significant: "We recognize that the combatant troops to be dispatched in July may have to include troops with insufficient training, but we consider the present emergency is such as to justify a temporary and exceptional departure by the United States from sound principles of training, especially as a similar course is being followed by France and Great Britain." The truth was, the eight divisions that had arrived in May had been hardly trained at all. Entirely apart from the inadequacy of the training program in the United States, run as it was by a tiny handful of professional soldiers themselves lacking in realistic military experience, the Allied demands for immediate shiploads of men by the hundreds of thousands brought over many who had not even had a chance to fire their rifles.

As soon as the dust had settled, a new battle broke out, between Foch and the British over shifting the D.A.N. The general state of the British Army became the center of discussion. Lord Milner, seeking to show that Foch exaggerated the manpower problem, cited figures on divisions as of the moment:

101 French
2 Italian (en route)
4 American (apparently not counting the Second and Third, just being committed)
11 Belgian (but very small)
53 British (including, according to Lord Milner, "2 skeleton," and not counting the British divisions cut up in "Blücher")

Clemenceau and Foch jumped on Milner's figure for British divisions—if the British really had fifty-one divisions in Flanders and Picardy, why did Haig need the D.A.N.?

Milner and Lloyd George quickly retracted—instead of "2 skeleton" the number was actually "10 skeleton," but Haig's intention was to fill up eight of these with Americans. That was why he had to keep the D.A.N. for the time being, and the Americans permanently.

With this admission came a shift in alliances around the table, Pershing turning anti-British and Haig switching from an anti-French to an anti-Lloyd George position. If Lloyd George would give him the B-men and the British Empire troops from the east, he would let Pétain and Pershing have their own men back. He reminded the Prime Minister that the War Office had stated that not even forty-three British divisions could be maintained under existing manpower policy, and that the number would be reduced by the end of summer to twenty-eight! In other words, the British Army in France would in the next three months fall to half its March 21 strength.

The disclosure was a shocker. Lloyd George went into full retreat, to the extraordinary extent of agreeing that Foch send his own expert to London to look into the British manpower question, a concession that promised the long-sought release of the B-men. Even Clemenceau, who never ceased prodding Foch to prod the British, was satisfied.

The decision on shipping was transmitted to Washington, supported by a "personal and confidential" message from Pershing to Secretary of War Baker to help justify the demand for undertrained Americans on the basis of the gravity of the military situation: the Germans had taken fifty thousand prisoners and eight hundred guns, had smashed up seventeen Allied divisions, and were blocked at the Marne only by a mix of exhausted and decimated French formations and part of the American Third Division. Pershing in fact went so far as to claim that only the Americans had succeeded in stopping the Germans—"the French were not equal to it." In terms of numbers, that was true, but Pershing omitted to mention that the Americans were in the line at the tip of the salient for the very reason that this was the least sensitive point. The principal American contribution to the battle was actually that of the three divisions in Lorraine that had freed French divisions for the Marne.

By June 2, the second day of the Council's meeting, the immediate crisis was once more over. Fighting around the rim of the Marne salient was fierce but local, and Foch was confident of its outcome. "The storm is still blowing all around the house," he said. "The roof tiles are flying off, the walls are shaking, but the foundation is holding, and that's what counts." During a luncheon break he strolled in the Versailles gardens with Balfour, the elderly British foreign secretary, who politely inquired about his strategic plans. The generalissimo illustrated them with a series of smart gestures from the prize ring—the French rather than the British, for he employed his feet as well as his fists. His counteroffensive, Foch gave the startled Britisher to understand, would consist of hitting and kicking first here, then there, then here, permitting his adversary no time to recover.

Foch's assurance was little shared by the critics in the Chamber of Deputies. Clemenceau's constant attendance at the front had given scope to the opposition, which planned its own major offensive for the Palais Bourbon on June 4. An opposition leader, Franklin-Bouillon, proposed an often discussed, never used, parliamentary device—a "Great Ministry" of all the leaders, that would be free to weigh peace negotiations in the scales of the military balance. Transparently, the "Great Ministry" was a means of breaking Clemenceau's grip on power. The sitting was anticipated with utmost interest not only in Paris but at Avesnes, where staff officers scanned the French newspapers daily for signs of weakening.

In a noisy, violent session, the opposition demanded peace negotiations on the one hand and on the other the dismissal of Foch and Pétain. Clemenceau refused to give them either. Repeatedly interrupted, at one moment driven from the tribune, he stoutly maintained his defense of the two generals and called on the Deputies to "rise to the height demanded by duty, a recommendation not needed by the soldiers. . . . I have told you, from the beginning, that we should have to pass difficult, hard moments, cruel hours. The cruel hours are here. The question is whether we have the stature to support them. . . . For four years, our effectives have declined, our front has been held by a line grown ever thinner, with Allies who have themselves suffered enormous losses, [against whom] arrived a new mass of German divisions at full strength. Withdrawals have been necessary, large for the British Army, with incredible losses, serious and dangerous for the French Army. . . . The men have fought one against five. . . . Yet we shall not surrender. . . . French and English effectives are becoming exhausted, but the Americans are coming."

The old Tiger reiterated what he had said to General Mordacq, driving back from the front: "We are giving ground, but we shall never surrender. . . . We shall be victorious, if the public authorities are equal to their task. . . . I am fighting before Paris, I shall fight in Paris, I shall fight behind Paris."

At Avesnes, Ludendorff read the report of the speech. "Proud, bold words," he noted with chagrin, and wished he had Clemenceau behind him instead of Hertling and Kühlmann.

Even Romain Rolland, in Switzerland, found himself moved by "this old man, however opposite to mine the ideal he incarnates, who carries on his shoulders the most terrible burden that has fallen on France for centuries, and, after passing several days at the front, comes to defend himself against a violently hostile Chamber, without once departing from either his lucidity or his sincerity." The lonely pacifist in Geneva even had some feelings for Foch and Pétain, whose generous and eloquent defense Clemenceau had made. "Their ambitions, their hatreds, are theirs alone," he wrote, "but misfortune is common to us all."

Despite his parliamentary triumph, Clemenceau did not feel the opposition was entirely wrong, and in any case it had to be given something. In addition to endorsing the sacking of General Duchêne, the wrong-headed commander of the French Sixth Army, he removed Franchet d'Esperey, the commander of the Northern Army Group. Realizing that Franchet was not really at fault, and further that he was one of the abler generals, he did not send him to Limoges, the retirement home of disgraced generals, but to Salonika, in exchange for General Guillaumat, a respected commander who was now entrusted with the defense of Paris, which had been declared in the war zone. In effecting their exchange, Guillaumat and Franchet d'Esperey had an interesting conference at which Guillaumat revealed that the Allied Salonika army, widely regarded as a ragtag, bobtail outfit with scant military value, was actually capable of taking the offensive against the Bulgarians opposite it.

Clemenceau was not through with the generals. When the nation was in danger in 1793, Clemenceau's ideological forebears, the Jacobins of the French Revolution, had mercilessly weeded out elderly generals in favor of younger ones. Clemenceau insisted that Foch do the same, and several sexagenarian commanders were placed on the retirement list by the sixty-seven-year-old generalissimo deferring to the seventy-six-year-old Premier.

III

THE MARNE

16

DIVISION IN THE GERMAN CAMP

On June 4, Ludendorff ordered "Blücher" broken off in favor of the second stage of the planned offensive, "Gneisenau-Yorck," farther west. The same thing that had happened with "Michael" and "Georgette" had recurred; the first blow of a one-two punch had been so successful that the second had had to be delayed and reduced in size. The strategic aim of "Gneisenau-Yorck," in the Matz River valley west of Soissons, was defined as breaking down the Soissons shoulder of the Marne salient and capturing Compiègne, eleven miles distant. Such an advance would alleviate the transport constriction in the salient, and would pin French reserves by posing a threat to Paris.

The attacking force was Hutier's Eighteenth Army, well rested since its "Michael" victory. Opposed to it was the French Third Army, which had moved into this sector in March as part of the general leftward movement of the French Army in support of the British. With twenty-four divisions against thirteen, and six hundred batteries against three hundred, Hutier enjoyed a promising numerical advantage, though hardly that of Boehn on May 27. Allowing time to move the heavy guns, D-day was set for June 9. Prince Rupprecht was notified that "Hagen" would have to be correspondingly postponed—that is, into July.

Shortly before the bombardment opened, a disconcerting surprise burst in the form of French counterbattery fire along the attack front. The enemy had evidently gotten wind of the preparations, necessarily carried out with more haste and less secrecy than those for "Michael" and "Blücher." Yet the thunderous concert of Colonel Bruchmüller once more accomplished its purpose; the French infantry proved again to be massed in the forward trenches, where they could be punished severely. The skillfully led shock troops followed the barrage for an advance of over six miles along a seven-and-a-half-mile front, on the left moving halfway to Compiègne. But the following day, June 10, little further progress was made, despite a special effort on the left. The French formations had remained intact despite their first-day losses, and were now containing the offensive without the intervention of more than local—corps and army—reserves.

That was bad news; worse came the following day. Against the west side of the new salient, at the unlikely hour of 11 A.M., enemy tanks and infantry suddenly appeared, almost without preliminary bombardment. Five French divisions were identified and over a hundred tanks counted.

Hutier's right fell back before the onslaught; and German reserves had to be shifted quickly to meet the threat. By the end of the next day, June 12, the line was stabilized, but Hutier's offensive, momentarily so promising, was completely stalled. A hastily improvised attack by the right wing of the German Seventh Army, called on by Ludendorff to give aid to its neighbor, was stopped in its tracks by artillery fire alone.

The Kaiser was so disappointed he had only a chocolate mousse for lunch.

Ludendorff was also disappointed, but he refused to despair. He studied his situation, with all its complex elements interrelating like three-dimensional chess: his manpower shortage, compounded by a virulent flu epidemic; the exhaustion of Allied reserves, alleviated by the Americans; the supply constriction on the Marne and the renewed build-up for "Hagen" in the north; the slowness of the Russian grain shipments and the prospects of the upcoming Austrian offensive on the Piave. On June 14 he gave up on the Hutier offensive on the Matz and directed the Army Group Crown Prince Wilhelm to begin long-range preparations for a new full-scale offensive operation to be launched in the Marne salient "about July 10." Meantime, "artillery and trench-mortar action will be maintained on the recent attack front from Montdidier to the Marne" because "it is worthwhile to have the Entente believe that the attack on Paris is being continued."

Next day, he turned from the map of the Western Front to that of Italy.

His hope was explicit: that the Austrian offensive would hurt the Italians badly enough for the latter to call for help from their western Allies, and that the call would be answered by the re-routing of American divisions from France to Italy. Thus the dangerously shifting balance of reserves on the Western Front would be redressed in Germany's favor, and Ludendorff would retain his freedom to maneuver.

The first reports on the Austrian offensive were good. The Austrians had crossed the Piave River at several points, on a broad front extending from the headwaters of the Brenta to the Adriatic coast. Momentarily, optimism once more pervaded the red-brick house in Avesnes. But the second day's fighting was less satisfactory; the Italians were holding tenaciously along the right bank of the Piave, keeping the Austrian bridgeheads isolated from each other. In the end, the Austrians had to recross the river (June 23.).

It was another disappointment, but Ludendorff had the courage to swallow it. Foreseeing a prolonged Austrian defensive in Italy, he called on the Austrian General Staff to send some Austrian divisions (realistically he hoped for no more than three or four) to France. As a further annoyance, he had to order emergency measures to keep the Austrian civilian population from robbing grain trains en route from Rumania to Germany.

On June 20, Ludendorff issued new general orders to the Army Group Crown Prince Wilhelm, outlining the new major offensive to be launched in mid-July. Instead of aiming south and west, toward Paris, it would strike in the opposite direction, south and east, on either side of Reims. This would improve both the chances of surprise and the chances of avoiding the main masses of Allied reserves in the battle's first stage. The troops at the tip of the salient, those nearest Paris, would stage a crossing to reestablish the bridgehead won by Captain Matthaei's battalion and since lost to French counterattack. But contrary to the dreams of German soldiers and the fears of Paris civilians, their mission would not be an advance on the capital. It would, in fact, take them in the opposite direction.

Nevertheless, though the capture of Paris formed no part of the plan, the offensive promised an enormous strategic prize. The design was a giant pincer movement by the three German armies around Reims that would crumple the entire eastern face and corner of the salient, encircling and destroying the French Fifth and Fourth Armies.

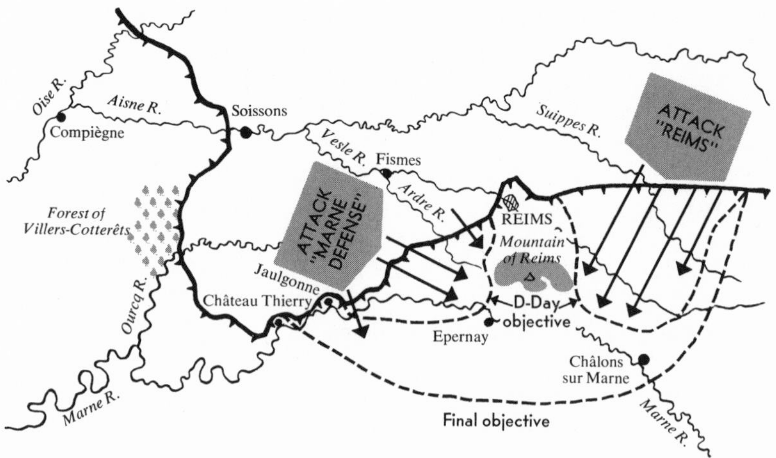

Ludendorff's plan for July 15 offensive to cut off and capture Reims.

The offensive of the German Seventh Army, forming the right-hand pincer, was code-named *Marnewehr* ("Marne Defense"), that of the First and Third Armies, forming the left-hand pincer, "Reims." Following a double Bruchmüller barrage that would annihilate the enemy front lines, the storming infantry would advance on two broad fronts, leaving Reims itself behind, defeating the French reserves, and joining hands in the region of Epernay–Châlons.

Rapid execution was of first importance. The enemy's front-line divisions had to be pulverized and overrun without a stop, as in "Michael" and "Blücher," his local reserves eaten up, and deep penetrations made all along the two fronts on the first day. Such an advance would net a huge bag of prisoners, not only from the overrun divisions, but from the cut-off garrison of Reims itself. All available French, American, and even British reserves would be drawn in, and the whole eastern end of the Allied front driven far back, with the loss of Verdun. Then, while the French tried to re-form their shattered front, the German reserve mass accumulated for "Hagen" would be turned loose against the British, who would be forced to fight alone. That the logistical problem of the Marne salient would vanish was incidental.

"Immediately following" the Reims attack, artillery, trench mortars, and air squadrons would be concentrated on the Flanders front for an attack "possibly . . . a fortnight later." (In the June 14 orders, the two dates had been specified as July 10 and July 20.) The hope was that "if the offensive at Reims succeeded, there would be a very decisive weakening of the enemy in Flanders"—that is, the D.A.N. would at last disappear, and British reserves might be pulled south.

Preparations were ordered "exactly similar" to those for the previous major offensives. Once again, the Paris guns would play a part. In the middle of the salient southwest of Fère-en-Tardenois, a new rail spur had been laid. New guns, fresh from Essen, would here be emplaced only fifty miles from Paris.

To relieve the Seventh Army headquarters of the burden of directing nine army corps, a new field-army headquarters was inserted on the west side of the Marne salient, Ninth Army headquarters, withdrawn from Rumania.

Because Rupprecht's reserves could not be touched again, lest "Hagen" be imperiled, the Marne offensive had to be entrusted to the same troops that had been through "Blücher." The available replacements from the Class of 1919—that is, the nineteen-year-olds called up the previous year—had already been used up in Hutier's "Gneisenau-Yorck" failure. Consequently, the hour had come for the Class of 1920, boys unlucky enough to pass their eighteenth birthdays in the first half of 1918. They barely sufficed to bring the shattered battalions up to reasonable strength for attacking, and they could not be considered the equal of veteran troops.

Ludendorff also received reports of a decline in the spirit of the older men. The once unquestioning, even eager, obedience to orders was giving way more and more visibly to a reluctance and even resistance, with multiplying instances of shirking and desertion. To Ludendorff's intense annoyance, the Reichstag had made the military code more lenient, so that the sentence of close arrest no longer meant that the miscreant was tied to a fixed object. "There were many men in the Army who deserved no mercy whatever," Ludendorff felt.

There were other signs. Several hundred Alsace-Lorrainers, soldiers whom the Germans had by preference kept on the Russian front, had since their transfer west organized an attempt at mass defection by way of the Netherlands. There was even a spirit of resistance detectable among the Bavarians, who had the effrontery to speak of the war as "a Prussian affair."

The enemy showed a disquieting awareness of the German morale problem; his air force showered the German lines with leaflets, promising that as prisoners German soldiers would be well treated and well fed.

Despite all such portents, the thunderclap that came from Berlin on June 24 was totally unexpected.

Early in the month (June 3) Ludendorff had read a

thoughtful memorandum prepared by Colonel Haeften, the head of the military section of the Foreign Office, which had stressed the importance of turning battlefield advantage to political account: "We cannot afford any longer to drift before events and to wait until one fine day the political fruits of our victories fall into our lap. . . . Unless our statesmanship sets to work on a definite plan before the conclusion of the military operations, there is no prospect of a peace of statesmanship."

"Peace of statesmanship" was a felicitous generality that won Ludendorff's endorsement. Unfortunately it masked a serious failure of communication. Haeften thought that in his assent to the memorandum Ludendorff was expressing a readiness to compromise on Belgium, whereas Ludendorff actually intended nothing of the sort. The confusion was compounded when the Colonel made his report to Berlin: Hertling and Kühlmann jumped to the conclusion that Ludendorff was now ready not only to relinquish his Belgian prey but to acquiesce in a direct peace feeler. Ludendorff's real thought, evidently not made clear to Haeften, was that the government should secretly sound out the Allies through a neutral government, and find out if they were ready to make peace on Ludendorff's terms.

Both Hertling and Kühlmann had developed deep misgivings about the course of the war. Even before the Matz check and the Austrian defeat, Hertling had received a surprisingly pessimistic letter from his fellow-Bavarian Crown Prince Rupprecht, recommending peace negotiations and the sacrifice of Belgium. Nonmilitary voices were also timidly raised; a handful of newspapers suggested that the time had come to spell out Germany's war aims, and they even put special, if delicate, emphasis on "those affecting England"—in other words, Belgium.

Hertling happened to have a speech scheduled in the Reichstag for June 24. At the last moment the elderly Chancellor asked Kühlmann if he would substitute. The notice was so short that Kühlmann had to skip lunch to prepare his text, but he accepted with alacrity. For several weeks he had been nurturing his own peace feeler through a German-British Red Cross meeting at The Hague. General Smuts had just made a conciliatory speech in Glasgow, and it occurred to Kühlmann that Ludendorff's apparent yielding on Belgium supplied the opportunity to take a decisive step. What he had in mind was a statement that would both signal the British that his cautious approach at The Hague was serious, and prepare the German public for a negotiated peace.

It was ticklish, but Kühlmann courageously made the attempt. In a discourse carefully sprinkled with the familiar clichés about Germany fighting in self-defense, the Allied war aims being the only obstacle to peace, new battlefield victories to be anticipated, he first disappointed his hearers by omitting to predict that the new victories would bring the end of the war. On the contrary, he intimated that the war would go on endlessly. He complained that "as long as every advance coming from the one side is interpreted by the other as a . . . trap, or misleading offer aimed at sowing discord among allies," it was impossible to advance the cause of peace. Then, maintaining his studiously ordinary tone, Kühlmann dropped a very quiet bombshell: "Without any exchange of opinions in this coalition war of such enormous dimensions, and in consideration of the overseas powers taking part, an absolute finish of the war can scarcely be expected by mere military decisions alone and without any kind of diplomatic discussions."

"Quite right," exclaimed the Left, in the record of the minutes, and "Hear, hear."

The critical passage seemed to have gone unnoticed by the Center and Right. Hertling, seated next to Kühlmann, waited a few minutes and took his leave, asking Kühlmann to call him if anything further happened.

Neither Hertling nor Kühlmann noticed the absence from his seat of one of the leaders of the Right, Count von Westarp. Westarp was a close friend of Ludendorff. No sooner had Kühlmann finished than Westarp found a telephone and had himself put through to Avesnes. The connection took time, and before Westarp finished his conversation, Kühlmann himself had left the Reichstag to return to the Foreign Office. Kühlmann was at dinner when he learned that Westarp had launched a sharp attack on him.

The debate resumed next day, with the Right, now fully alerted, angrily demanding explanations. One Conservative leader, Stresemann, wanted to know if the Supreme Command had told the government that decisive military successes were no longer obtainable. Another, Posadowsky, was clumsy enough to condemn Kühlmann for an excess of candor, thereby implying that Stresemann's hypothesis was correct.

Thus the debate had the effect of aggravating the very objection Westarp and Ludendorff had to Kühlmann's speech, its character as a confession of military weakness. In Ludendorff's eyes, such a confession would have been useless and harmful even if the tide of battle had actually turned, and Ludendorff was convinced that it had not. If the German Army was stretched taut, so was the enemy. Large masses of enemy reserves had been drawn to the Marne, and there was evidence that the French D.A.N. in Flanders was at last pulling out. The tactical situation was thus turning in Germany's favor.

True, the Americans were arriving at a more rapid rate than had been believed possible, and the Italian victory on the Piave assured that the flow would continue. According to Ludendorff's information, about fifteen American divisions had crossed in April-May-June, bringing the number in France to about twenty (the real totals were seventeen and twenty-three respectively). They were expected to concentrate in the Lorraine-Vosges sector, where Ludendorff thought they could be tied up by minor diversionary attacks that he had ordered in his June 14 directive. The Americans, he calculated, could give little help beyond what they were already giving to Pétain, whose French reserves were now once more used up. He remained convinced that "Reims" and "Marne Defense" would redouble the pressure on Pétain and force Foch to weaken his northern sector. Then "Hagen" would fall on the British and squeeze them back to the Channel.

In the light of Ludendorff's assessment, that the British were about to be driven from Europe, Kühlmann's open call for negotiations was unpardonable.

Once more, the First Quartermaster General, backed to the hilt by the Field Marshal, overpowered the civilian government. The frail old Reconciliation Chancellor came limping to rear headquarters at Spa to apologize.

Nothing would satisfy Ludendorff short of an absolute surrender. He dictated a point-by-point definition of German war aims on Belgium: "Belgium must remain under German influence, so that she cannot again fall under Anglo-French domination. . . . Flanders and Wallonia [must be] united by personal union and economic arrangements . . . customs union, community of railways, etc. . . . with Germany. [There must be] no Belgian Army. . . . A long period of occupation [will be ended only by] Belgium's attaching herself to us as closely as possible."

In other words, *Anschluss*. Ludendorff also specified that Kühlmann had to go.

The task of dismissing the Foreign Minister was left to the Kaiser. At Spa, the Supreme Warlord had a villa, requisitioned from a Belgian industrialist, surrounded by a spacious park. Kühlmann was summoned thither on July 9, and Wilhelm took him for a stroll. "Kühlmann," he said at last in a tone of regret, "our ways must unfortunately separate."

Kühlmann was prepared. He had heretofore avoided any mention of his Netherlands-Red Cross peace feeler to the impulsive and indiscreet Warlord, but now he told him the story. Very soon, Kühlmann disclosed, he might be called to Holland to begin secret, substantive peace talks. He even had a Dutch castle, Amerongen, picked out as a site. It belonged to their mutual friend Count Bentinck.

To Kühlmann's astonishment, the Kaiser brushed the whole matter aside—if Kühlmann wanted to pursue talks in Holland he could do so on his own, as a special emissary. Kühlmann pointed out warmly that the whole purpose of his speech had been to show the British government that German public opinion was ready for peace negotiations, and that his resignation in the wake of nationalist criticism would torpedo the whole project. The Kaiser admitted that in that case there would be little point in Kühlmann's proceeding on his own. But as Foreign Minister he was finished.

Hertling returned to Berlin to explain to the Reichstag that the Foreign Minister had resigned for complicated reasons that could hardly be put into words.

Despite Hertling's meekness, Ludendorff was far from satisfied with the Reconciliation Chancellor. When he voiced his preference for someone stronger, a Lloyd George or a Clemenceau, his chief of staff, Colonel von Thaer, abruptly made a proposal. Wouldn't it be simplest for Ludendorff himself to take the reins of government?

For once, Ludendorff was completely taken aback. "No, oh no!" he exclaimed. "No thought of it!"

Yet the idea did not seem so outrageous as to forbid discussion. He pointed out the difficulty: "Completely aside from the fact that His Majesty would never consider it, I am the totally wrong person. Shoemaker, stick to your last. As a soldier, I will succeed. How shall I go before parliament as chancellor?"

That was the real question. Even the Kaiser's hostility was a detail; what was impossible to imagine was Ludendorff successfully managing the Reichstag. But that difficulty merely forced Thaer's logic, and he voiced the answer with military succinctness: "Dictatorship—only solution! It's high time!"

Ludendorff shook his head. "Completely out of the question! Don't talk to me about such things!" But his objection was not on principle. "It will also never be considered; His Majesty would never do it!" A dictatorship without the backing of either the Reichstag *or* the Kaiser was manifestly impracticable.

Yet despite Ludendorff's categorical rejection, the fact that Thaer could openly make the proposal showed the viability of the idea in German Army circles, where in fact it had been discussed for a long time. After all, a dictatorship would be merely an extension and formalization of the power Ludendorff already wielded. Given the proper combination of events, Thaer's proposal could easily come into being.

One component of such a combination would be a new clash between the Supreme Command and the Berlin government. Another, not so obvious, might well be a battlefield victory on the Western Front, which would, as Czernin foresaw, complicate rather than simplify the negotiation of peace.

17

THE ALLIES CONCERT THEIR PLANS

While Ludendorff was imposing his implacable will on his reluctant associates, the Allied leaders were struggling more democratically to reconcile their own differences. In ten days in the middle of June, first Haig and then Pétain appealed to their governments, in accordance with the Beauvais agreement, over the head of Foch. The crux of their respective complaints was the same: Foch's assignment of the reserves. Pétain wanted the whole D.A.N. back, plus the five American divisions training with the British. Haig did not want to give up a single French or American soldier. The last straw for Haig was Foch's request that some of the British reserves should be prepared to return south of the Somme, where they would be available for use on Pétain's front if necessary. In addition, Haig, backed by Lord Milner speaking for Lloyd George, wanted new assurances that Foch would hold the Channel ports even if Paris were threatened. At a conference at the Boulevard des Invalides (June 7), Foch swore once more that he would defend both.

Foch was more opposed than the British themselves to a withdrawal of the British armies from Flanders. He had been thinking the same thought that had occurred to Hindenburg —if the Channel coast were abandoned, German shells would fall on English soil, and the B-men, at this moment about to cross the water to reinforce Haig, would be held back.

A week and a half later (June 17), Pétain was coupling his demand for the D.A.N. with an insistence on application of the letter of Directive No. 4, with which an instruction written by Foch seemed to conflict; Foch wanted both the First and the Second Position strongly held.

The dilemma of the Allied reserves seemed virtually hopeless on paper, as long as only the number of ready-to-fight combat divisons was considered. But the picture was radically altered when another factor was introduced, the manpower in the process of arriving in France. The flow came not only from America but from Britain. Lloyd George's release of the B-men was at last taking tangible shape in loaded cross-Channel ferries, while the transfer of British Empire troops from the East continued. At the same time, the arrival rate of the Yanks was such that Foch could give Pétain five more American divisions while letting Haig keep five.

The one critical question was, could the Germans be held through June and July, until Haig had absorbed his new troops and a substantial number of American divisions could complete training? If the question could be answered affirmatively, the D.A.N. could be brought back to the French front and additonal British divisions could even be borrowed from Haig.

Early in June, two small portents appeared on the southern rim of the great Marne salient: first, the French counterattack that wiped out the bridgehead south of the Marne (the one taken by Captain Matthaei's battalion, which had meantime been relieved); and second, a combined French-American attack, (using part of the U.S. Third Dvision) that captured Hill 204, an important height northwest of Château-Thierry.

Then came the fight for Belleau Wood. The U.S. Second Division was given the mission of clearing the Germans from a little mile-square wilderness that proved to be almost as full of machine guns as trees. In three weeks' bloody fighting, with some help from the French and from the U.S. Third, the Second Division took the wood, along with 9,500 casualties. The Yank leadership and staff work did not shine. Outfits blundered into each other and lost contact with the enemy, but the fighting qualities of the troops commanded German respect. "The American 2nd Infantry Division can be considered a very good division," reported the Operations Bureau of the German Seventh Army. "The recruitment of the men must be qualified as remarkable; they are healthy, physically well constituted. Their spirit is fresh and full of naïve confidence."

A quirk of censorship led to a long-lasting misconception in many American minds about the battle. The censor forbade mention of any specific units, but permitted identification of branches of service—that is, Army or Navy. The correspondents seized the opportunity to identify the Second Division's Marine Brigade as "the Marines," heaping extravagant credit that by extension led to a lasting conviction on the part of many newspaper readers that the "United States Marines" had stopped the Germans single-handed and saved Paris. They had not done anything like that, but they had done enough to lead General Degoutte, the new commander of the French Sixth Army, to rename the woods "*Bois de la Brigade Marine*," to the lasting annoyance of the U.S. Army.

Far more important than Belleau Wood was the battle on the Matz, the offensive by Hutier known to the Germans as "Gneisenau-Yorck," by which Ludendorff had tried to break down the Soissons shoulder, June 9–12. The attack had fallen on the French Third Army, under General Humbert. Another resister of Directive No. 4, Humbert had tried to compromise on the question of First Position versus Second Position by making the rear trenches of his First Position his main line of resistance. That had taken half his infantry out of mortar range, but left the other half in, and this front half took heavy casualties. But though driven sharply back on the first day, the Third Army had remained intact, and had saved all its artillery. Humbert consequently did not suffer the fate of Duchêne, but was merely treated to a rare tongue-lashing by

Pétain. Over the next two days the Third Army stopped the offensive, the first time a major German offensive had been halted by the troops initially attacked. That in turn permitted the use of some of Fayolle's reserves for the counterattack on Hutier's flank that had disconcerted Ludendorff on June 11. The counterattack also vindicated Pétain's faith in tanks. General Mangin, who led the maneuver, was given five infantry divisions and 130 Schneiders and St. Chamonds. Where the infantry was held up by machine guns, the tanks rumbled forward and erased the nests with close-range blasts from their sawed-off 75's. They crossed trenches, invaded garrisoned villages, and fought off infantry counterattacks. They also illustrated once more their vulnerability to artillery fire; by nightfall fully half were casualties.

Foch, who had moved his headquarters to Bombon, southeast of Paris, was tremendously elated by Mangin's success, which he described as "astonishing." It was the first Allied attack on a scale this large since the year had begun, and despite its hastily improvised character—nothing remotely like the Bruchmüller-Hutier preparation—it had gained a respectable amount of ground, captured prisoners and guns, and most significant, had had a clearly recognizable strategic impact. Foch began at once to plan a major Allied offensive stroke.

The day before (June 10), he had received a letter from Haig of a character so different from Haig's representations at the Invalides conference that it seemed as if three months instead of three days had passed. Haig had evidently received improved assurances from Lloyd George, because he now declared that he could reconstitute all fourteen British skeleton divisions (ten from "Michael" and "Georgette," four from "Blücher") within a few weeks. Eight of the fourteen were to be filled with B-men. There were enough regular replacements ("A-men") to fill three more, and the remaining three would be rebuilt with battalions withdrawn from Palestine and Greece. In addition, three full divisions were coming back from the East. By late July, a British Expeditionary

Force of some sixty full-strength divisions would be ready for action.

On the same day, Foch received an offer from Pershing that both surprised and gratified him.

Colonel Bruchmüller's bombardment for "Gneisenau-Yorck" had extended far enough west to include the U.S. First Division, whose front lines at Cantigny had been battered by explosives and drenched in gas. An A.E.F. officer later recalled the weird sight of a mounted messenger galloping out of the poison fog, both horse and man wearing gas masks. The assault front was narrower, and the First received no shock troops. As the French to the east fell back, however, Pershing jumped to the conclusion that the Germans had produced another "Michael" or "Blücher" breakthrough, and hastened to Foch's headquarters to enact a rather grandiloquent repetition of his March 28 gesture. Volunteering to constitute himself the interpreter of United States opinion, he announced America's determination to throw her whole weight into the struggle at once without counting the cost.

Foch and Pétain needed no Americans to fight Hutier, but Pershing's offer was too good to be ignored. The total of American divisions in France already exceeded twenty, and the schedule promised twenty-five by mid-July. Quiet-sector duty for some of these—Pétain calculated that five of the oversize American divisions could replace six French—could help Pétain concentrate his own French Army for the upcoming battle. At the same time, five American divisions could be given Haig to tide him over till the B-men got there.

More significantly yet, several American divisions were now ripe for a larger role. The First and Second had seen serious combat, at Cantigny and Belleau Wood. The Twenty-sixth, Thirty-second, and Forty-second had had ample quiet-sector exposure. The Third Division, backed by French artillery, was in the line on the south bank of the Marne, at the tip of the salient. In addition, four to six divisions that had arrived in April or early May would be ready for anything by mid-July. Given a free hand to juggle the American divisions to suit the situation, postponing formation of Pershing's American Army, Foch could construct his reserve force, his "mass of maneuver," while assuring both Haig and Pétain adequate reserves of their own.

With Haig, Foch negotiated the return of the D.A.N. to the French zone, the move to be accomplished in stages, as Haig's reconstitution proceeded. The fact that five of the ruined British divisions had by now been filled up with B-men made Haig's diary entry of June 24 downright complacent: "General Pétain being short of reserves, at Foch's request I arrange to send him . . . three French divisions. . . . [The move] reduces our strength on the Kemmel front for the moment, and a certain amount of risk is, of course, run."

The whole D.A.N. was scheduled to arrive in the Marne area by July 10, reorganized as the French Ninth Army. Thus Ludendorff's hope of moving the French out of Flanders was fulfilled. However, it was fulfilled only technically, because in reality the rebuilding program of the British Army was making good the loss and even exceeding it; Haig went so far as to promise Foch that if all went well, a few British divisions could be made available for action in the Marne–Aisne sector by mid-July. In addition, General Díaz was sending two Italian divisions to partly compensate for British and French troops he still had in the line.

The burgeoning U.S. air force was also plugged into the Marne buildup. Colonel Billy Mitchell organized the "U.S. First Air Brigade," made up of four U.S. pursuit and three U.S. observation squadrons, plus French units, in the Toul (Lorraine) sector, and moved it to two airfields west and southwest of Château-Thierry. George Creel, the U.S. propaganda chief, had announced back in February that "the first American-built battle planes are today en route to the front in France," but in July the Americans were flying French Nieuports and hoping to get some of the new French Spads. The fifty-four American-piloted Nieuports flew the 140 miles to their new base at Tonquin on June 29, becoming part of an Allied concentration confronting a mass of German air power inside the salient that included the fighting squadrons of Her-

"Michael": a heavy German gun being moved forward by infantrymen and horses, March 21, 1918. CREDIT: IMPERIAL WAR MUSEUM

"Michael": British troops retreating through Aveluy, March 25, 1918. CREDIT: IMPERIAL WAR MUSEUM

Shock troops attacking, Spring 1918. CREDIT: WEHRGESCHICHTLICHES MUSEUM

"Michael": a German 10 cm. batt opens the way for German shock tro CREDIT: WEHRGESCHICHTLICHES MUSEU

Aftermath of "Michael": an old man waiting for customers in his wrecked shop, April 3, 1918, in Amiens. CREDIT: IMPERIAL WAR MUSEUM

"Michael": a ruined village between Peronne and St. Quentin jammed with Germans coming and going. CREDIT: WEHRGESCHICHTLICHES MUSEUM

"Georgette": a British field gun on the Lys canal at St. Venant, April 13, 1918. CREDIT: IMPERIAL WAR MUSEUM

"Georgette": the command post of a French infantry regiment on Mount Kemmel just before the attack of April 24, 1918. CREDIT: ÉTABLISSEMENT CINÉMATOGRAPHIQUE ET PHOTOGRAPHIQUE DES ARMÉES

"Georgette": British soldiers man a street barricade in Bailleul, April 15, 1918, just before the fall of the town. CREDIT: IMPERIAL WAR MUSEUM

"Blücher" offensive: French 75's taking position in a wheat field in front of Reims, May 31, 1918. CREDIT: ÉTABLISSEMENT CINÉMATOGRAPHIQUE ET PHOTOGRAPHIQUE DES ARMÉES

Germans defending a shallow trench against counterattacking French infantry. CREDIT: SÜDDEUTSCHER VERLAG

Pontoon crossing of a branch of the Aisne by a French raiding party during a lull in the German offensive of May, 1918. CREDIT: ÉTABLISSEMENT CINÉMATOGRAPHIQUE ET PHOTOGRAPHIQUE DES ARMÉES

"Blücher" offensive: devastated area, Aisne, June 1918. CREDIT: IMPERIAL WAR MUSEUM

German dead at Belleau Wood. June 29, 1918. CREDIT: U.S. SIGNAL CORPS

The U.S. First Division arrives on Lorraine front in French "40 and 8" cars, February 3, 1918. CREDIT: ÉTABLISSEMENT CINÉMATOGRAPHIQUE ET PHOTOGRAPHIQUE DES ARMÉES

A French captain showing American infantryman how to hold and throw live grenades, Chanoy, February 7, 1918. CREDIT: U.S. SIGNAL CORPS

The 42nd Division in front-line trenches, Neuvillers, May 10, 1918. CREDIT: U.S. SIGNAL CORPS

American troops training with the British, May 23, 1918. CREDIT: IMPERIAL WAR MUSEUM

Battle of the Marne: French soldiers of the Tenth Army in a captured dugout, July 18, near Longpont; in the foreground, a young German prisoner. CREDIT: ÉTABLISSEMENT CINÉMATOGRAPHIQUE ET PHOTOGRAPHIQUE DES ARMÉES

Battle of the Marne: French battery laying down rolling barrage in support of attacking infantry of the Tenth Army. CREDIT: ÉTABLISSEMENT CINÉMATOGRAPHIQUE ET PHOTOGRAPHIQUE DES ARMÉES

Battle of the Marne: French assault wave in German first-line trenches, Haricot de Vadenay, July 29, 1918. CREDIT: ÉTABLISSEMENT CINÉMATOGRAPHIQUE ET PHOTOGRAPHIQUE DES ARMÉES

Battle of the Marne: a French Saint-Chamond tank, Chavigny, July 18, 1918.
CREDIT: U.S. SIGNAL CORPS

Battle of the Marne: French troops passing British dead in the Woods of the Mountain of Reims, July 23, 1918. CREDIT: IMPERIAL WAR MUSEUM

Battle of the Marne: French infantrymen and tank in a captured German position near Courcelles, west of Reims (no date). CREDIT: MUSÉE DES DEUX GUERRES MONDIALES

"Battle of the Marne": a wrecked bridge over the Marne at Chateau Thierry. 150th U.S. Field Artillery in the foreground, July 25, 1918.
CREDIT: U.S. SIGNAL CORPS

mann Göring and Ernst Udet, and all three of the large formations the Germans called "Flying Circuses." On the morning of July 2 the Americans, who had found air combat in Lorraine rather tame, had their first taste of the Germans' best when eight of them reconnoitering the Marne ran into nine new Fokker D-VII's led by Udet. In a thirty-five-minute battle, two planes were shot down on each side. On July 5, Eddie Rickenbacker, formerly Pershing's chauffeur and now a fighter ace with six victories, ferried in the first of the new Spad 13's with which the American squadrons were being reequipped. Two days later, the Americans were moved from Tonquin to Saints, to make room for a British air brigade being added to the Allied aerial team fighting for control of the Marne sky.

At the last minute, Pershing, who perhaps felt that his generosity of June 10 had been a little rash, produced a small sour note by insisting that all American divisions coming over in July should go to the "American sector,"—that is, Lorraine —but it did not matter; Foch had enough Americans.

"*Depuis que je pratique la coalition, j'admire moins Bonaparte*" ("Since making coalition war, I admire Bonaparte less"), quipped Clemenceau after one of the argumentative inter-Allied conferences, but despite bickering, backbiting, and diary writing, the Allied leadership was cooperating with noteworthy efficiency. Troops had been moved when and where they had to be moved, and every ally had made whatever sacrifices were necessary.

As everyone knew, the supreme crisis was approaching. Whether it could be mastered no longer depended on the American shipbuilding program, the release of B-men, "amalgamation," or the return of troops from secondary fronts. Everything that could be done behind the battle line had been done. Now it was up to the vast mix of Allied soldiers and their commanders.

In a conference with Pétain and Clemenceau on June 17, Foch executed a strategic retreat over Directive No. 4, interpreting his own seemingly contradictory instructions in a sense favorable to Pétain. The issue was not entirely resolved, because Foch could not bring himself to a wholehearted endorsement of the Second Position as the place to concentrate the French Army. His reluctance was rooted in his longing to go over to the offensive. After three months of retreating, maneuvering, and parrying on battlefields chosen by Ludendorff, he felt that the moment was near to reverse the roles.

Pétain, who had long ago named June as the decisive month of the war, could not disagree. He suggested that the approaching German offensive should be first halted and then defeated by a counteroffensive. A parry, followed by a riposte.

Foch had no patience for so conservative a program. He wanted to plan an Allied offensive at once, fix a D-day, and get all the necessary preparations under way without regard for enemy plans. If the Boche struck first, good, if the Boche struck at the same moment, good, and if the Boche was still in the midst of his own preparations, good.

Foch's determination to launch an Allied offensive as soon as a sufficient mass of reserves could be assembled, coinciding with Ludendorff's plan to fight a battle of annihilation around the Reims shoulder, made inevitable a clash on a gigantic scale, dwarfing "Michael," "Georgette," and "Blücher." The locale of the Allied offensive was left undecided for the moment, but one sector under favorable consideration was the west face of the Marne salient.

As day followed day with local attacks, counterattacks, barrages, raids, air combat in and around the salient, the question of the place and time of the German offensive grew more and more critical. Much of the advantage or risk of Foch's offensive depended on how accurately Ludendorff's intentions could be read. Foch thought the German blow would fall in the north-central part of the front, between Château-Thierry and Arras. Pétain disagreed, believing that it would come between Château-Thierry and the Argonne Forest, east of Reims—a very accurate prognosis. On June 28, Pétain's G-2, taking into consideration the time the Germans would need to move reserves and heavy artillery north for an offensive there, or to equip the Marne front with all the new battery positions, observation posts, ammunition dumps, airfields, telephone centrals, and other support elements for an offensive there, made a guess at the date—July 15.

Air reconnaissance had been less than completely successful in unmasking the previous German offensives, and Pétain now put his faith in aggressive ground patrols. A raiding party that crossed the Marne near Dormans one night late in June brought back a valuable prize: a German officer of the engineers who had in his possession plans for crossings of the river at Mont-St-Père and Jaulgonne.

Further raids continued to accumulate evidence that the German attack front was indeed the one suspected by Pétain, and that its aim would be to pinch off Reims, whose strategic importance to Ludendorff needed no emphasis. If Pétain was correct, the key defensive sectors were those of the French Fifth and Fourth Armies, the former south, the latter east, of Reims. The Fifth was commanded by a corpulent but attack-minded general, Berthelot, whom Foch had especially chosen for his aggressiveness. The Fourth was commanded by Gouraud, the valiant, stubborn one-armed hero who had been among the loudest protesters against Directive No. 4. Yet Pétain was determined this time that his generals should conform. He was aware of practical difficulties, particularly in the case of Berthelot, whose troops had occupied their present positions for only a month and had not been able to complete the Second Position. Berthelot consequently had an excuse for keeping a large proportion of his infantry well forward, and he took it. Gouraud's army, on the other hand, had long been at its present locale, and had elaborate fieldworks covering not only First and Second Positions, but even an Intermediate Position.

Pétain's Directive No. 5, again prescribing the Second Position, was sent to Foch's headquarters for approval. When no immediate reply was received, Pétain's operations officer telephoned his opposite number at Bombon, who returned to the phone after a few moments with the word, "Approved, you can march." Directive No. 5 was at once signed and circulated to the army groups and army headquarters. Gouraud protested at once. The one-armed general beseeched Pétain, "How can you ask me to consent to give up an inch of ground confided to my honor?"

But Pétain now felt he could rule. In a dry tone familiar to his subordinates, he replied, "I leave you twenty-four hours to decide." Gouraud pulled his infantry back from the First Position, which he left manned only by a handful of volunteers.

The date named by French G-2 for the German offensive, July 15, put it three days ahead of the earliest practicable date for the Allied counterstroke. As the first week of July passed and G-2's estimate looked better and better, Pétain was relieved by and Foch resigned to the probable sequence of the two offensives.

The growing conviction that Ludendorff's blow would fall on both sides of Reims made the locale of the counteroffensive more and more inevitable. Mangin, now in command of the French Tenth Army on the west face of the salient, had pointed out the value of the Forest of Villers-Cotterêts as cover for the troop concentration. An offensive from here, directly following a German offensive from the opposite face, promised exceptional embarrassment for the enemy. Foch agreed with enthusiasm; even a moderate advance here would bring an immediate advantage by placing the rail lines and highways running south from Soissons under field-artillery fire.

On July 8, an order from Pétain's headquarters at Provins detailed the means available to the Tenth Army for its offensive: eight divisions to be added to the five Mangin already had, making thirteen. Of the eight new divisions, six would be French, and two American—the U.S. First and Second. In addition to the strong infantry contingent, the French 501st Tank Regiment, consisting of five groups of St. Chamonds and Schneiders, would be available to the Tenth Army.

The Sixth Army, on the Tenth's right, was also to participate in the offensive, with its left wing. The Sixth would be strengthened by one French and one American division (the Fourth) and by the 502nd Tank Regiment.

All along the threatened front, battle alerts were ordered nightly. Raiding was intensified even further. On the French Fourth Army front east of Reims, Gouraud insisted on prisoners being taken every single day. On the night of July 11–12, several deep raids brought back a number of Germans whose interrogation confirmed that the offensive was imminent, and made it all but certain that it would be on the night of July 14–15.

Foch read the G-2 report with satisfaction. Now he felt no compunction about calling on Haig for British reserves; there was no way Ludendorff could hit the British after first launching an offensive and then taking an Allied counterpunch. The Flanders front was safe at least till late July.

On July 13 he sent off a letter to Haig:

> In view of the turn that the impending battle in Champagne seems to be taking I call on you for British reserves. I ask you to send four divisions to the French front to begin with. . . .
>
> Detrainment in the region Revigny-Vitry-le-François. . . .
>
> I ask you furthermore to prepare four other divisions to follow the first four if the exigencies of the battle require.
>
> I will be happy to meet as soon as convenient to discuss the situation with you.
>
> *Foch*

Only one question remained unanswered, When exactly was H-hour, the moment of attack?

18

JULY 14

Children, old people, and the sick had been evacuated from Paris as the city braced for a possible siege. A million gas masks had been collected in Orléans for shipment to the capital. Nevertheless, on Bastille Day, crowds thronged to cheer marching contingents of French, British, Americans, Italians, Belgians, Serbs, Greeks—practically every ally—while overhead, fighter planes buzzed, not as part of the celebration, but to guard against German bombers. None appeared, and Badaboume remained silent, as Paris enjoyed its tense holiday.

The Paris authorities had organized the parade of Allies in alphabetical order, a device that put the American contingent first. Drawn from the various regiments of the First Division, the khaki-clad battalion carrying the Stars and Stripes drew tumultuous applause as it led the way down the Avenue des Ternes and the Rue du Faubourg St-Honoré—bypassing the Arc de Triomphe–Champs-Élysées–Concorde route, reserved for the eventual Allied victory parade. The doughboys had had the pleasure of a truck ride into Paris. The previous two nights, the First had put in hard marches, twenty to twenty-five miles, moving south from its reserve position near Beauvais.

Only the top officers of the First thought they knew what the move meant, that the First was to be brigaded with the U.S. Second to form Pershing's first American Army corps, a large step toward an American Army.

There were now seven American divisions in and around the Marne salient, though only two were actually in the line. The Third was now practically complete, its artillery having just joined it. Its line had also been shortened. The division was gathered in a compact mass at the tip of the salient, from a point just east of Château-Thierry to the Jaulgonne Bend. Its front line consisted of empty foxholes along the southern bank of the river; these were occupied every night by one platoon from each company in the line, and evacuated at dawn. The main line of resistance was three to four hundred yards back, where the Paris–Metz railway ran on a high embankment, giving good cover. Across the river, steep hills sloping to the water's edge screened the enemy.

The other American division in the line was the Twenty-sixth (Yankee), now occupying Belleau Wood. Two untried divisions, the Twenty-eighth and the Fourth, newly arrived and minus their artillery, lay in reserve positions, southeast and southwest of Château-Thierry respectively. Near the Fourth was the airfield of the American pursuit group. On Bastille Day, a flight returned with Quentin Roosevelt missing. Four days earlier, Teddy Roosevelt's son had gotten separated from his flight and had survived a strange adventure. Attaching himself to the tail end of what he thought was his own group, he had awakened to the discovery that he was flying in company with German Fokkers. He had shot down the Fokker in front of him and dived for home. Today he was not so lucky; a German radio broadcast reported him shot down over the salient and buried with military honors. This same day the American Observation Group made a deep penetration in the face of hot antiaircraft fire and fighter opposition to bring back photos of German activity in the salient.

This and other aerial reconnaissance confirmed the fact that the attack was imminent.

Six of the seven American divisions were clustered in the line or in reserve around the salient. The seventh American division was in an entirely different area, sixty miles away. But this one, the Forty-second (Rainbow) Division, was actually in the most critical position of all. It was in the reserve line of General Gouraud's French Fourth Army, east of Reims, one of the two armies expected to take the brunt of the German offensive, the other being the French Fifth Army, around and south of Reims, and containing no American units. During the past ten days the Rainbows had kept their picks and shovels busy biting into the stubborn Champagne chalk, deepening trenches and completing dugouts of the Second Position. Its advanced posts were within easy rifle range of the Intermediate Position, whose trenches Gouraud had made his main line of resistance, and clearly visible off in the northern distance was the ridge where the German shock troops were gathering. The night before the fourteenth of July, every man had stood to his post; when Bastille Day dawned without the Boche attack, the Forty-second was given a holiday, with football games organized against teams from the neighboring French outfits.

Besides the seven American divisions in and around the Marne salient, twelve others were in the line or in reserve in quiet sectors, helping free French and British divisions for the Marne. Eight more were in various stages of training, travel, or debarkation; their presence in France had significance in the light of Foch's intended counterstroke, whose success would demand more troops to keep it going.

Despite the active presence of so many American troops, Pershing was left with no role in the battle. He spent the day distributing prizes to French schoolchildren at Chaumont, receiving in turn the present of an illustrated history of France for his son. (In Washington, Colonel House spent the day in an equally peaceful activity, drafting a charter for the League of Nations.)

On the afternoon of July 14, Foch drove to Provins for a last-minute conference with Pétain. There the generalissimo formally approved Pétain's conception of Mangin's offensive of July 18 as a counterstroke to Ludendorff's blow, now defined as probably falling on both sides of Reims, extending east as far as Mont Teton, and including a Marne crossing to protect its right flank. Defensive preparations, including the strengthening of the front with batteries of heavy artillery echeloned in depth, were complete except for one thing: Pétain wished he had information on the German H-hour. He still hoped to get it.

Meantime, for Mangin's attack on the eighteenth to jump off on time, the troops had to be started for their final positions now. Orders were therefore cut in Provins for the transfer of the new American III Corps (First and Second Divisions), commanded by General Bullard, to the French Tenth Army. Unfortunately, the new American corps headquarters was not yet ready to function in combat, and at the last moment the two big American outfits were grouped in the French XX Corps, along with the French First Moroccan Division. Everything was done in a spirit of pell-mell improvisation. The U.S. Second Division got under way on the verbal order of a French motor-transport captain.

Mangin's Tenth Army had now grown to four corps with a total of seventeen divisions, and its tank force had been augmented by a sixth group of heavy tanks and a full regiment of Renaults. The two leftmost corps of the French Sixth Army would also participate in the offensive; its two rightmost corps were expected to be involved in the defensive battle.

On the evening of the fourteenth, the Kaiser's special train halted at a point northeast of Reims, behind the attack front of the German First Army. Here a camouflaged tower eighty feet high had been constructed for the Supreme Warlord's personal observation post. A few miles in front, his son Crown Prince Wilhelm mounted a similar tower to watch the opening of his army group's offensive.

At 7:55, off to their left, a heavy French box barrage singled out a piece of the German front line. Minutes later, a company of the French 366th Infantry, 132nd Division, dashed across No-Man's-Land and flung themselves into the German forward posts. As the rest of the company covered with rifle and machine-gun fire, its commander, followed by a sergeant and three men, pressed on into the German line. Surrounding a deep dugout, they hurled grenades and ordered the occupants to come out.

The daring raid paid off handsomely—twenty-seven Germans emerged from the dugout, to be hustled back to the French lines. So large a catch on the eve of an offensive could hardly fail to produce intelligence results, and this one did not fail. Within an hour, Captain Gauché of Fourth Army G-2 was saluting General Gouraud with explicit information:

"The enemy preparation will begin at twelve ten and the infantry will attack at three forty."

"Are you certain, Gauché?" asked the general.

"I'm certain," said Gauché.

By 9:30, telephones and runners had carried the message to all elements of the French Fourth Army, and through General Headquarters to the neighboring Fifth Army and the Sixth, along the Marne.

All up and down the front, extending in a vast curve sweeping from east of Reims to Château-Thierry, the battle alert was on. Opposite, the German infantry was crowding into the forward trenches or marching through the darkness to reach them. Along the north side of the Marne, the men filed into the woods at least six to eight hundred yards from the river, on the forward slopes of wooded hills extending down to the water's edge. The woods were dense thickets of trees too slender to give protection, but thick enough to make passage nearly impossible. There were no dugouts, trenches, or foxholes. Flags planted to indicate the line of departure of the attack were invisible. In the interest of secrecy, the officers had seen the forward positions only once, by daylight. The troops stumbled forward as best they could, crashing into trees, losing their footing, as intermittent enemy artillery fire fell among them.

Across the river, the Americans and French waited tensely in foxholes along the water's edge, behind the railway embankment, and in whatever other natural or contrived shelter they could find. Along the front of the French Fifth Army, many troops were exposed in forward positions with no more than hastily dug foxholes. East of Reims, however, Gouraud's Fourth Army was in deep dugouts in the Intermediate Position and the Second Position behind it. In places where they had been digging in the chalk, the soldiers looked like white specters in the moonlight. Up in the First Position, scattered groups armed with automatic weapons and signal flares waited at the outpost line, with the mission of signaling the advance of the German infantry and then fighting to the last man.

A half hour before midnight, the entire artillery of the Fourth Army suddenly opened with a deafening roar on the trenches and battery positions opposite.

The men in the observation posts could see the earth light up with splotches of red and yellow where the shells burst, while to the rear the sky was white with gun flashes. Rocket flares rose from the German trenches with varicolored messages of distress.

The Second Battle of the Marne had begun.

19

JULY 15

On his tower platform north of Reims, the Kaiser saw and heard the flashes and reports from the enemy line, but attached no particular significance to them. Artillery fire had risen and fallen unpredictably during the past several days and nights of incessant raiding. If any of the officers with the Supreme Warlord found the French fire disturbing, they said nothing.

On his own observation tower nearer the front, the Crown Prince, more sophisticated in military matters than his father, was concerned at the prolonged volume of the enemy fire. He asked his artillery officer what he thought. The officer answered that the French fire seemed of "normal intensity."

"I don't agree," said the Crown Prince. "I think it's more violent."

Here and there along the southern horizon a German munitions dump blew up, lighting the night sky.

In both the Kaiser's and his son's observatories an officer with watch in hand counted down first the minutes, then the seconds, to the German barrage: "Fifty . . . forty . . . thirty . . . twenty . . . ten . . ."

With a roll of thunder that presaged the apocalypse, Colonel Bruchmüller's bombardment opened, its 6,400 guns drowning out the sound of the French fire. Eagerly, the Kaiser watched the jumping white curve of the horizon, which

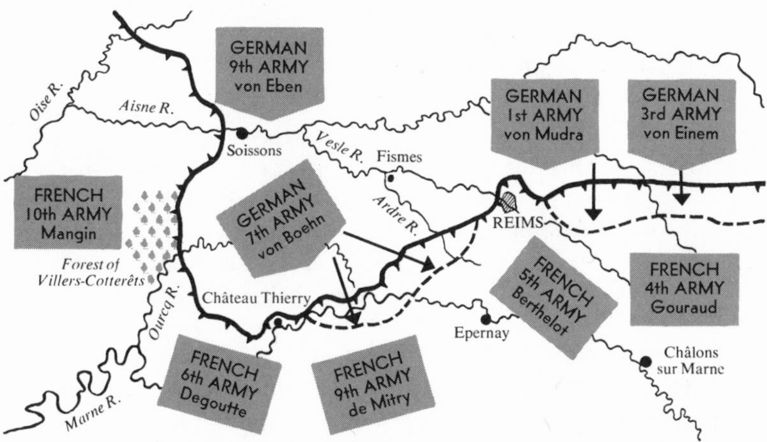

Battle of the Marne, July 15–17.

Ludendorff had promised would be the first gleam of his sunrise of victory.

The German attack direction was threefold: the First and Third German Armies, strung out east of Reims, were to attack southward to form the left-hand pincer in the encirclement of Reims; the left of the Seventh Army, stretching from Reims to the southwest, was to attack in a southeasterly direction, toward Épernay, forming the right-hand pincer; the center of the Seventh Army, consiting of two corps (Kathen and Wichura), was to attack south across the Marne, to provide flank and rear protection for the troops to the north attacking toward Épernay.

To the men of the Rainbow Division in their reserve position in Gouraud's Fourth Army, the fury of the German bombardment completely dwarfed that of the barrage begun earlier by their own side. Nothing they experienced afterward, at St-Mihiel or in the Argonne, came close. The first shower drenched the rear sections in gas, while explosions tore up the landscape and filled the air with shrieking splinters. In the large, deep shelters there was no room to sit; the men all stood, jammed so tight they could scarcely turn around. Air grew foul and candles went out. Soldiers stationed on the dugout steps tried to fan air down to their fainting comrades below. The officers finally hit on the expedient of moving the men in a circle, out one dugout entrance and in the other. Outside, some of the stumbling, gas-masked, half-blinded figures took shell splinters and fell gasping in the trench, but mass suffocation was averted. The packed-in, slowly circling line of men felt the impact of the shells as that of a giant jackhammer pounding the earth with machine-gun rapidity.

Wire communications disappeared at once, and could not be reestablished despite heroic efforts by the signalmen crawling out over and over again to repair lines.

Throughout the rear position, the French artillery fought from the open. In front of L Company of the 168th Infantry, the crew of one 75 astonished the Americans by accompanying its work amid the din with *Quand Madelon: "Pour le repos . . .* [crash!] *le plaisir* [slam!] *du militaire* [bang!]." In the midst of a phrase, a whirring enemy shell blew gun and crew to bits.

For ten minutes, along the entire front of over sixty miles, the German field artillery and heavy artillery rained down on all depths of the Allied line. For the next hour (for an hour and a quarter east of Reims, owing to a refinement of Colonel Bruchmüller's calculations), the heavy artillery concentrated on the rear, or battery positions, exclusively. Next came a period of concentration on rear infantry positions. Finally the climax: the 2,200 mortars joined in for two solid hours of deluging the forward infantry positions—that is, the trenches of the French First Position.

The effect of the barrage was very different at different points of the long line. In Gouraud's Fourth Army, sheltering in the chalky dugouts of the Intermediate Position, casualties were light. In several parts of the line held by Berthelot's Fifth Army and Degoutte's Sixth, on the other hand, forward positions were heavily manned and shallowly dug, and suffered accordingly.

On the extreme right of the German offensive, the barrage tore up the south bank of the Marne, and German engineers began pulling boats and rubber rafts from under cover. To the shock troops huddled in the woods it seemed as if the German bombardment here had at first overwhelmed that of the Allies, but then the Allied fire began to grow ominously in intensity, at times surpassing the German.

What had happened was that the French XXXVIII Corps, on the extreme left of the attack front, had ascertained that the assault was directed only against its rightmost division, the U.S. Third, and immediately concentrated its entire corps artillery fire in the threatened sector. As the German shock troops pushed their way through the thickets, splinters from the exploding shells darted and glowed like comets. Then the familiar dull clump of another kind of projectile brought the cry "Gas!" A horse-drawn battery advancing toward the river received a direct hit, completely blocking the path. Horses writhed on the ground, and munitions boxes exploded.

The commanding officer of the Fifth Grenadier Regiment of the German Thirty-sixth Division sent a patrol from his headquarters to ascertain the situation. It found that the first battalion, attacking on the right, against the Americans (of the Third Division), had been badly cut up by artillery fire on the paths, and the American machine-gun fire was so heavy that a crossing was impossible. The rafts had been left a hundred yards short of the river.

On the left, however, two other battalions had reached the river and crossed in assault boats. Pulling themselves up the steep bank on the far side, they encountered barbed wire, invisible in aerial photographs. Behind it were trenches, and suddenly they were face to face with the enemy in the pitch blackness. But the defenders, survivors of the bombardment, fell back, and the shock troops were able to form up for the advance. They were barely in time—the officers checking their watches found that the rolling barrage had already begun to move ahead of them. Pressing on against increasing fire, they gained the railway embankment several hundred yards south of the Marne. North of them, other shock troops had crossed, and the engineers were building pontoon bridges.

Transmitted to the rear by runner and to higher headquarters by telephone, the news soon reached Avesnes, and from there returned south to the Kaiser in his forward observation post: the Seventh Army was across the Marne!

At the same time the First and Third Armies, around Reims, reported that they had already occupied the enemy's First Position!

The delighted Warlord ordered the breakfast baskets to be broken out.

As day dawned south of the Marne, German engineers were building pontoon bridges east of Dormans. The shock troops had taken several villages and much of the railway embankment, and were beginning to ascend the southern slopes of the valley. On the German extreme right, the Sixth Grenadiers were advancing after crossing the river, when through the morning mist and the tall grain in the wheatfields, enemy columns were seen. The color of their uniforms was made out—khaki. A quick change of front brought the American counterattack to a halt, but the threat put an end to the advance, and the Grenadiers were pinned where they lay.

The Germans' problem was to improvise a line, mostly in the open, extending from their crossing points in the Jaulgonne Bend eastward, to connect with the thrust up the Marne valley toward Épernay and Châlons. Their bridges and boat crossings were under every kind of fire, including air bombardment. Crossings farther west, to relieve the pressure, were found to be impossible. Lying prone in the wheatfields, the Americans had shot up two assaulting companies after letting them come into close range.

Jaulgonne was a hot corner, one of the hottest of the battle, or even of the whole war. Yet on Ludendorff's map at Avesnes it was not really all that important. The attack direction, after all, was not toward Paris. On the contrary, most of the Seventh Army was turning its back on Paris. Any kind of defense line that would protect the southern flank would be satisfactory; the Marne itself could provide flank protection for the main thrust of the eastward offensive, between the Marne and the Ardre.

It was on this broad attack front, the right-hand pincer, and on its mate, the left-hand pincer east of Reims, that Ludendorff and Hindenburg fixed their eyes.

A German platoon leader, Hans Zöberlein, of the Bavarian Twelfth Division, Corps Schmettow, described his experience this day on the Marne–Ardre front:

> The day began dim, but gradually the sun came through. . . . Our observation balloons had already been pushed ahead. Near Romigny we saw two fat sausages slowly rocking in the breeze. A few flyers circled them in the usual balloon patrol. . . . Suddenly a balloon burst into flame and a parachute blossomed next to it. Now the observer jumped from the other balloon. Those were enemy flyers circling the balloons. . . . But *we* were making the offensive, not the French! [The aircraft were the new Spad 13's, and to the further surprise of the Germans, their markings proved them to be flown by Americans.] In Romigny a column of prisoners trudged toward us [—and turned out to be Italians].
>
> Directly before us, on the road, a French battery planted one shell after another. From this road one looked out toward the valley [of the Belval stream] whose trough blended westward with the basin of the Marne. In the deep hilly woods to the south

> rocked the noise of the battle. . . . Farther on in the cover of a forest path we met the other battalions of our regiment. We threw ourselves down beside them in the underbrush. . . . The *Oberleutnant* spread out a map; many dark spots of forest marked the broad basin of the Marne. "Today we will go about so far," he said. "We're still about six or seven kilometers from the Marne. . . . Reims will be cut off. That is our main objective. We must succeed, if all the French reserves are not right here."
>
> "Fifth Company, march!" I plunged ahead after my company, leaving the woods for the ruins of Champlat. In two great shell holes lay German tanks. . . .
>
> The field of our morning preparation fire was crossed. . . . Discarded [enemy] supplies and weapons lay about. . . . [German] field kitchens were operating in the open field. If the flyers saw those! . . . An ammunition column pushed us from the road. Artillery that had finished its firing program rattled past, returning to its base. [At dusk, French planes came over and bombed the woods.]
>
> We heard that we were to spend the night here and tomorrow at daybreak deploy for the attack. The division in front of us had suffered heavy casualties, the situation of the new line was not known in the confusion of the forest. . . . Tomorrow, the 16th of July, would be a hot day.

On the whole, the Seventh Army offensive between the Marne and the Ardre was going well. One stubborn enemy outfit (the French Fortieth Division) was holding out despite both its flanks being bent back. By mid-morning, French reserves were identified in the battle. The question was, How many reserves did the French have available to plug the holes here?

That depended on the success of the other pincer. If the attack east of Reims did as well as the one south of the city, French reserves would quickly be devoured.

There, along the broad attack front of the German First and Third Armies, stretching more than thirty-five miles eastward from near Reims, where the thunderous barrage had deafened the Rainbowers for three hours and a half, the rocket flares signaling the infantry assault leaped into the sky on the dot of 4:40 German time (3:40 French time). The shock troops in their forward trenches had taken casualties from the enemy barrage that had preempted H-hour, but with no river barrier in front of them, they crossed a No-Man's-Land of pockmarked chalk in a matter of minutes to plunge into the trenches of the enemy First Position. In previous offensives, this had been the decisive event, and the battalion commanders were quick to send back runners with the triumphant news, which promptly reached the Kaiser in his tower. But something was wrong this time. The front-line trench of the French First Position was all but empty—only at intervals was there a single man, living or dead, armed with rocket flares. As the shock troops clambered out of the trench and plunged forward, a tremendous hail of artillery fire enveloped this very area, the enemy's own First Position, in explosives and gas. Minutes later, the attackers reached the rear trench of the First Position. But instead of being filled with sprawled bodies, this trench too was nearly empty—save here and there, where well-concealed automatic weapons suddenly began spitting, while the rain of artillery shells of all calibers never ceased.

The volume of large-caliber fire received was an especially ominous sign, because heavier guns, with their longer ranges, could be echeloned in greater depth. German artillery observers had already noted this, along with the fact that nature had deserted to the enemy—the prevailing wind was from south to north, permitting the French artillery to recover quickly from Colonel Bruchmüller's gas while treating the German artillery in its turn to a bath of phosgene, chlorine, and mustard.

Not till after 7 A.M. did the first attackers reach the French Intermediate Position. Here, unexpectedly, they ran into a terrific machine-gun and rifle fire that could only mean the enemy main line of resistance. Disorganized and decimated, the shock troops were unable to advance. All along the line the scattered groups halted, fell back, and sought refuge in shell holes and in the trenches and dugouts of the French First Position, now awash with gas.

Six miles back, the Kaiser was in the middle of his victory breakfast when a staff car pulled up at the foot of the tower and the Crown Prince came running up the steps.

"Well, what's going on at the front?" called out the Kaiser.

Finding his father in so cheerful a mood, the Crown Prince hesitated a moment, but finally said quietly, "That's what I came here about. They don't want to believe it, but I have the feeling that we're bogged down." "They," naturally, were Hindenburg and Ludendorff.

The Crown Prince was dead right. As he spoke, renewed assaults were breaking against Gouraud's heavily manned Intermediate Line. Here and there a footing was gained, but counterattacks were prompt and decisive. In front of the U.S. Forty-second Division, a penetration was reported. Two companies of Alabamans of the 167th Infantry joined two French companies in recovering the position. Three battalions of other Rainbow regiments moved into the line and fought off attacks all morning. Farther to the right, the shock troops drove the French out of the village of Perthes, but were driven out in their turn. By 9 A.M. the German attacks were losing their punch, the German bombardments dwindling.

Rudolf Binding pictured the day of hell for the German infantry in Champagne:

> Under a merciless sun, which set the air quivering in a dance of heat, and sent wave after hot wave up from the burning soil, the treeless, waterless chalk downs lay devoid of all color, like stones at white heat. No shade, no paths, not even roads; just crumbling white streaks on a flat plate. Across this wind rusty snakes of barbed wire. Into this the French deliberately lured us. . . . Our guns bombarded empty trenches . . . only in little hidden folds of the

> ground, sparsely distributed, lay machine-gun posts, like lice in the seams and folds of a garment, to give the attacking force a warm reception.

As the attack had become disjointed, the German artillery fire no longer related to the infantry's struggle; command posts and headquarters units, complacently moving up to their assigned advance positions, found themselves suddenly left in the open, under enemy fire, waiting for the infantry in front of them to move forward. Everything piled up—supply units, reserves, rear-echelon outfits, with enemy artillery ceaselessly raining down explosives and gas.

In contrast to the merry looting of English dugouts on March 21, nobody had anything to eat or drink all day.

In his headquarters in the dragoon barracks at Provins, Pétain was gratified by Gouraud's successful defense, though not by a word or gesture did he betray self-satisfaction at the dramatic vindication of Directive No. 4. On the contrary, he was entirely taken up with the problem created on his other front, southwest of Reims, where army generals and corps commanders had through lack of time or desire failed to apply No. 4.

There were five army corps holding the line from Reims to Château-Thierry, divided between the French Fifth Army of General Berthelot and the French Sixth Army of General Degoutte. Of the five, the one at the top of the line, the First Colonial Corps, around Reims, was so far not under attack, though it had received some of the bombardment. At the bottom of the line, the XXXVIII Corps was only partly under attack—on its right, in the sector held by the American Third Division. In addition to the corps artillery, Allied bombardment squadrons had been dispatched to rain bombs on the Germans' pontoon bridges in the Jaulgonne Bend.

But between these two anchors the line had given way. North of the XXXVIII Corps, the commander of the III Corps, who had resisted Directive No. 4, had been caught with too many battalions in the forward positions. Much of the infantry of his two front-line divisions had been slaughtered, and now he had only their remnants and his own reserves to man the Second Position. The four companies of the U.S. Twenty-eighth (Keystone) Division in the line with the French 125th shared the fate of the French front-line outfit, and in addition either did not receive or did not understand orders to retreat; as a result, most of the Pennsylvanians who survived the barrage and the attack were taken prisoner. The rest of their two regiments (109th and 110th Infantry), originally in reserve, found themselves suddenly on the front line.

Pétain had had the XXXVIII Corps send its own reserve division to attack the flank of the developing pocket south of the river.

Farther north, two of Berthelot's corps, the French V and the Italian II, had also been ordered to man forward positions in strength and had suffered accordingly. Berthelot had already put in all his own reserves. From the sector south of the Marne, west of Dormans, a confusion of messages pouring back from the front line gave little reassurance that the situation could be stabilized soon: "Boche are advancing south to Hill 243. . . ." "The 20th Division is defending its 2nd Position. . . ." "There are six bridges west of Dormans, two very large ones between Dormans and Tréloup. . . . A large column of vehicles is waiting to cross. . . ." "The Boche are probably surrounding the 2nd Position from La Chapelle-Monthodon to Comblizy. Left regiment: Leading battalion disappeared. . . . Colonel killed. 2 bn. commanders wounded. . . ." "At 10:05 A.M. the Boche were on the Patis–Nesles-le-Repons road. . . ."

Pétain did not sense another Chemin des Dames, but if the German eastward thrust reached Épernay, Reims could not be held, because the main road and rail line would be in German hands. Could the First Colonial Corps, garrisoning Reims, be pulled out? Would even Gouraud's Fourth Army be safe? Finally, was it certain that Gouraud, despite the morning's results, would not need reserve help himself?

The situation differed considerably from that of May 27;

Pétain had his reserve army at hand—the French Ninth Army, basically constituted from the D.A.N. returned from Flanders. Three divisions of infantry and one of cavalry he was able to turn over at once to Maistre, the successor to Franchet d'Esperey as commander of the Northern Army Group, which had recently been renamed the Northeastern Army Group. A fourth (the French Tenth Division) he kept in hand for the moment; it was all he had. A fifth (the French Fourteenth Division) was en route, but would not arrive till the next day. Neither would the two British divisions that Foch had successfully commandeered from Haig. The question was, Where could he turn for reserves for the next forty-eight hours? The answer was obvious: the "mass of maneuver" building at this moment in the Forest of Villers-Cotterêts, opposite the west face of the salient, for Mangin's counteroffensive.

He sent off a telegram to Fayolle, whose Reserve Group had been renamed the Northern Army Group: THE BOCHE HAS MADE A POCKET SOUTH OF THE MARNE. SUSPEND THE MANGIN OPERATION TO ALLOW ME TO SEND YOUR RESERVES SOUTH OF THE MARNE. He called for the immediate march of one infantry division and one cavalry corps.

At noon he ordered Maistre to mount a counterattack against both flanks of the Boche pocket.

Meantime Foch quit his headquarters at Bombon to meet Haig. During the night the Field Marshal had received a telephone message from London about Foch's request for British divisions for the Marne. The War Cabinet (Lloyd George and his chief colleagues) was worried, and suggested to Haig that "if you consider the British Army is endangered or if you think that General Foch is not acting solely on military considerations, they [the War Cabinet] rely on the exercise of your judgment, under the Beauvais Agreement, as to the security of the British front after the removal of these troops. General Smuts, on behalf of the Imperial War Cabinet, will proceed to G.H.Q. today to confer with you on your return from Beauvais."

The very question had arisen at the June 7 meetings at the

Boulevard des Invalides, when Haig had asked whether, in case of a request from Foch for British troops south of the Somme, he could check with London before complying. Foch had successfully argued for Haig's prior compliance with the request and secondary notification of London. But Lloyd George had had a second thought, and on June 22 had had Milner tell Haig that if he feared the British Army would be imperiled by such a request from Foch, he should check with London first, before complying.

On July 13, Haig had hit on a judicious compromise. He had ordered two of the four divisions Foch requested to entrain at once, but held the other two up till he could talk to Foch. Foch had therefore arranged a luncheon meeting on the fifteenth at the village of Mouchy le Chatel.

Foch left Bombon at 9:30 A.M. Unlike Pétain, he was untroubled by the Boche pocket south of the Marne. He was sure that Gouraud's block of the left German pincer was solid, and that Berthelot would eventually master the right pincer. Arriving at Mouchy le Chatel ahead of Haig, he decided to drive to the nearby town of Noailles, headquarters of General Fayolle, commander of the Northern Army Group, of which Mangin's Tenth Army, gathering in the Forest of Villers-Cotterêts, was a part. Fayolle, Foch's old schoolmate of nearly sixty years earlier, met him on the doorstep of his headquarters. "How's your attack—is it going ahead all right?" asked Foch.

Fayolle's face was troubled. "No, it isn't. General Pétain has just ordered me to suspend the movements because he needs the troops to support the defensive battle." Foch ran up the steps, Weygand behind him. Reaching Fayolle's office, he dictated an order to be telephoned to Provins:

> *For General Pétain.*
>
> It must be understood that until there are new developments that you let me know about, there can be no question in any way of slowing up, much less stopping, the Mangin preparations. In case of urgent and absolute

need, you will take from there troops absolutely indispensable, informing me at once.

Foch

It was a distinctively Foch-like message, full of impetuosity and offense-mindedness, but taking care to make the necessary reservation. Foch was impetuous, but he had also seen a lot of war.

Foch drove on to Mouchy to meet Haig. At lunch (sent ahead by Foch), he was in excellent spirits as Haig explained his objections to giving up his reserves. British Intelligence had detected heavy batteries moving into Crown Prince Rupprecht's sector, while prisoners and deserters had given information on a German offensive in Flanders said to be scheduled for July 18.

Foch took little stock in that rumor. He pacified Haig with the promise that the second set of two British divisions, those Haig was holding up pending the conference, would be kept near the Allied juncture, ready to return at once if Haig needed them.

At Provins, Pétain received Foch's message a little after 12:30. He read it with care, and took note of the loophole, the permission to "take from [Mangin] troops absolutely indispensable" if the need was sufficiently urgent. The urgency had in fact abated slightly since Pétain had sent his order to Fayolle. The German thrust toward Épernay was slowing, and the failure of the attack against Gouraud was becoming more and more evident. It was unlikely that any reserves would have to be saved for the Fourth Army. After debating Foch's order, Pétain decided to cut back his request to Fayolle to the single infantry division (the French 168th), which was drawn not from Mangin's Tenth Army but from Degoutte's Sixth.

Through July 15, Mangin's concentration proceeded. The U.S. First Division, which had marched south from Beauvais, now lay in the "Dammartin billeting area," north of Meaux on the Paris–Soissons road. On the afternoon of July 15, with everyone hoping for another few days' rest, or possibly even leave on the Riviera, after the strenuous five weeks at Cantigny, the First suddenly received orders to entruck at once. The orders were accompanied by the trucks; the staff had to race around the countryside to round up the men from the villages, barns, and farmyards. The First was sufficiently experienced to know what needed to be done—mainly find extra trucks somewhere so that the rolling kitchens, normally animal-powered, could keep up with the troops. Kitchens and men were loaded, headquarters closed, villagers bade goodbye, and within two hours of receipt of the order, the infantry of the First Division departed in a thousand French trucks—whither, they had no idea. Artillery and supply trains moved separately by secondary roads reserved for animal-drawn traffic.

That afternoon at Provins the tension heightened again as the Germans, responding to Ludendorff's orders, renewed their attacks by both pincers. Once more the French Fifth Army was heavily attacked in the woods between the Marne and the Ardre, and along the Marne valley toward Épernay, while all along the front of the French Fourth Army the shock troops scrambled out of their shell holes and the trenches of the French First Position behind a new rolling barrage.

At 4:45, Pétain sent a message directly to Foch. He asked permission to postpone the Mangin offensive for twenty-four hours, and requested that the U.S. Second Division, already moving toward the Forest of Villers-Cotterêts, be returned to become a reserve for the defensive front.

Scarcely had he sent off the message when he received one from Gouraud:

"At 1700 hours [5 P.M.], the first parallel of the position of resistance is in our possession on the entire front of attack."

There was no longer the slightest doubt—Gouraud had won a smashing defensive victory, even if in spite of himself. A thoroughly prepared Bruchmüller-Hutier offensive, mounted by twenty-five divisions, had been stopped without the loss of a gun, scarcely the loss of a prisoner, with heavy casualties inflicted on the attackers, and without a dent in the main line of resistance.

All available reserves could be concentrated against the enemy's right-hand pincer.

At almost the same moment, a report came from the French Sixth Army headquarters on the fighting south of the Marne:

"At the latest reports the front held by us at 1500 hours [3 P.M.] had not changed. . . . No part of our front was broken. . . . In the course of counterattacks . . . the American Third Division took 400 prisoners, including one battalion commander."

Even between the Marne and Ardre, where the battered divisions of the French Fifth Army were still outnumbered despite the arrival of reinforcements, the Germans showed signs of tiring.

In a telephone conference with Foch, Pétain agreed that Mangin's counteroffensive could go as scheduled on the eighteenth, that the two days intervening would see the final containment of the German attack. He canceled his request for the U.S. Second Division.

To support a new counterattack against the flank of the Germans south of the Marne, he sent a detachment of the new little Renault tanks. The attack jumped off at 7 P.M. and pushed the Germans sharply back into the Condé woods they had come from.

The inability of the Germans to free the Marne crossings from heavy artillery fire by evening created a serious supply constriction for the troops on the extreme right of the great offensive. German Seventh Army headquarters, after checking with the Supreme Command, sent an order to Corps Kathen, whose troops were battling south of the river:

"Corps Kathen will take up the defensive. After nightfall the elements of the 10th Inf. Div. south of Mont-St-Père will be withdrawn across the Marne. Thereafter the 10th Div. will be strongly echeloned in depth north of the Marne. . . ."

Far to the north, behind the disastrous Champagne attack front, Rudolf Binding was making his way back to his own headquarters. As he led his horse in the pitch blackness he wondered if there was "any remedy for human folly." In his dugout he opened his diary and began his entry:

"July 15: I have lived through the most disheartening day of the war."

20

JULY 16

Shortly after midnight, July 15–16, the Army Group Crown Prince Wilhelm received a telephone message from Avesnes:

"The Seventh and First Armies will continue the attack on the 16th, and the Third Army as well, but only on its right. The Army Group will place the center of gravity of the advance of the Seventh Army along the north of the Marne in order to force the enemy to evacuate the Reims arc. Since troops will continue to be sent to Army Group Rupprecht, the attack of the Third Army will be narrowed. The principal effort in the attack east of Reims will be made by the First Army."

The German Third Army, which had carried the brunt of the attack on Gouraud's Intermediate Position the day before, and had spent the night bringing in its thousands of wounded, was excused from more than a token participation in the resumption of the offensive. Some of its formations, especially its heavy artillery, would be started north for "Hagen."

Ludendorff was also abandoning the attempt to advance eastward simultaneously on both banks of the Marne. The concentration of French reserves and the heavy fire on the Marne crossings made that design now seem too ambitious for the Seventh Army. The narrowing of the front automatically scaled down the possible depth of penetration, and the hope of capturing Châlons was given up. But the basic strategy remained the same, with Épernay the target of the drive and the pinch-off of the Reims corner the hoped-for booty.

Early in the morning of the sixteenth, the wheatfields and woods along the Marne, the thicketed ravines of the Mountain of Reims, the chalk plains of Champagne, echoed with the roar of artillery and the rattle of automatic weapons as the lines of field gray rose from their holes and concealment and formed up for the attack.

On the right, south of the Marne, the Germans hung on grimly against the counterattacking Allies. Driven out of ruined villages and blackened farms, they counterattacked in turn and won some of them back. Only on the extreme right corner, where the German Tenth Division had been pulled back across the Marne, did they really give up ground, as the American Third Division topped off its rocklike stand by reoccupying the corpse-strewn river bank. Over the pontoon bridges, continuously repaired by German engineers, Allied planes flew to add their bombs to the pounding of the artillery. Fighter planes rose on both sides of the river to streak the leaden sky with dogfights.

Hans Zöberlein's regiment was supposed to reach Venteuil, on the Marne, five miles from Épernay, that day, but in furious fighting in the alternating woods and wheatfields to the west, they were stopped. Zöberlein was slightly wounded in the foot, but had to take over command of the company when the *Oberleutnant* was hit. As night fell,

> the click of spades sounded up and down the line. We were digging in. Scouting parties went to look for wounded. . . . Our medic-corporal, Ferdl, reported nine dead, twenty-six wounded, four missing. "That was a business today, all day long! If it goes on this way, to-

morrow at this time the regiment will be broken up! . . . They say the offensive isn't going so well. Today only our division won territory."

Medic-corporal Ferdl's information was not far wrong. The fighting to the south and the north had raged bitter and bloody all day long, with woods and hills taken, lost, and retaken, but with meager results. It was obvious that the French were putting their reserves in here, south of Reims.

At Seventh Army headquarters and at Avesnes, it was increasingly clear why the French reserves were available in numbers south of Reims: the German First Army, mounting the new offensive east of the city, was having no better success than had the combined First and Third the day before. The improvised barrage, executed by artillery depleted by the pounding of French counterbattery fire, was incapable of clearing a path even on the narrower attack front. The shock troops made a game effort, dodging through a No-Man's-Land littered with the bodies of their comrades, dragging machine guns and mortars forward, here and there pressing up to the resistance line before melting away in the hail of fire.

They resorted to trickery, appearing in front of the Rainbow Division in French helmets and uniforms, and flying shot-down, re-patched French Spads to attack Allied observation balloons. Such ruses accomplished no more than the sacrificial attacks, as General Douglas MacArthur, Rainbow chief of staff, noted in his report. Wherever along Gouraud's line the shock troops gained temporary footing in the Intermediate Position, they were quickly driven out by counterattacks.

To add to German difficulties, Allied air squadrons had seized control of the sky over the whole Marne salient. From a new position in its very center, the Paris gun hardly dared fire a shot, beautifully camouflaged though it was. Though the shorter range promised a gun life of two hundred rounds, the crew managed only four shots, making thirteen in the two days in the new position, a pattern of firing that puzzled the artillerists in Paris but accomplished little else.

In the dragoon barracks in Provins, Pétain studied the incoming reports from the defensive fronts. Gouraud's reassurances were prompt and categorical: nothing remained to be done but to repossess the old First Position as an outpost line, an operation Pétain sanctioned for later in the day.

From the other sectors, the stream of bulletins to higher headquarters was distinctly more favorable than on the previous day:

"12 noon, from the 73rd Div.: Situation of the division: Public laundry at St-Agnan (incl.)—Grange-aux-Bois (excl.) —north edge of Janvier Farm clearing—Maison-Rouge. The [counterattack] will be resumed at the hour set."

"12:45 P.M. from the 77th Div.: The Germans have attacked the plateau on the east and northeast of Chêne-la-Reine. Request at least two infantry regiments and a regiment of heavy artillery."

"1:20 P.M. French 18th Inf. Div.: Regiment on the left is making normal progress. Nine prisoners of the 2nd Jaeger and of the Hussars of the Guards. . . ."

"1:25 P.M. French 20th Inf. Div.: The Boche are evacuating the small woods north of Montleçon; we are entering in pursuit."

"1:40 P.M. French 18th Inf. Div.: Our left regiment is advancing . . . north of Clos-Milon Farm. More prisoners.

"Left bn. of right regiment is advancing. Right bn. has halted. Prisoners. 1st Foot Guards."

"2 P.M. French III Army Corps: St-Agnan reported retaken."

By early afternoon, it was evident that the line was holding in the Marne valley, where several divisions of the reserve Ninth Army had been thrown in. Pétain now added Ninth Army headquarters (General de Mitry) to take charge of the whole sector, formerly divided between the Sixth and Fifth Armies.

To the north, between the Marne and Ardre, the fresh reserves promised to master the German offensive if they had not already done so. The first two British divisions, those sent by Haig in immediate response to Foch's request of July 13, were detraining at this moment, and the second two were en route from the north. Pétain asked Foch to send him those also.

Foch was even less worried than Pétain. He refused to send the second pair of British divisions, assigning them instead to detrain north of Paris.

That of course was in line with his promise to Haig to keep them in a place whence they could return promptly to the British front in case of need. But to Foch this was a secondary detail. He wanted them north of Paris, west of the Marne salient, so that they could be added to Mangin's Tenth Army, now rapidly concentrating in the Forest of Villers-Cotterêts.

Foch was convinced that Gouraud's solid repulse of the German First and Third Armies, being completed this very evening by counterattacks to repossess the First Position, had been decisive for the defensive battle. If a little ground was still being lost toward Épernay, the two British divisions Pétain already had were more than enough to tip the scale.

He heartily seconded a proposal from Mangin, transmitted by Fayolle, that the Tenth Army should jump off on the eighteenth with no prior artillery preparation whatever.

The Germans, he felt, were overdue for a little surprise of their own.

Early that morning, the men of the American First Division, after riding all night, had their trucks halted and received the order to climb out and march into the nearby woods. There they breakfasted, slept, and stayed under cover. With dusk, they fell in on the roads and marched east through what some officers now knew was the Forest of Villers-Cotterêts, on the western face of the Marne salient.

All morning in the red-brick house at Avesnes, Ludendorff, like Pétain, studied a stream of reports from the front. Reluctantly, he concluded that east of Reims there was nothing to be done except cut losses. At noon, he ordered the offensive there canceled, the troops to go over to the defensive. He specified that as many of the shattered divisions as possible should be moved back to army-group and General Headquarters reserve, while all heavy artillery, trench mortars, and aircraft not needed for the defensive position were to be put on the waiting railway cars and headed north. At the other end of the line, batteries not needed by Corps Kathen in its new defensive role north of the Marne were likewise loaded for shipment to Rupprecht for "Hagen."

Yet Ludendorff clung desperately to the belief that another push between the Marne and the Ardre would topple Reims. Even the narrowest pinch-off of the city would be of immense value both logistically and psychologically. What if, after his brutal expulsion of Kühlmann from the government barely a week ago, the great offensive whose prospects he had extolled to Hertling and the Kaiser were to prove a flat, unqualified failure?

Even impassive Hindenburg was growing uneasy and becoming a prey to fantasy. He wrote later that he believed the fate of Reims "hung by a thread," and that the city's fall might "make a very great impression" on the enemy. The wish was father to the thought. Yet it hardly mattered; with the armies at grips all along the vast arc of front, there was nothing to do but fight, on the defensive where necessary, on the offensive where possible. The only alternative was to abandon the whole Marne salient. That, at Avesnes on the evening of July 16, remained unthinkable.

21

JULY 17

Guns still blazed from the Jaulgonne Bend to the Mountain of Reims on the morning of July 17, but it was evident very early, on both sides of the battlefront, that the result achieved so immediately by Gouraud's French Fourth Army had now been achieved, more slowly and at far greater cost, by Berthelot's Fifth. Incessant French counterattacks were holding the Germans between the Marne and the Ardre, while south of the Marne the German withdrawal began to take on urgency.

Tense, desperate Ludendorff, holding to a rigid self-control, drove to German First Army headquarters at Rethel. His intention was to get the attack east of Reims renewed in order to supplement the Seventh Army's now painfully laborious push south of the Ardre. The First Army's chief of staff convinced him that it was out of the question—"several days" of fresh preparation were needed to bring up ammunition, reorganize shattered units, rest demoralized men. Farther east, the corps commanders of the German Third Army were so far from any thought of renewing their offensive that they expressed concern over the possibility of Gouraud's launching an attack against their exhausted formations.

The German Seventh Army was now fighting alone, and it had its hands full. At 5:30 P.M. on the seventeenth, its chief of staff, Colonel Reinhardt, telephoned army-group headquarters to emphasize the pressure on the two corps (Wichura, and Conta, on Wichura's left) still south of the Marne from the enemy counterattacks and from the ceaseless pounding of the bridges—"seventy per cent of the bridge trains have been destroyed." Unless a withdrawal was begun promptly, a catastrophe might develop.

The Crown Prince's headquarters passed the message up to Avesnes. With utmost reluctance, Ludendorff agreed, though he still held off on issuing the order. He had decided to give the First Army the breathing space its chief of staff pleaded for, and had defined the front for the renewal of the offensive on July 21 as "the boundary between the Seventh and First Armies," just south of Reims. He still hoped that the Seventh Army would manage to penetrate far enough east in the next twenty-four hours to topple the city.

On this day, Hans Zöberlein's regiment was the spearhead of the advance. It captured Grand Pré farm in the morning and held it against repeated counterattacks.

> In the afternoon of the 17th, enemy artillery fire broadened. Then came the order: 'At 6 o'clock the left neighboring regiment will attack. Our regiment will advance with them, 5th Company behind the open left wing of the battalion.' Cursing, we got up and crouched in the underbrush, ready for attack. Behind the Bois du Roi a pitch-black thundersorm broke out.

The regiment plunged forward in the midst of the driving rain, which lifted as suddenly as it came. As the sun setting over the Marne valley bathed the battlefield in a double rainbow, the German attack broke and fell back. Instead of fresh attack orders, a warning was received of enemy concentrations near Reims and on the Marne, ending ominously, "The line is to be held at all costs."

It was now clear to everyone from the German soldiers on

the line to Supreme Headquarters that no further progress could be made without rest, reorganization, and fresh artillery preparation.

Ludendorff gave in and signed the order for the Seventh Army to withdraw from south of the Marne. The artillery could start pulling out immediately, with the main troop movement to be carried out on the night of the nineteenth. But even while renouncing Épernay, he clung to Reims, as if to a dream. Unless the city fell, a general withdrawal was inevitable. What would they say in Berlin? Militarily, he needed a strong defensive position here while he launched "Hagen," but beyond that, how could he justify this battle? The enemy's reserves must be at the point of exhaustion; one more push would surely bring the prize. He decreed a three-day pause to rest the troops and bring up ammunition.

He was not far wrong about the reserves. Pétain had thrown all his French reserves into the battle, had put all available American outfits into the line, and had only his two newly arrived British divisions in hand. He appealed once more to Foch to send him, if not the second set of two British divisions already en route, which Foch had earmarked for Mangin, then still others which Foch had asked Haig to have ready to move in a contingency.

But Foch had just received a letter from the British demanding that all British divisions be returned "forthwith" to Haig. The letter, though signed by Haig, had actually been drafted in London, where the impending German attack in Flanders seemed more and more threatening. Haig added a verbal message of his own to the effect that if the British divisions were needed "to exploit a success" they should of course be used. Haig, however, had slight expectation of any such contingency arising from Foch's planned counterattack, in which he took little stock. He pointed out that his British Second Army, the probable target of the next German offensive, had only fifteen divisions, of which two were "half-trained American" and one a "second-class" British division.

Foch answered Haig by asserting that the scale of the German Marne-Reims offensive precluded any large-scale offensive elsewhere "for the moment." That "for the moment" failed to reassure either Haig or Lloyd George, but what Foch really meant was that Ludendorff could not strike in Flanders until after the Mangin counterstroke, now just one day away. Unlike Haig, Foch anticipated serious results from the counterattack, results that might change the whole strategic picture.

Including both Mangin's Tenth Army and the left of the French Sixth Army, the attacking force he had ready to go now consisted of twenty-three divisions, including four of the double-strength American divisions. In line against them were only nineteen divisions, of which only eleven were in the front line. It was the first time in 1918 that an Allied force had mustered a clear numerical superiority. Foch could only satisfy Lloyd George, Haig, and Pétain by giving up the superiority, and with it the offensive. He chose not to satisfy them.

He also chose to keep his plans to himself. To the anxious queries of Clemenceau and Poincaré, he returned soothing generalities, with never a hint of his offensive plans.

The concentration of Mangin's forces was proceeding on schedule, though hardly with parade-ground smoothness. Roads into the Forest of Villers-Cotterêts were jammed with an incredible tangle of men, animals, guns, wagons, trucks, and tanks. In a series of corps- and division-headquarters meetings, Mangin virtually abandoned normal cover for movement, in favor of making sure the attacking units got to the line of departure in time. Yet surprise remained not only desirable but, Mangin thought, probable. There was little German air reconnaissance on this side of the salient; indeed, the German air squadrons, battling heroically against the odds, had been almost driven from the sky. There was also little German raiding, in sharp contrast to the incessant French raiding of the week before July 15. It looked as if the

Boche were content to use the west side of the Marne salient as a rest area. The only really important Allied order in respect to secrecy was one forbidding preparatory fire before H-hour, fixed at 4:35 A.M. At that moment, preparatory fire was to begin on the Sixth Army attack front, while on the front of the Tenth Army, the entire assault force would go straight into the attack behind the rolling barrage.

The twenty-three attacking divisions were distributed in two waves, front-line and reserve, over a front of over twenty miles, from the Aisne River in the north to the southwest corner of the salient.

On the Tenth Army front, eleven divisions were in the front line, with six in reserve. On the Sixth Army front, five divisions were in the line, with one in reserve. The Tenth Army was also supplied with most of the tanks—123 Schneiders and 90 St. Chamonds, and 130 little Renaults. The Sixth Army, whose role was basically that of flank guard, had only one regiment of 125 Renaults and a groupment of 10 St. Chamonds. The entire cavalry corps of three divisions was tethered behind the Tenth Army to exploit a possible breakthrough, and most of the sixty-seven air squadrons available lay on fields behind the Tenth.

The most strenuous efforts of men, trucks, and horses were required to get the artillery into position. The 75's and their crews could be packed into trucks, but the 105's and 155's had to be hauled, part way by horses, finally by trucks quitting the roads to drag the heavy guns into the forest. In the village of Mortefontaine, through which the U.S. First Division was marching to its jump-off position, a soup kitchen was set up in the street to feed anybody hungry among the crowds of men piling through.

The previous night, as a precaution against air reconnaissance, the First had had to quit the moonlit road and march in the fields, but tonight this was unnecessary. The thunderstorm that had soaked Hans Zöberlein and his comrades fighting on the eastern face of the salient, some thirty-five miles away, had moved west, or a second storm had materialized, because as the First Division marched, visibility was suddenly blotted out and sound drowned in the crash of thunder and pelt of rain, with only lightning flashes to illuminate the blackness. The men were immediately soaked to the skin, as the pitch darkness heightened the confusion.

Artillery and caissons were given the middle of the road, while the infantry slogged along on the muddy shoulders. Suddenly a new roar was added to the din, and the guns, trucks, and caissons had to pull over, forcing the riflemen off into the fields. Down the middle of the road lumbered a column of big Schneider tanks. On top of each tank rode five doughboys armed with picks, shovels, axes, and crowbars. They were engineers of the U.S. First Division, assigned to help make sure the tanks made it to the line of departure. After the tanks came heavy trucks loaded with field-hospital equipment, and a scattering of Dodge staff cars, motorcycles, Signal Corps reel carts, one-mule machine-gun carts, ambulances, and supply wagons. To many of the First's worried officers, the confusion seemed beyond salvation, yet hour by hour units turned off the road (sometimes at the wrong place), and the batteries crashed and blundered to their firing positions. As traffic thinned, the French front-line guides were met, and finally only the infantry was marching, with the road to itself.

The U.S. Second Division had worse luck. It could have used the First's soup kitchen. Since its departure the previous night from its reserve position west of Château-Thierry, many of its outfits had not had a bite to eat. As night fell, it still had a long march to make it to its departure line at the eastern edge of the Forest of Villers-Cotterêts. The few roads through the woods were swamped with the division's men and vehicles, and the infantry battalions roamed helplessly through the maze of paths, soon turned by the thunderstorm into black, dripping tunnels.

Despite the enormous commotion, Mangin was justified in his optimism over the chance of surprise. At the headquarters of the German Ninth Army opposite there was no expectation of a large-scale enemy offensive. Headquarters of the German Seventh Army, preoccupied with its mounting peril south of the Marne, gave even less thought to this side of the salient. An identical obliviousness reigned at the Crown Prince's headquarters and at Avesnes.

The Germans on this face of the salient were aligned for defense, but protected by only sketchy field fortifications, and lacking in depth. Each front-line division of the Ninth Army had its nine battalions in three rows, the second constituting the main line of resistance and the third the artillery covering

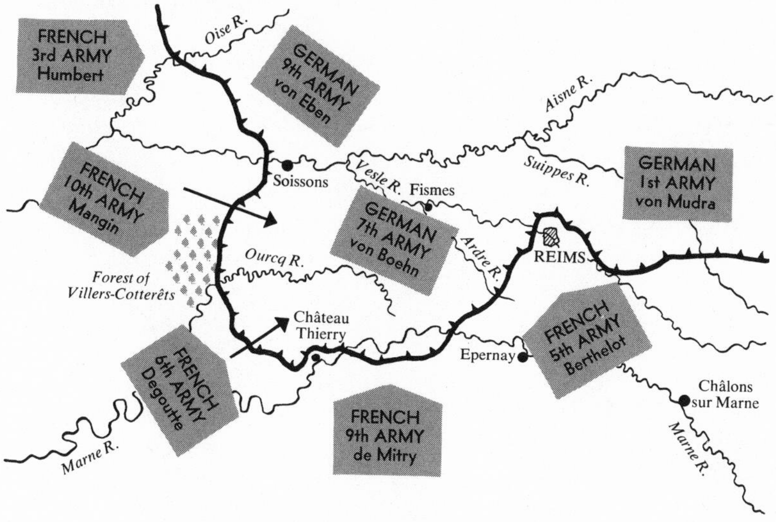

Allied counter-offensive of July 18.

line. But the effect of Mangin's many local attacks had been to compress the Germans' first two lines together, so that the forward line now lay only some five hundred yards in front of the main line of resistance, with the artillery less than a mile farther back. The total net effect was that the lines were too close together for any of the three to keep out of field-artillery and mortar range, and too thin to provide intense small-arms fire anywhere. The right wing of the German Seventh

Army, which had not been similarly harassed, was more deeply echeloned.

Ludendorff was so little concerned with the possibility of an enemy offensive that on the evening of the seventeenth he left Avesnes to go not to the Marne front, but in the opposite direction, to Tournai, in Flanders, where the headquarters of Prince Rupprecht was located. He had a conference scheduled for next morning, July 18, with Rupprecht's staff to settle details of "Hagen," whose D-day he now calculated as August 2. That would give time to launch the July 21 assault on Reims, tidy up the Marne salient, move the heavy artillery, and scrape together the last possible reserves of infantry for the offensive that would win the war.

Among the German rank and file on the west face of the Marne salient the rumor was rife that Reims had already fallen. The belief that victory was imminent may have contributed to carelessness. From the Forest of Villers-Cotterêts, the men in the front line could hear the sound of motors. Then the thunderstorm broke, drowning out the noise, and everyone sought shelter.

22

JULY 18

In the predawn gray on the other side of No-Man's-Land the men, animals, guns, tanks, and vehicles converged through the dripping forest. There was much hurry-up-and-waiting, and little sleep, but by 4:30 A.M. most of the batteries, infantry battalions, and tanks were miraculously in place. One regiment of the U.S. First Division was not quite on the line of departure, and most of the U.S. Second was still panting through the Forest of Villers-Cotterêts, battalions crisscrossing into each other, and even the French guides losing their way. The Second's regimental commanders, waiting at their forward command posts, watches in hand, were sweating—if the attacking elements failed to jump off on time, the divisions advancing on the right and left would have their flanks open to enfilading fire from the Germans in the gap. The French on the front line sent every available man back to find the Americans, and at the last possible moment, the doughboys and Marines began to appear. The Second Battalion of the 23rd Infantry, spearheading the attack in its sector, double-timed the last few hundred yards, making it to the forest's edge just as the tremendous crash of artillery up and down the line signaled H-hour (4:35 A.M.). The rest of the Second Division caught up just in time, and started out across an open plain covered with waving wheat.

The bombardment broke not only on the attack front, but as a diversion on several other fronts, as far off as the chalk plains of Champagne. On the attack front it immediately became a barrage, moving forward at the rapid rate of fifty-five yards a minute. Before the German first line, the shadowy figures of men and tanks materialized without warning out of the tall wheat blanketed by the morning mist. The first line was overrun at once, and the second line, barely a third of a mile back, almost as rapidly. Only the third line was able to offer spotty resistance. Difficult terrain features were bypassed, and nearly everywhere else the offensive went through the entire position of the German front divisions. The German gunners fired till they were overrun, and guns were captured all along the line.

Thomas Boyd, of the Second Division's Marine Brigade, described his platoon's adventure that morning in *Through the Wheat,* one of the first of the war novels.

> The platoon reached the first machine-gun nest almost without knowing it. There were three Germans, their heavy helmets sunk over their heads. . . . Pugh, a little in the lead, drew a hand-grenade from his pocket, pulled out the pin, and threw it in their faces. . . . One German fell flat, another grasped at his arm . . . while the last man threw his hands above his head. . . . The line pushed on.
>
> The fighting grew more furious. Germans, surprised, were hiding behind trees and firing their slow-working rifles. . . . Some member of the platoon offered his version of an Indian war whoop. . . . Other men calmly and methodically worked the bolts of their rifles back and forth, refilling the chambers as they were emptied of each clip of five shots. From time to time a man dropped, thinning the ranks and spreading them out to such an extent that

contact on the right side of the moving line was lost.

Farther on in the woods a small trench had been dug, but through the fierceness and unexpectedness of the attack most of the enemy had been driven from it. . . .

Bodies lay gawkily about on the grass. One, headless, clutched a clay pipe between its fingers. Another lay flat on its back, a hole in its stomach as big as a hat. A heavy leather pack, which a shell had struck, was the center of a ring of packages of Piedmont cigarettes . . . salvaged from some dead American. . . .

The trees became sparse. Ahead, over an interminably long wheatfield, the platoon could see the horizon. There were no Germans in sight. The platoon . . . faced in the direction from which they had come and combed the woods for machine-gun nests which they might have passed unnoticed during the attack. In their hunger the men forgot even to look for pieces of German equipment which they might sell to Y.M.C.A. men. . . . But each leather German pack was searched for food, and canteens were picked up, shaken, and either thrown down with disgust or hastily put to the men's lips and greedily drained of whatever might be in them. Loaves of black bread, in spite of the mouldy look, were devoured; an occasional comb of honey was found.

The Tenth Army's front was apportioned among four corps, from north to south the I, the XX, the XXX, and the XI. The first three made extraordinary progress in the first hours. The I Corps, whose left was on the far side of the Aisne, overran the German division opposite, destroying two thirds of it, while executing a difficult turning movement to preserve the connection with the line north of the Aisne. To its south, the XX Corps overpowered two German divisions, capturing nearly all the German artillery. The XXX Corps overran one enemy division and part of a second. Only the XI Corps,

Mangin's southernmost, reported slow going. The reason was not hard to find; on the XI's front the rugged terrain made it impossible to use tanks. Elsewhere, the tanks waded into machine-gun nests with their sawed-off 75's banging and their own machine guns rattling. Reaching the German third line, they succeeded in penetrating between insufficiently alert German batteries and knocking them out with flanking fire. In the wheatfields, the tank gunners could sight above the tall grain which handicapped the German machine gunners.

The Sixth Army, executing its flank-guard mission, did not advance until after an hour and a half's artillery preparation, when it occupied the enemy front line. Here the German second line was much farther back, and the two attacking corps halted to bring up their own artillery for a fresh preparation.

As the mist vanished before the rising sun, the German Army could be seen for the first time in full retreat, with lines of prisoners filing back to the Allied rear areas.

It was not yet apparent to everyone, but the main success of the day had already been won. Fayolle, the army-group commander and Mangin's immediate superior, concluded by 9:30 that the prompt arrival of German reserves was making impossible a real breakthrough. Pétain arrived, and the two generals drove to Bonneuil, where Mangin's headquarters was located. There they were told that the general was at his "observatory."

Mangin, a flamboyant type, had had a platform built in a treetop close behind the front, a tower rather less commodious than the Kaiser's. While congratulating the army commander on the success of his attack, Pétain did not conceal his dissatisfaction with Mangin's unconventional notion of a forward headquarters. "Here you don't command anything," he told him. Mangin protested that he had his staff at hand, ready to gallop forward with orders, and asked Pétain for more reserves. "No," said Pétain. "Return to your headquarters."

Mangin obeyed, but made up his mind to try Foch for the reserves.

Optimistically, he ordered his three cavalry divisions to advance through the infantry, and committed his Renault tanks. But German reserves were already on the scene. The earliest were half devoured by the battle before they could establish a line, but ultimately, absorbing the front-line remnants, they managed to form a solid front of resistance. The Allied tanks and infantry, having outrun their artillery, had to attack without support, in broad daylight, and in many places against positions of natural strength. The Schneiders and St. Chamonds especially began to take losses from direct artillery fire. The half-mile-wide Missy-aux-Bois ravine, on whose eastern edge the Germans had planted 77-mm. guns, stopped the U.S. First Division and the French 153rd on its left. The U.S. Second Division was also in trouble at a ravine, in front of the key village of Vierzy.

By noon, the Germans were holding strongly along most of the line and even appeared to have the offensive stopped. The Allied artillery's leapfrogging procedure—one battery at a time advancing—had left it far behind, and the cavalry exploitation Mangin dreamed of did not materialize. The horse regiments had difficulty crowding through the narrow paths of the Forest of Villers-Cotterêts, and arrived to find the front too thoroughly jelled. Some of them charged anyway, but they were cut to pieces by machine-gun fire.

In contrast, the tanks continued to distinguish themselves despite casualties. On the First Division front, machine-gun fire came from a deep cave. The leading battalion bypassed it, and the support battalion drew fire. It was impossible to approach through the open ground in front of the cave mouth, and the second assault wave was being held up. An officer spotted a tank nearby and summoned it. The tank waddled up to the cave "like a huge turtle," as an eye witness put it, machine-gun bullets rattling off its armor, its own guns blazing away, and disappeared into the cave. Presently it backed out, followed by a column of German infantry that numbered six hundred men, including a colonel.

A group of St. Chamonds led the 18th Infantry, on the right of the First Division, all the way to its final objective. A group of Schneiders helped the Moroccans capture a succession of objectives, clearing out the machine-gun-infested ravines and shooting up the German-held villages. Some of the Renaults from the reserve got into action with the U.S. Second Division late in the day, also with good effect. Renaults of the Sixth Army helped the French Second and Forty-Seventh Divisions gain all their objectives.

Despite the help of the tanks, the infantry fighting was bitter and bloody through the long afternoon. Strong German reinforcements blocked the approaches to Soissons, now an immensely sensitive point to the Germans because its rail line provided the main artery not only for bringing supplies into the salient but for getting material out of it. Nevertheless, the French 153rd Division finally cleared the deep end of the Missy ravine, the U.S. First captured Brieuil on the eastern slope, while the Moroccans, the U.S. Second, and the French to the south pushed their lines ahead.

Night fell with the German defensive front intact about four to six miles east of its original front line.

The tanks had taken even heavier casualties, proportionately, than had the Allied infantry. Of 223 tanks engaged with the Tenth Army, sixty-two were knocked out by artillery fire and forty more disabled by mechanical trouble. Casualties among the tank personnel ran to 25 percent.

But the effect of this offensive could not be measured in terms of ground gained, or the value of its sacrifices in terms of losses taken. One of the war's rare decisive events had occurred. The truth was infinitely more evident from the German than from the Allied side. Over on the opposite face of the salient, Hans Zöberlein and his surviving comrades were preparing to meet French counterattacks in the steaming wheatfields when from the west they heard the rumble of a barrage, spreading from Soissons to the Marne. "We listened, astonished," recorded Zöberlein. Suddenly the whole battle situation was reversed; instead of attacking to pinch off Reims, the Germans were themselves attacked on all sides of the salient.

Ludendorff was in the midst of his conference with Rupprecht's staff at Tournai when a telephone message was brought to him that a large, unexpected enemy tank attack had pierced the German line southwest of Soissons. The same message added that not only had the local reserves been committed, but the Army Group Crown Prince Wilhelm had already sent to the battlefield, using all the motor transport available, all the reserves of the Seventh Army and the army group that were in the process of reorganization for the attack up the valley of the Ardre on July, 21. The last hope of capturing Reims was thus dashed in an instant, and the problem of extricating the Seventh Army troops south of the Marne was suddenly rendered critical. The only reserve in that sector, the battered Tenth Division, whose survivors had been pulled back across the Marne three nights before, had been committed to the new battle. The whole situation in and around the great Marne salient, which for three days had been turning slowly, inexorably, against Ludendorff, had now in three hours swung sharply in favor of the Allies.

The exigencies of the battle in the Marne salient and the buildup for "Hagen" had left Ludendorff only one single division in General Headquarters reserve, the Fifth, northeast of St.-Quentin. This he ordered to Soissons at once by rail.

He terminated his conference at Tournai, as he wrote later, "in a state of the greatest nervous tension," and returned to Avesnes.

When his train pulled into the station at two o'clock, Hindenburg was on the platform to meet him. En route to the red-brick house, the Field Marshal reported the latest news. So far, a dozen German divisions had been destroyed or seriously weakened, and in the light of the afternoon renewal of the enemy attack, there was no guarantee that even the addition of the Fifth Division, plus one (the Seventy-sixth) scraped from the thinly held eastern sector, would suffice to hold the new line. Permission had been granted Boehn to pull all his troops back north of the Marne, and the German Ninth Army had been ordered to concentrate all efforts on holding Soissons.

Once more Ludendorff made a hard decision, the hardest of the year.

From the precious reserves he had succeeded by the strenuous efforts of the past weeks in collecting for Rupprecht, he ordered one division (the Fiftieth) to move south at once, and another (the Twenty-fourth) to be held in readiness.

At 5 P.M., the Kaiser was announced. Hindenburg went out to meet the Supreme Warlord and conduct him into the operations room.

The old Field Marshal expressed the supposition that the Kaiser wanted to learn their opinion of the causes of the painful situation that had developed. The Kaiser assented.

Ludendorff spoke. He admitted that insufficient attention had been given the possibility of an enemy offensive on the western face of the salient. He thought greater vigilance on the part of the Ninth Army might have averted the peril, and added that perhaps the troops of 1914 would have pulled themselves out of it.

The Kaiser wanted to know if the troops had failed to resist sufficiently. Ludendorff replied, "We thought the reserves capable of more resistance."

He went on to reveal the immediate extent of the damage. The Marne would have to be abandoned and a new defensive line constructed, shallower and easier to hold, before any thought could be given to a renewed offensive. In other words, a retreat much like that of 1914.

The Kaiser did not hide his agitation at the idea of a retreat. He had counted at least on holding all the ground won. When Ludendorff pointed to the shortage of reserves, Wilhelm finally gave voice to a reproach, reminding Ludendorff that just four days earlier he had voiced a forecast of unlimited optimism.

Ludendorff replied that the hazards of war were often unexpected.

True enough, but hardly justification for his confident prognosis of victory, furiously maintained against rising civilian skepticism, reiterated on the eve of battle, and now exposed as no more than a gambler's false prescience.

Perfunctorily, Ludendorff offered his resignation, which the

Kaiser perfunctorily declined. For that, it was either too early or too late.

The summation of the German Army Group Crown Prince for July 18 summarized what had happened in lucid terms. It stated that Mangin's attack

> almost completely shattered the divisions of the Ninth Army along a broad front between the Aisne and the Clignon brook.

The enemy success was attributed by Seventh Army headquarters to surprise, numbers, and tanks:

> The enemy was in a certain sense fortunate in attaining a practical surprise. . . . During the early morning hours of July 18, two deserters . . . stated that between 5 and 6 A.M. a French attack on a large scale would be started against the German front between the Aisne and the Marne. Noise of motors . . . seemed to indicate that tanks were going into positions of readiness. These were the only signs which indicated that an attack on a large scale was imminent.
>
> It now appears that we did not appreciate fully the number of his troops. . . . We expected that our successful advance on Reims would compel French GHQ to throw the forces it had intended for the west front of the Seventh Army and the south part of the Ninth Army into the Epernay-Reims-Châlons battle to avoid annihilation there. This calculation was based first on the assumption that our offensive would overrun a weak and surprised army without interruption, in other words, that a catastrophe would develop in the Reims arc, into which the hostile reserves would be drawn. This first assumption was based on a second, which was that the number of divisions opposed to the Army Group German Crown Prince [Wilhelm] was so low that a simulta-

> neous concentration in the Villers-Cotterêts woods and a strong occupation of the Reims front was out of the question. . . .
>
> Both assumptions were wrong. . . .
>
> Finally, we had underestimated the offensive value of tanks. . . . Armored tanks, employed in mass heretofore unknown and technically highly developed, preceded the infantry . . . in long, connected lines. Our defense had not been prepared for this mass employment on a broad front . . . our infantry felt helpless opposite the fire-disgorging, rapidly moving machines and lost their nerve.

Chancellor Hertling later found a way to summarize the battle both more succinctly and more melodramatically: "The history of the world," he wrote, "was played out in three days."

By a bizarre coincidence, a Munich publisher chose this moment to announce publication of the first volume of a vast scholarly work—Oswald Spengler's *Decline of the West.*

23

RETREAT FROM THE MARNE

Through the night of July 18–19, the Germans could hear the noise of French tank crews repairing their shot-up vehicles, and at dawn the attack recommenced all along the western face of the salient. Even though fully alerted, the defenders once more had their hands full as the lines of tanks and waves of infantry followed the barrage across the wheatfields and through the patches of woods, while overhead roared flights of Bréguet bombers to hit German rear areas.

At the end of a long, bloody day's fighting, the German Ninth and Seventh Armies had retreated another two and a half to three and a half miles on most of the front. They still hung onto the Soissons–Château-Thierry road, but the Allied advance was now dangerously close to cutting it. Boehn and the Crown Prince agreed that a general pullback of the troops in the whole southern part of the salient was unavoidable.

That night the Germans south of the Marne carried out their planned withdrawal to the north bank with skill and secrecy. The French and Americans opposite were entirely unaware of what was taking place, and next morning followed up a violent bombardment with an infantry attack that discovered empty trenches.

That day (July 20) the French Ninth and Fifth Armies, the latter reinforced by two British divisions, extended the attack front all around the salient. Yet the Germans held firmly in the east and gave ground only slowly in the west. Several Allied divisions, including the U.S. Second, had to be relieved. Once more, it almost appeared as if the counteroffensive might be halted.

But once more the ground gained was no indicator of the significance of the fighting. On this day, the third of the offensive, Ludendorff took the painful step of "provisionally" canceling "Hagen," the reserves for which were draining steadily south to the Marne.

The German defense continued to show stubborn strength through the next two days (July 21–22), to a point where Hindenburg suggested the possibility of planning a counterattack west of Soissons to catch Mangin's left flank. But Ludendorff was being pulled in the opposite direction by Boehn and the Crown Prince, who felt that their exhausted troops could not hold securely short of the Aisne and Vesle rivers. Ludendorff was also thinking of the Austro-Hungarian ally, on whom a general retreat from the Marne salient could not fail to make a dangerous impression. For the moment, he prescribed a retreat behind the Ourcq, anchored on Fère-en-Tardenois. That night (July 22) he notified the Army Group Crown Prince Rupprecht that it would have to supply several fresh divisions at once to replace worn-out divisions of the Army Group German Crown Prince.

The German defensive showing made little impression on Foch, who dictated a memorandum to Weygand for presentation to Haig, Pétain, and Pershing. The three Allied generals gathered at Foch's Bombon chateau on July 24, and Weygand read Foch's views aloud. All three were considerably taken aback at the optimism and ambition of the program laid down: "The moment has come to abandon the general defensive attitude forced upon us until now by numerical inferiority and to pass to the offensive." There followed a whole series of attacks, up and down the length of the front, to free lateral rail lines, recover coal fields, secure the Channel ports, and reduce the St. Mihiel salient, this last an operation to be entrusted to a new "American Army." Foch foresaw local German retreats, which he urged should not be permitted to take place unmolested. Haig protested that the British Army was not yet ready, Petain that the French Army was worn out, and Pershing that the American Army did not yet exist. "Temporary weaknesses," said Foch, and in the end they all agreed.

That same day Ludendorff thought the apparent jelling of the front presented the glimmer of an opportunity to seize back the initiative. Instead of Hindenburg's attack west of Soissons he reverted to the pinch-off of Reims. The attack was designed as an assault by a single corps of the German First Army against the heights west of the city. If it succeeded, this blow could be followed by Hindenburg's.

But once again Reims proved a nut impossible to crack; the attack (by Corps Borne) on July 25 ended in yet another bloody check. Meantime, just when they appeared to be stopped, the persistent attacks of the French Tenth, Sixth, and Fifth Armies broke through in several places and threatened the Ourcq defense line.

Foch had been able to maintain the pressure far longer and harder than Ludendorff had thought possible. Where two American divisions had been withdrawn (the First after five straight days' attacking), three more (the Fourth, Twenty-sixth, and Thirty-second) had appeared. Besides the two originally south of the Marne (the Third and the Twenty-eighth), another (the Forty-second, transferred from Gouraud's Fourth Army without any intervening rest) had come in. Four British divisions were also identified, two on each side of the salient, while over forty French divisions had participated thus far. And the pressure was unrelenting.

Once more Ludendorff was forced to surrender to realities. The pinch-off of Reims was abandoned for good, Hindenburg's counterattack west of Soissons was shelved, and "Hagen" renounced without qualification. All effort had to be concentrated on withdrawal to a defense line that could be held—for how long, or for what purpose, was unclear, but there was no time now even to think about that. Ludendorff ordered an immediate pullback of the Seventh Army to an intermediate position en route to the Aisne-Vesle line.

On the night of July 25, after a harrowing eleven consecutive days in the line, Hans Zöberlein's regiment was relieved and started north.

As they waited for midnight to begin their march, Zöberlein and his comrades

> secretly thought about the remarkable fate that we Germans for a second time in this war came to grief on the Marne. . . . The moon shone pale. . . . The posts stood still, in a dream. Cries for help reached us: "*De l'eau—de l'eau—sanitaire!*" Crouching shadows moved over the field. A cool, light breeze drove the stench of corruption enemywards. . . . All supplies which we could not take back and the weapons of the dead and wounded were buried. We hunted for boxes of cartridges in the road, where even nearer than yesterday the entrenching line of the French could be seen. . . .
>
> Midnight. Time to leave, to escape the annihilating fire at daybreak. The Sixth Company remains behind to cover the retreat. The first group starts off, ten minutes later the second, and then after a few rifle salvoes the rest. We leave the ruined glade, climbing over the numerous shell holes in the underbrush. Here and there rises a sandy mound in which a rifle is stuck, a steel helmet over its butt. There they lie buried, those who would never come back from the battle of the Marne. . . .
>
> Along the road back to Romigny the column passes, rattling artillery, the riders in the blowing rain bent over in their saddles, the cannoneers hanging on the limbers of the guns. Between slouch the dispersed fragments of infantry, the remnants of

> companies, guns slung round necks, tarpaulins over heads against the rain, the knapsacks underneath bulging with the effect of a line of comic hunchbacks. Wagons stand waiting to take away supplies. . . . The long lines of infantry file in the gray morning out of the woods, over the open field, without haste. . . . Behind us thunder the engineers' demolitions. The engineers soon come running down the slope, followed by the infantry rearguard. . . . Only our dead remain behind.

On August 2 the French recaptured battered Soissons, while the U.S. Thirty-second Division struck the last blow of the battle by taking, losing, and retaking Fismes, on the Vesle between Soissons and Reims. The Marne salient was erased.

Pétain notified Foch that the French Army was "at the end of our effort," with morale good, but the troops "very tired." German intelligence was well aware of this situation; its report to Ludendorff listed only eight French divisions in reserve. All spring, such a report had been exciting news at Avesnes, but this time it meant nothing, because Foch had no fewer than thirty-eight non-French reserve divisions—seventeen British, fifteen American, two Italian, and four Belgian.

On the German side, there were hardly any reserve divisions, and the divisions in the line were falling alarmingly in rifle strength. The official field strength of battalions had been reduced from 850 to 700 men, but despite the breaking up of ten divisions, the actual, or fighting, strength fell far below the 700 figure.

As ominous as the dwindling numbers of the Army was the rise of opposition to the war among the rank and file. "The soldier at the front had begun to think politically," observed Hans Zöberlein. "It happened in all the trenches and barracks. The failure of the offensive brought . . . open discussion, silenced before by victory. Now it began to appear that those who had prophesied a bad end were right; we would not win the war! The people had no desire that this war of the Kaiser and a handful of capitalists should be won."

Another German soldier retreating through the ruined villages of the Marne salient expressed a different insight in a letter home. After describing how a French civilian funeral party was dispersed by a bombardment that tore up the cemetery, he added the thought: "It is good that the war isn't raging in our own country."

Even the havoc visited on the French tanks by the German artillery brought no advantage, as another aspect of Ludendorff's decision of the previous winter became apparent. Tank production was difficult to get started, yet once started it could be kept up and even increased with ease. Within a short time, the French would be able completely to replace their Marne tank losses, while a German tank program, launched now, could produce no serious results even by autumn.

Besides, the British had a tank program going. Winston Churchill had made good on his promise to Haig, and by midsummer Haig appreciated it. The British Army had not been engaged now for three months; it had had time to absorb B-men, troops from the East, and Americans. Sixty divisions at full strength, backed by a large accumulation of tanks, it was ready for a major offensive against a now seriously weakened enemy.

Foch and Haig agreed on an attack by Rawlinson's British Fourth Army east of Amiens, where the Germans had been sitting since "Michael." Haig had had an amalgamation problem of his own, because the Canadian government insisted that its troops had to be used together as the Canadian Corps. But on August 8 the Canadian Corps and the Australian Corps, four divisions apiece, spearheaded a surprise assault made like Mangin's without artillery preparation. It broke through German defenses even less alert and no better dug in than those of July 18. The performance of the British tanks was even better than the French had been, thanks to a little-noticed minor attack by the Australians on July 4 that had gained valuable lessons in tank-infantry coordination.

There were 324 heavy tanks in the assault wave, and 160 light (Whippets) for exploitation (along with cavalry, which again proved useless). The Australians, Canadians, and tanks advanced up to seven miles on the first day, with British and French on either side going nearly as far. Hundreds of guns were captured along with thousands of prisoners and even a divisional staff. Elated Foch committed another French army, the Third, farther east, and though the Germans once more recovered and held, was more than ever confirmed in his certainty that the tide had decisively turned.

As for Ludendorff, one aspect of August 8 impressed him above all, and caused him to label it a "black day for the German Army"—the unmistakable, visible, audible signs of the erosion of German morale. The stricture Ludendorff had made against the troops who had given way on July 18 was this time far better documented, if no more merited by the heroically long-suffering German front-liners. Many surrendered willingly, even in large groups. Especially revealing were the epithets with which troops leaving the front greeted those relieving them: "Scabs!" "Strikebreakers!" Some of the cries came from proletarian militants who had been drafted after the January strike in Berlin, but the expressions exactly fitted the front-line soldiers' feeling after the defeat on the Marne: the war was lost, and to keep fighting at this stage was a crime.

> Summer of 1918—[wrote Erich Maria Remarque later] Never has life in its niggardliness seemed to us so desirable as now. . . . Summer of 1918—Never was so much silently suffered as in the moment when we depart once again for the front line. Wild, tormenting rumors of an armistice and peace are in the air; they lay hold on our hearts and make the return to the front harder than ever. Summer of 1918—Never was life in the line more bitter and more full of horror than in the hours of the bombardment, when the blanched faces lie in the dirt, and the hands clutch at the one thought: No! No! Not now!

Not now at the last moment! Summer of 1918—Breath of hope that sweeps over the scorched fields, raging fever of impatience, of disappointment, of the most agonizing terror of death, insensate question: Why do they not make an end?

24

WHY NOT PEACE?

Why did they not? Besides the soldiers, many others were asking. On August 13–14, a Crown Council was held. At the request of the Supreme Command, it took place at rear headquarters, the Hotel Britannique in Spa, Belgium. From Berlin came the Kaiser, Chancellor Hertling and the new foreign minister, Admiral von Hintze. From the field came the German Crown Prince, and from Vienna came a large delegation: young Emperor Karl, his own new foreign minister, Count von Burián, and Baron Arz, chief of the Austro-Hungarian General Staff.

Karl, his minister, and his general had carefully prepared their program in advance. Baron Arz was to explain that the state of the Austro-Hungarian Army forbade extension of the war into the winter, while Count Burián was to disclose an imminent Austrian intention to publish a peace proposal. Hertling, Hintze, and the Kaiser also came to Spa with the intention of concerting a peace project they had discussed, consisting of a carefully stage-managed diplomatic intervention by a neutral country.

But Ludendorff at once took command, just as if the Marne

had never happened. In separate meetings and in the general conference, he persuaded everyone that the war was not lost after all. It was true, he admitted, that contrary to his earlier promise, it was not won, and in fact, the prospect of defeating the enemy in the field, in the sense in which the Russians had been beaten, had to be abandoned.

But the defensive battle offered excellent prospects of wearing the enemy out: "We can no longer hope to break down the fighting spirit of our enemies by military action," but "we must set as the object of our campaign that of gradually wearing down the enemy's fighting spirit by a strategic defensive." This could be accomplished, according to Ludendorff, provided everyone did his utmost. Specifically, he wanted the "home front," as he called it, to be subjected to strict discipline, and from the Austrians he wanted as many troops as they could manage to send to the Western Front.

It was an incredible performance, and within its limits incredibly successful. Baron Arz and Emperor Karl were completely hypnotized, and promised to send Austrian divisions to France. Count Burián was less convinced, but agreed to suspend the projected Austrian peace proposal. Chancellor Hertling and Foreign Minister Hintze were encouraged by Ludendorff's optimism to the point where they agreed that it would be best to postpone their project until after "the next success" on the Western Front.

Ludendorff did not object to the idea of seeking mediation through the King of Spain or Queen Wilhelmina of Holland; in fact he specifically endorsed the idea. His thought was that such a channel could be used to induce the Allies to state their real war aims—that is, the minimum for which they would settle. He had no intention whatsoever of making peace on the basis of the Fourteen Points. On the contrary, he expressed his conviction that Germany could still keep Belgium! So far from considering such concessions as a degree of autonomy for Alsace-Lorraine, he still intended to annex the Longwy-Briey basin, and of course Luxembourg.

Hindenburg ended the conference on a note of astonishing optimism: "I hope that we shall after all succeed in maintaining ourselves on French soil and thereby in finally enforcing our will on the enemy."

Behind the strange performance of the two generals lay one obvious conscious factor: the desire to put as good a face on things as possible for the benefit of the Austrians. Beyond this lay the psychological need for self-justification, certainly strong in the case of Ludendorff. Having promised victory with increasing assurance to counter mounting skepticism, he could not easily turn completely around. This psychological factor was doubtless heightened by the abruptness of the military reversal, deriving from the timing of the two D-days, "Reims-Marne Defense" on July 15 and Foch's counteroffensive on July 18. Largely as the result of coincidence, the entire initiative had changed hands in a single day, something unheard of before in the war. It was difficult to accept the fact that so swift a transformation could be irrevocable.

Yet by August 14 enough time had gone by to permit an objective evaluation. Crown Prince Rupprecht was writing to Prince Max of Baden at this moment in a very different sense from that expressed by Hindenburg and Ludendorff: "By the mistaken operation beyond the Marne and the series of heavy reverses which followed, absolutely fatal both materially and morally, our military situation has deteriorated so rapidly that I no longer believe we can hold out over the winter; it is even possible that a catastrophe will come earlier."

Even granting the psychological basis, there was missing from the analysis put forward by Hindenburg and Ludendorff a purely intellectual element of decisive importance: an appreciation of the difficult politics of making peace. Perhaps because Ludendorff had always thought solely in terms of total victory, he was unable to come to grips with the frustrating mechanism of peace by negotiation. The sort of peace maneuver he envisioned, to ascertain the Allies' minimal demands, presupposed a solidly reestablished stalemate on the Western Front. A mere local German tactical success would not suffice. The other side of that political equation escaped him too: if a stalemate were not reestablished, the diplomatic balance must rapidly tilt against Germany.

In any case, the formula of waiting for "the next success" was quickly proved a fantasy. Four days after the Spa conference (August 18) Mangin's French Tenth Army, rested for only two weeks, attacked between the Oise and the Aisne. Once more the Allies scored a brief, rapid advance, taking guns and prisoners; once more German reserves had to be thrown in pell-mell. ("Another black day," recorded Ludendorff.) Mangin's offensive had not even died when Byng's British Third Army struck (August 21), capturing Bapaume and unhinging another part of the German defensive line. On August 26, Horne's British First Army, rested since April, attacked east of Arras with similar success. On September 1, an Australian force captured Péronne; on September 2, the Canadians broke through the old, solidly built Drocourt–Quéant defensive line.

The conduct of the war had simply passed out of Ludendorff's hands. It was now in those of Foch.

One morning Colonel Mott, Pershing's liaison officer with Foch, met the generalissimo, since August 6 a marshal of France, returning from mass in the village church of Bombon. "As I saluted him he paused as though inviting me to speak, and I ventured the remark that the Germans seemed to be getting more than they could stand. He came up close to me, took a firm hold on my belt with his left hand, and with his right fist delivered a punch at my chin, a hook under my ribs, and another drive at my ear; he then shouldered his stick and without a single word marched on to the château." It was the same pantomime, a little more vigorously applied, with which Foch had explained his plans to Balfour at Versailles two months earlier.

There was nothing particularly Napoleonic about Foch's strategy of a stream of blows up and down the front, but it answered the purpose. Haig caviled with military correctness over the American-planned offensive against the St-Mihiel salient in Lorraine, which made little chess-game sense, but the campaign was no longer a chess game and it did not matter where the Allies struck. Foch compromised by letting Pershing fight his St-Mihiel battle and then make a difficult switch north to the Meuse-Argonne, where the American effort would be more related to the other Allied offensives. That the Germans were already pulling out of St-Mihiel when Pershing's Americans and French jumped off on September 12 also did not matter; over the next two days they still captured prisoners and guns.

All that really mattered was that the sands had run out; Foch now had plenty of Americans and plenty of tanks.

On September 7, the townspeople of Avesnes were stirred to a lively curiosity that soon turned to delight: all day long and into the evening, automobiles and trucks passed back and forth between the railway station and the houses where the Germans were billeted, officers and baggage in the autos, soldiers and looted furniture in the trucks. Someone inquired at the *Kommandantur* what was going on, and received the reply: "The climate of Avesnes is too cold for the General Staff."

The forward headquarters was now too far forward, and was withdrawing to Spa. The Kaiser's train pulled out for the last time, while with stately tread, Jenny the elephant marched north on foot.

Ludendorff's maps were pinned up in his old suite at the Britannique, one floor above Hindenburg's. On September 15, a map to which he had paid scant attention, that of the Balkan front, suddenly registered a major shock. Czar Ferdinand of Bulgaria had insistently warned that his Bulgarian Army could not hold against a determined offensive. Franchet d'Esperey, the general exiled by Clemenceau to Macedonia after the Chemin des Dames disaster, had been clamoring for permission to launch an attack, which for varying political reasons London and Rome had opposed. Clemenceau, converted by Foch to the project, won his Allies' consent and telegraphed Franchet on September 10. On the fifteenth, Franchet's French-Serb spearhead stabbed clean through and menaced the whole Bulgarian Army with immediate catastrophe.

The same day, two months after the Marne jump-off, the long-threatened Austrian peace offer was addressed to the

United States. Beguiled by the aggressive attitudes of Ludendorff and Hindenburg, Emperor Karl had held off for a month before giving in to the hardheaded arguments of Count Burián. To fulfill the letter of a promise to Kaiser Wilhelm, he notified the latter, but then had the offer published before Wilhelm could enter a protest.

The stratagem did Karl and Burián no good. Secretary of State Lansing wasted no time in returning a coldly negative reply. The Allies were no longer interested in dealing with Vienna.

Karl's move at least helped dispel some illusions. In Berlin on September 20, the Social Democrats called on Chancellor Hertling for an immediate request for armistice, a no-annexation peace, and complete democratization forthwith—in short, a revolution. Foreign Minister Hintze was able to start his project for enlisting Queen Wilhelmina as a mediator, thanks to a tardy and reluctant acquiescence from Ludendorff, who was frantically promising the Bulgarians military help. Too late; the Bulgarians asked Franchet d'Esperey for an armistice.

On the Western Front on September 26, Pershing's new American Army struck the Hindenburg Line, Ludendorff's *Siegfried Stellung*, while Gouraud's French Fourth Army, quitting the trenches that won the Marne battle, applied pressure west of the Argonne Forest. Next day, three of Haig's British armies began an intensive bombardment, clearly a prelude to assault, against the Hindenburg Line in the north.

The American-French advance and the British bombardment continued on September 28. At six o'clock that Saturday evening, in the Britannique, Ludendorff descended to Hindenburg's suite. Gloomily the two generals canvassed the situation, and agreed that an armistice was indispensable. They were thinking of an armistice of the eighteenth-century variety—a pause in which the troops could profit from a breathing spell and then, if necessary, resume combat. Hindenburg, phlegmatic but astonishingly optimistic, thought that a peace offer now might still permit annexation of the

Longwy-Briey basin. Ludendorff, his nerves on edge to the point where he actually spoke sharply to the old Field Marshal, was a shade more realistic; he thought that in the West peace had to be made on the basis of the Fourteen Points, but that the eastern booty could be kept. As a gesture to the western Allies, he proposed that the air force's project of bombing Paris and London with incendiary bombs should be canceled.

He turned his anger on the Berlin government. Recalling the Crown Council in these rooms six weeks earlier, he convinced himself that he had called on the politicians there to make peace at once. Now it was a matter of urgency; no delay was possible.

Next day (Sunday, September 29), the Kaiser, Hertling, and Hintze arrived once more at the Britannique. Peremptorily, Ludendorff demanded to know what had been done about his request for the initiation of peace negotiations.

Admiral Hintze was taken aback. He was in the midst of maneuvers for a diplomatic intervention by Queen Wilhelmina, but he believed the enterprise to have originated with himself. In any case, given the short space of time, the move had not yet borne fruit.

Ludendorff brusquely announced that an armistice must be concluded immediately. How quickly was immediately? Within twenty-four hours, said Ludendorff.

Hintze, Hertling, and the Kaiser were equally dumbfounded. The notion of arranging an armistice through diplomatic channels "within twenty-four hours" was simply fantastic. Such a time context implied not a negotiation but a surrender.

For seventy-five-year-old Hertling it was the last straw. He had dreamed of being the Reconciliation Chancellor who would bring Germany a profitable peace that would head off revolution; now in rapid succession he was confronted with revolution and defeat. Next day (September 30), the Reconciliation Chancellor resigned.

The Kaiser, rather surprisingly, proved more flexible than the Chancellor. Manfully swallowing the idea of a constitutional revolution that reduced him to a figurehead, he agreed to the demands of the Reichstag leaders and published a decree pledging democratization. He then asked his cousin Prince Max of Baden to form a government.

Prince Max, at the moment at Dessau, accepted, and by the time he arrived in Berlin found his government virtually formed by agreement among the Reichstag parties. The great problem was the ultimatum from the Supreme Command. To beg the enemy for an armistice on his first day in office, he felt, would be a capital blunder, and he could not believe that the military situation had overnight turned so hopeless that this open a confession of weakness was needed. He suspected that Ludendorff was seeking to maneuver against the democratic revolution in Berlin.

But Prince Max's attempts to delay were vain in the face of the uncompromising insistence of both Hindenburg and Ludendorff. Ludendorff sent six telegrams on October 1, and the next day Hindenburg arrived in person to tell the Crown Council that "there appears to be no possibility . . . of winning peace from our enemies by force of arms." That night (October 2) Ludendorff sent a special emissary, Major von dem Bussche, to brief the leaders of the Reichstag on the military situation. The major's exposition laid stress on the exhaustion of German reserves, the shrinking of the infantry battalions, and the rapidity with which the situation at the front, where the long-prepared defense systems of the Hindenburg Line were under violent siege, was deteriorating. In sum, the major pictured the German Army as no longer able to defend itself. "The enemy's tanks have been unexpectedly numerous. . . . Every twenty-four hours can impair the situation and give the enemy an opportunity to discover our present weakness."

The politicians were thunderstruck. Despite defeats and withdrawals, despite the collapse of Bulgaria and the threatened defection of Austria, they had no idea that things were at this crisis stage where, as Major von dem Bussche said in so many words, hours counted. How could it all have happened so quickly?

Prince Max and his foreign minister—still another new one, a Dr. Solf—helplessly drafted a note to President Wilson, the most amenable-looking of their enemies, checked it out with the Supreme Command, and sent it by way of Switzerland on the night of October 3–4. The Swiss envoy presented it in Washington on October 6. It asked for "steps toward the restoration of peace" and cited the Fourteen Points as a "basis for peace negotiations." Meantime Prince Max, who had always argued that the authoritarian structure of the German government was in Allied and especially American eyes an obstacle to peace, set on foot in the Reichstag unequivocal moves toward immediate, full democratic government.

Wilson's reply was encouragingly prompt and mild. He asked if the German government meant that it accepted the substance of the Fourteen Points, and if it was prepared to withdraw its military forces entirely from Allied soil. On the second point, Prince Max consulted the Supreme Command—was there any objection to a prompt evacuation of France and Belgium?

To answer, Ludendorff came in person to Berlin, arriving October 9. He raised no objection to the proposed evacuation, but astonished Prince Max by asserting that the situation had taken a sudden turn for the better—morale and supply improved. In reply to a direct question from Dr. Solf as to whether the front could hold out for three more months, he gave a curt No, but later he voiced the strangely contradictory anticipation that "I hope to have six hundred tanks in the spring."

There seemed as little justification for Ludendorff's startling new optimism as there had been for his previous urgent foreboding. The Hindenburg Line was breached in many places, one important town after another had fallen—Cambrai, Péronne, St.-Quentin, Laon. If Pershing's American offensive east of the Argonne Forest had temporarily stalled, there was scant comfort for the Germans in the new American Army's problem, which consisted in having so many troops on the battlefield that they got in each other's way.

Puzzled and profoundly distrustful of the First Quartermaster General, Prince Max thought it might be wise to call a council of war and hear from all the generals. Through Hindenburg, Ludendorff protested vehemently, and the idea was dropped.

On October 12 a new note was sent to Wilson, pledging the evacuation of France and Belgium.

Wilson had meantime heard from his allies, who were none too pleased either with the German approach to Washington or with Wilson's magisterial acceptance of the role of Allied spokesman. The second of the Fourteen Points, that on freedom of the seas, had caused apoplexy in the British Admiralty, while the French had been deeply pained by Wilson's omission of reparations for the ravages of invasion.

Wilson's second note, in reply to Prince Max's reply, consequently exhibited a distinctly cooler tone: No arrangement could be accepted that did not "provide absolutely satisfactory safeguards and guarantees of the maintenance of the present military supremacy of the armies of the United States and of the allies in the field." Furthermore, submarine warfare must cease at once (a U-boat skipper with a bad sense of timing had just sunk a passenger ship), the German Army must stop destroying things as it retreated, and finally, by unmistakable implication, the Kaiser must go.

It was evident that the Allies felt the game was in their hands. Kühlmann was vindicated; every delay imposed by the Supreme Command since his June 24 speech had served only to reduce Germany's bargaining position. Now there was hardly a counter left on the German side of the table.

For the first time, Ludendorff began to see where his manic fixation on total victory had led. He now had to ask himself what history would say. When on October 17 a new conference was held in Berlin, he startled the harried civilians even more than he had at Spa. He flatly denied attaching a twenty-four-hour time limit—whose silliness was certainly apparent—to his September 29 request for armistice negotiations. Even more amazingly, he now expressed himself as quite satisfied with the position at the front. The manpower problem no longer looked grave; he had assurances of a much larger recruitment than he had thought possible. The truth behind this claim was that the War Office had stated that by sacrificing industry's needs, with consequent fatal effects on war production, it could give him a total of 600,000 men very shortly, and after that no more at all. Meantime the average field, or paper, strength of German battalions had slipped to 508, while the real strength of divisions had fallen below 3,000. This detail Ludendorff did not mention.

Two years earlier, Ludendorff had backed the German Navy's demand for unrestricted U-boat warfare. Now the Navy found a way to repay him. Admiral Scheer, chief of naval operations, supported Ludendorff's bluster by pronouncing the Navy absolutely opposed to the termination of submarine warfare.

Prince Max and the civilians groped for some sort of sense in the foolish, clipped phrases of their epauletted colleagues, and thought they found some: a simple, cowardly desire to escape blame for the debacle that, thanks to them, now clearly threatened.

Prince Max, gentlemanly but not weak, was astonished at Ludendorff's effrontery. From the Kaiser he obtained the cessation of U-boat warfare, and on October 21 reported this in a new note to Wilson.

But the continuing Allied battlefield successes, from Flanders to the Argonne Forest, and the confirmation of German weakness implicit in the armistice negotiations, had now removed the basis for two-sided bargaining. In his third note, on October 23, the American President warned that the United States did not mean to deal with "the military masters and monarchical autocrats of Germany" except on the basis of surrender.

It was the turn of Ludendorff to be taken aback. His obliviousness to the technical difficulties of making peace, to which his shallow military dogma of war had blinded him, had now completely victimized him. While imposing the peace of Siegfried the conqueror on Russia and grasping for Belgium, the Netherlands, and northern France, while planning the control of Eurasia by the Master Race and dreaming of world conquest, he had assumed the Fourteen Points to be a safe last-resort retreat line—a basis for negotiation, which he could use in case of defeat, offering to relinquish some of his occupied territory in return for the qualification of some of Wilson's points. It had not occurred to him that defeat automatically eliminated negotiation concerning the Fourteen Points and introduced instead the threat of their modification against Germany. He had scarcely noticed that in Wilson's reply to Emperor Karl, who had hopefully sent his own note to Washington on October 6, the American President had coolly canceled one of his points (Point 10) and in its place pronounced the death knell of Austria-Hungary.

As if instantly to convert Wilson's pronouncement into concrete reality, the Italian Army launched an offensive on October 24 in whose face the seething, mutinous, multinational Habsburg army disintegrated.

To Ludendorff and Hindenburg, the American President now appeared a master of deceit who had replied graciously to the German peace offer in order to entrap Germany in one concession after another until, casting aside his mask, he demanded total surrender.

To such treachery they could find no other answer than a fight to the last man. To this end they issued a proclamation to the Army (October 25) branding the American demands unacceptable to "us soldiers."

Only two men as insensitive, not to say humorless, as Ludendorff and Hindenburg could at this stage, after the frightful suffering they had imposed on the front-liners all spring and summer, have employed such an expression as "us soldiers." Only two men disconnected from all reality save "military" could have failed to realize that the war was entirely out of their hands.

When Prince Max threatened to go over their heads to get the opinions of other generals, Hindenburg and Ludendorff thought to counter by journeying once more to Berlin to bully the Kaiser. Prince Max forbade their coming; they came anyway, but the Kaiser, showing better sense than theirs, gave them no support. When an acrimonious exchange broke out, Ludendorff found himself again offering his resignation, which the Kaiser this time accepted.

Hindenburg, reverting to his role of patriotic statue, stuck to his post to the bitter end, which was to be excruciatingly drawn out to November 11, making it a year to the day since Ludendorff had overruled his generals and laid down the plan for *Friedensturm* in the conference at Mons.

The delegation sent to sign the armistice at Rethondes was headed by Matthias Erzberger, the too-clever politician who had drafted the Peace Resolution and interpreted it to admit the dismemberment of Russia. Now everything was lost—Poland, the Baltic states, Belgium, Luxembourg, the Longwy-Briey basin, Alsace-Lorraine, the Polish Corridor. The Fourteen Points, as Hindenburg had said, were fit only to be dictated to a completly beaten enemy—exactly what, thanks to Ludendorff's decisions, invariably endorsed by Hindenburg, Germany had finally become.

In Wilson's last notes, a fifteenth point had been added to the fourteen: America and her allies, the professor-president coldly implied, could not deal with a Germany headed by a Kaiser. The Social Democrats and their allies demanded abdication, and on November 9 a cavalcade of limousines carrying the Supreme Warlord left Spa for the Netherlands. In Holland, the Kaiser found refuge at the home of a sympathetic friend—Count Bentinck's Castle Amerongen, the site Foreign Minister Kühlmann had picked out months earlier for his secret peace talks with the British government.

On the morning of November 11, under the spell of the impending armistice, the Western Front was passive except for artillery fire. But in a sector just north of the Meuse River, a few miles short of the French-Belgian border, a battalion of the French 415th Infantry had been called on to deliver the last attack of the war, an assault crossing to seize a bridgehead over the Meuse, in case the Germans refused the armistice. The battalion carried out its mission, crossing the Meuse in the early hours of the morning, taking heavy casualties, digging shallow holes under German machine-gun fire. As a result, it heard nothing of the armistice until a runner from regiment suddenly flung himself down with the news, along with an order: "At 1100 hours all buglers will sound the 'Cease-fire.' "

There was only one bugler, Delaluque, in the battalion, and he was in the front line. A runner found him and the two succeeded in crawling back to the shell hole that served as Captain Lebreton's command post. The captain gave him his orders.

"Right, Captain," agreed Delaluque. "There's only one trouble—I've forgotten the tune of 'Cease-fire.' "

Captain Lebreton shouted the tune, which, like bugle calls everywhere, had been converted to a vocal mnemonic: "Your shooting was so bad . . . you don't get . . . any pass, my lad!"

Sprawled above him, Delaluque repeated it to be sure he had it, then drew his battered bugle from his knapsack, where he had carried it since 1914. Next, the search for the mouthpiece. Captain Lebreton looked at his watch—10:57. A Boche machine gun kicked up dirt close by. Delaluque brought out spools of thread, a meat-can opener, finally the mouthpiece, stopped up with bits of candle wax and tobacco. He cleaned it out while the captain impatiently gazed at his watch.

At exactly eleven, Lebreton's hand went up. In accordance with orders, Delaluque raised himself slowly, till his head and bugle were in full view of the enemy, closed his eyes, and blew.

With the first notes, all firing stopped. Delaluque stood up all the way and blew on.

Still, not a shot. Instead, faintly, from across the fields, came the sound of other bugles—German.

The war was over.

LUDENDORFF

The old-fashioned military historians who first dealt with World War I treated it as a sort of gigantic combination of chess tournament and football game. Reviewing Ludendorff's performance in 1918, they concluded that he lost because he was "more of a tactician than a strategist," that is, because his attention was too narrowly fixed on the immediate battlefield in each of the successive battles. Had he coordinated "Michael" and the other offensives with sufficient niceness, according to this theory, he could have won.

Several wars later such a point of view seems absurdly pedantic. There is no reason to believe World War I generals were stupider than most, and among World War I generals Ludendorff ranks as an able and even a gifted leader. If he was less than perfect in his battlefield calculations, perfection must be judged as either impossible to attain or a matter of luck.

Ludendorff's real trouble goes far deeper, and both illuminates and is lighted by the subsequent history of the twentieth century. Nearly all generals are conservative and nationalist, and not a few carry their political views to extremes.

Some have actually embodied them in governments— Pétain, Franco, Admiral Horthy. Their conservative dictatorships have had only limited historical significance; indeed Franco's regime may ultimately be remembered for bringing Spain peace and Pétain's for saving French Jewry from Hitler's Final Solution.

Ludendorff is something else entirely. Prefiguring Hitler in his racist dream of world dominion, he came close to creating a German super-empire that, complemented by a German-backed anti-Bolshevik dictatorship in Russia, would have stretched from ocean to ocean. The course of history that might have followed a decisive German victory on the Marne can hardly be conjectured, but it seems likely that the Ludendorff dictatorship advocated by Colonel von Thaer might have come about simply through the tremendous enhancement of Ludendorff's prestige. Such a dictatorship would have been a very different thing from the tame regimes of Franco and Pétain. A final Punic war between German Europe and the Anglo-Saxon powers would almost seem to follow, with the first stage at least a siege of Britain.

The true and meaningful explanation of Ludendorff's defeat in 1918 is surely to be found in the extravagance of his ambitions rather than in errors of battlefield judgment. Those ambitions not only exceeded his means, but outran common sense. The spectre of Ludendorff's super-empire, even though not fully visible to the Allies, looked menacing enough to provoke a superlative combined effort from battered France, war-weary Britain, and aloof America. Foch's slogan for his general offensive, "*Tout le monde à la bataille,*" echoed the sentiment of the aroused democratic world, which put aside all other considerations to fight.

Whether a tactically successful outcome to "Marne Defense" and "Reims" would have brought German victory in 1918 may some day be ascertained by computer simulation and game theory, that is, by a sophisticated version of the kind of war game Colonel Wetzell played at Spa in February to test the capacity of the French motor transport system. The sharp turn in the tide of numbers by July at least raises doubts. The British Army, intended target of "Hagen," was much stronger than it had been in March and held a much shorter line. Even a fresh tactical success in Flanders would not, in August, automatically have brought British evacuation. As Clemenceau thought, further retreat was entirely possible for the Allies as long as the Americans kept coming.

There is a mystical quality in Ludendorff's demonic urge to victory, a gambler's psychosis that plays tricks with the odds. Here too Ludendorff prefigures Hitler, and 1918 foreshadows World War II.

A far more trenchant analysis of "*Friedensturm*" than that of the postwar military critics was made in the German Reichstag in the 1920s. The majority resolution of the subcommittee investigating the loss of the war was bland, concluding delicately that "The Government relied upon the judgment of the Supreme Command . . . [because] it had at its disposal no personality capable of opposing the will of the Supreme Command." But a minority resolution, introduced by Deputy Eichhorn, drove home two telling points: "The Supreme Command acted as pacemaker of the policy of conquest [including] . . . the renewed demand for the annexation of the whole of Belgium," and "The German Government, the Reichstag and the people were systematically deceived by the Supreme Command . . . advocates of peace by mutual agreement were treated as traitors."

Ludendorff after the war entered the political arena, first taking part in the "Kapp putsch" of 1920 and then joining Hitler in the Munich "Beer-Hall putsch" of 1923. In 1925 he ran for president of the German republic on the National Socialist ticket. By the time Hitler achieved power—ironically enough with the aid of Hindenburg, drafted into politics against his inclinations—Ludendorff had broken with him. The trouble was over Ludendorff's insistence that Christianity be abolished in favor of a pagan cult based on the gods of Wagner and the *Niebelungenlied*, a cultural revolution that Hitler deemed inexpedient. Ludendorff died in 1937, embittered, but spared the second and even greater catastrophe visited on Germany and the world by the pursuit of his idea.

BIBLIOGRAPHY

Sources of Eyewitness Accounts

There are a wealth of eyewitness accounts of the battles of 1918. Those used in this book include:

Binding, Rudolf, from his war memoir published in English as *A Fatalist at War,* trans. by Ian F. D. Morrow. Boston, 1929.

Boyd, Thomas, from *Through the Wheat,* by Thomas Boyd. New York, 1923.

Gaudy, Georges, from *Souvenirs d'un poilu du 57e régiment d'infanterie,* Paris, 1921–23; excerpts trans. in *Promise of Greatness, the War of 1914–1918,* ed. by George Panichas. New York, 1968.

Matthaei, Captain Fritz, and Captain Hans von Pranckh, from *Im Felde unbesiegt, der Weltkrieg in 29 Einzeldarstellungen,* by Gustav von Dickhuth-Harrach. Munich, 1921.

Oberer, August, Nicholas Schulenberg, and Heinrich Zellner, from *Der Deutsche Soldat, Briefe aus dem Weltkrieg,* ed. by Rudolf Hoffmann. Munich, 1937.

Zöberlein, Hans, from *Der Glaube an Deutschland, ein Kriegserleben von Verdun bis zum Umsturz,* by Hans Zöberlin. Munich, 1931.

American Battle Monuments Commission, *American Armies and Battlefields in Europe.* Washington, D.C., 1938.

Asprey, Robert B., *At Belleau Wood.* New York, 1965.

Bernstorff, Count Johann-Heinrich von, *My Three Years in America.* London, 1921.

Bethmann-Hollweg, Theobald von, *Reflections on the World War.* London, 1920.

Binding, Rudolf, *A Fatalist at War,* trans. by Ian F. D. Morrow. Boston, 1929.

Blake, Robert, ed., *The Private Papers of Douglas Haig, 1914–1919.* London, 1952.

Boyd, Thomas, *Through the Wheat.* New York, 1923.

Brissand, André, *1918, pourquoi la victoire.* Paris, 1968.

Buchan, John, *A History of the Great War,* Vol. IV, *From Caporetto to the Armistice.* London, 1922.

Bullard, Robert Lee, *Personalities and Reminiscences of the War.* New York, 1925.

Bundesarchiv, *Der Weltkrieg, 1914–1918,* Vol. XIV, *Die Kriegführung an der Westfront im Jahre 1918.* Berlin, 1944.

Chandler, Charles de Forest, and Lahm, Frank P., *How Our Army Grew Wings: Airmen and Aircraft Before 1914.* New York, 1943.

Churchill, Winston, *The World Crisis, 1916–1918.* London, 1927.

Clemenceau, Georges, *Grandeur and Misery of Victory,* trans. by F. M. Atkinson. London, 1930.

Craig, Gordon, *Politics of the Prussian Army, 1640–1945.* London, 1955.

Crozier, Emmet, *American Reporters on the Western Front, 1914–1918.* New York, 1959.

Cruttwell, C. R., *A History of the Great War, 1914–1918.* London, 1934.

Czernin, Count Ottokar, *In the World War.* New York, 1920.

Debergh, François, and Gaillard, André, *Les chemins de l'armistice.* Paris, 1968.

DeWeerd, Harvey A., *President Wilson Fights His War: World War I and the American Intervention.* New York, 1968.

Dickhuth-Harrach, Gustav von, *Im Felde unbesiegt, der Weltkrieg in 29 Einzeldarstellungen.* 2 vols. Munich, 1921.

Dill, Marshall, Jr., *Germany, A Modern History.* Ann Arbor, 1961.

Dooly, William G., Jr., *Great Weapons of World War I.* New York, 1969.

Doumenc, Commandant, *Les transports automobiles sur le front français, 1914–1918.* Paris, 1920.

Duroselle, Jean-Baptiste, *From Wilson to Roosevelt, Foreign Policy of the United States, 1913–1945,* trans. by Nancy Lyman Roelker. Cambridge, Mass., 1963.

Edmonds, Brigadier-General Sir James E., ed., *History of the Great War Based on Official Documents.* London, 1939.

Encyclopædia Britannica, 1972 edition.

Essame, H., *The Battle for Europe, 1918.* London, 1972.

Evelyn, Princess Blücher, *An English Wife in Berlin: A Private Memoir of Events, Politics and Daily Life in Germany Throughout the War and the Social Revolution of 1918.* London, 1921.

Faulkner, Harold Underwood, *American Economic History*. New York, 1923.

Feldman, Gerald D., *Army, Industry and Labor in Germany, 1914–1918*. Princeton, 1966.

Fischer, Fritz, *Germany's Aims in the First World War*. New York, 1967.

Fuller, John Frederick Charles, *Armament and History*. London, 1946.

Gatzke, Hans W., *Germany's Drive to the West*. Baltimore, 1950.

Gaudy, Georges, *Souvenirs d'un poilu du 57e régiment d'infanterie*. 3 vols. Paris, 1921–23.

German Offensive of July 15, The. Marne Source Book. Leavenworth, Kansas, 1923.

Gibbs-Smith, Charles H., *The Aeroplane: An Historical Survey*. London, 1960.

Glaise-Horstenau, Edmund von, *The Collapse of the Austro-Hungarian Empire*, trans. by Ian F. D. Morrow. London, 1930.

Görlitz, Walter, *Hindenburg*. Bonn, 1953.

—— *History of the German General Staff, 1657–1945*, trans. by Brian Battershaw. New York, 1964.

——, ed., *The Kaiser and His Court, The Diaries, Note Books and Letters of Admiral Georg-Alexander von Müller, Chief of the Naval Cabinet, 1914–18*, trans. by Mervyn Savill. London, 1961.

Gough, Sir Hubert, *Memoirs*. London, 1954.

G.S.O., *G.H.Q. (Montreuil-sur-Mer)*. New York, 1920.

Guinn, Paul, *British Strategy and Politics, 1914 to 1918*. Oxford, 1965.

Hagood, General Johnson, *The Services of Supply, A Memoir of the Great War*. Boston, 1927.

Hankey, Lord, *The Supreme Command, 1914–1918*. London, 1961.

Hanssen, Hans Peter, *Diary of a Dying Empire*, trans. by Oscar Osburn Winther. Bloomington, Ind., 1955.

Harbord, James G., Major-General, *Leaves from a War Diary*. New York, 1925.

Herbillon, Colonel, *Souvenirs d'un officier de liaison pendant la guerre mondiale: du général en chef au gouvernement sous le commandement du General Joffre*. Paris, 1930.

Heywood, Chester D., *Negro Combat Troops in the World War, the Story of the 371st Infantry*. New York, 1928.

Hindenburg, Paul von, *Out of My Life*, trans. by S. A. Holt. London, 1920.

Hoffmann, Rudolf, ed., *Der Deutsche Soldat, Briefe aus dem Weltkrieg*. Munich, 1937.

Horne, Charles F., ed., *The Great Events of the Great War*, Vol. VI. New York, 1920.

House, Colonel Edward M., *Intimate Papers*. 2 vols. New York, 1926.

Hudson, James J., *Hostile Skies, A Combat History of the American Air Service in World War I*. Syracuse, 1968.

Isorni, Jacques, and Cadars, Louis, *Histoire véridique de la grande guerre*. 4 vols. Paris, 1968–70.

Jones, Ralph E., Rarey, George H., and Icks, Robert J., *The Fighting Tanks*. Old Greenwich, Conn., 1969.

Juillard, René, ed., *La grande guerre*. 3 vols. Paris, 1960.

Jünger, Ernst, *In Stahlgewittern, ein Kriegstagebuch*. Berlin, 1937.

Kühlmann, Richard von, *Erinnerungen*. Heidelberg, 1948.

Kürenberg, Joachim von, *The Kaiser, A Life of Wilhelm II, Last Emperor of Germany*, trans. by H. T. Russell and Herta Hagen. New York, 1955.

Laffargue, André, *Foch et la bataille de 1918*. Paris, 1967.

Liddell Hart, B. H., *Foch, The Man of Orleans*. Boston, 1932.

——, *A History of the World War, 1914–1918*. London, 1935.

——, *Reputations Ten Years After*. Boston, 1928.

Lloyd George, David, *War Memoirs, 1918*. Boston, 1937.

Loewenberg, Peter, "Psychohistorical Origins of the Nazi Youth Cohort," *American Historical Review*, December 1971.

Lord Riddell's War Diary, 1914–1918. London, 1933.

Ludendorff, Erich, *The General Staff and Its Problems: The History of Relations Between the High Command and the German Imperial Government as Revealed by Official Documents*, trans. by F. A. Holt, Vol. II. New York, n.d.

——, *My War Memories, 1914–1918*. London, 1921.

Lutz, R. H., *The German Revolution, 1918–1919*. Stanford, 1922.

——, ed., *Fall of the German Empire, 1914–18, Documents of the German Revolution*. 2 vols. Stanford, 1932.

Maurice, Major-General Sir F., *The Last Four Months, The End of the War in the West*. London, 1919.

Max of Baden, *Memoirs*, trans. by W. M. Calder and C. W. H. Sutton. 2 vols. London, 1928.

McAuley, Mary Ethel, *Germany in War Time, Personal Experiences of an American Woman in Germany*. Chicago, 1917.

Memoirs of Marshal Foch, trans. by Colonel T. Bentley Mott. Garden City, N.Y., 1931.

Memoirs of the Crown Prince of Germany. London, 1922.

Messenger, Charles, *Trench Fighting, 1914–1918*. New York, 1972.

Miller, Henry W., *The Paris Gun*. New York, 1930.

Ministère de la Guerre, État-Major de l'Armée, Service Historique, *Les armées françaises dans la grande guerre,* Vols. VI, VII, VIII, X. Paris, 1923–1938.

Mitchell, William B., *Memoirs of World War I*. New York, 1960.

Mock, James R. and Larson, Cedric, *Words that Won the War, the Story of the Committee on Public Information, 1917–1919*. Princeton, 1939.

Mordacq, General Jean, Jules Henri, "Le commandement unique," *Revue des Deux Mondes,* April 15, 1929.

——, *Les légendes de la grande guerre*. Paris, 1935.

Nobecourt, R.-G., *L'année du 11 novembre (1918)*. Paris, 1968.

Norman, Aaron, *The Great Air War*. New York, 1968.

Novak, Karl Friedrich, *The Collapse of Central Europe*. London, 1924.

Ogorkiewicz, R. M., *Armour: The Development of Mechanized Forces and Their Equipment*. London, 1960.

Panichas, George A., ed., *Promise of Greatness: The War of 1914–1918*. New York, 1968.

Paxson, Frederic L., *America at War, 1917–1918*. Boston, 1939.

Pershing, John J., *My Experiences in the World War*. New York, 1931.

Pierrefeu, Jean de, *G.Q.G. Secteur I, Trois ans au grand quartier général par le rédacteur du communiqué*. Paris, 1920.

Pitt, Barrie, *1918, The Last Act*. London, 1962.

Poincaré, Raymond, *Au service de la France, neuf années de souvenirs, Victoire et Armistice, 1918*. Paris, 1933.

Recouly, Raymond, *Le mémorial de Foch: mes entretiens avec le maréchal*. Paris, 1929.

Remarque, Erich Maria, *All Quiet on the Western Front,* trans. by A. W. Wheen. Boston, 1929.

Renouvin, Pierre, *La crise européenne et la première guerre mondiale*. Paris, 1969.

Repington, Lieutenant Colonel Charles à Court, *The First World War, 1914–1918,* Vol. II. London, 1921.

Rolland, Romain, *Journal des années de guerre, 1914–1918*. Paris, 1952.

Roosevelt, Quentin, *A Sketch with Letters,* ed. by Kermit Roosevelt. New York, 1921.

Rosenberg, Arthur, *The Birth of the German Republic, 1871–1918,* trans. by Ian F. D. Morrow. New York, 1931.

Rothwell, V. H., *British War Aims and Peace Diplomacy*. Oxford, 1971.

Ryan, Stephen, *Pétain the Soldier*. New York, 1969.

Seldte, Franz, *Vor und Hinter den Kulissen*. Leipzig, 1931.

Simonds, Frank H., *History of the World War*, Vol. V. Garden City, N.Y., 1920.

Society of the First Division, *History of the First Division During the War, 1917–19*. Philadelphia, 1922.

Stallings, Laurence, *The Doughboys, The Story of the AEF, 1917–1918*. New York, 1963.

Suarez, Georges, *Briand, sa vie, son oeuvre, avec son journal et des nombreux documents inédits*, Vol. IV, *Le pilote dans la tourmente, 1916–1918*. Paris, 1940.

Suffel, Jacques, ed., *La guerre de 1914–1918 par ceux qui l'ont fait*. Paris, 1968.

Swope, Herbert Bayard, *Inside the German Empire*. New York, 1917.

Taber, J. H., *The Story of the 168th Infantry*. Washington, D.C., 1925.

Terraine, John, *Douglas Haig, The Educated Soldier*. London, 1963.

Thomas, Shipley, *The History of the AEF*. New York, 1920.

Thoumin, Richard, *The First World War*. London, 1960.

Tschuppik, Karl, *Ludendorff: The Tragedy of a Military Mind*, trans. by W. H. Johnston. Boston, 1932.

U.S. Army in the World War, 1917–1919, Vol. V, Champagne-Marne, Aisne-Marne. Washington, D.C., 1948.

Valluy, J. E., and Dufourcq, Pierre, *La première guerre mondiale*. Paris, 1968.

Wedd, A. F., ed., *German Students' War Letters*. London, 1929.

Weygand, General Maxime, *Foch*. Paris, 1947.

Wheeler-Bennett, John W., *The Nemesis of Power*. London, 1964.

Williams-Ellis, Major Clough, and Williams-Ellis, A., *The Tank Corps*. New York, 1919.

Willoughby, Charles Andrew, *The Economic and Military Participation of the United States in the World War*. Fort Leavenworth, Kans., 1931.

Zeman, Z. A. B., *A Diplomatic History of the First World War*. London, 1961.

Zilliacus, Z., *Mirror of the Past, A History of Secret Diplomacy*. New York, 1946.

Zöberlein, Hans, *Der Glaube an Deutschland, ein Kriegserleben von Verdun bis zum Umsturz*. Munich, 1931.

INDEX

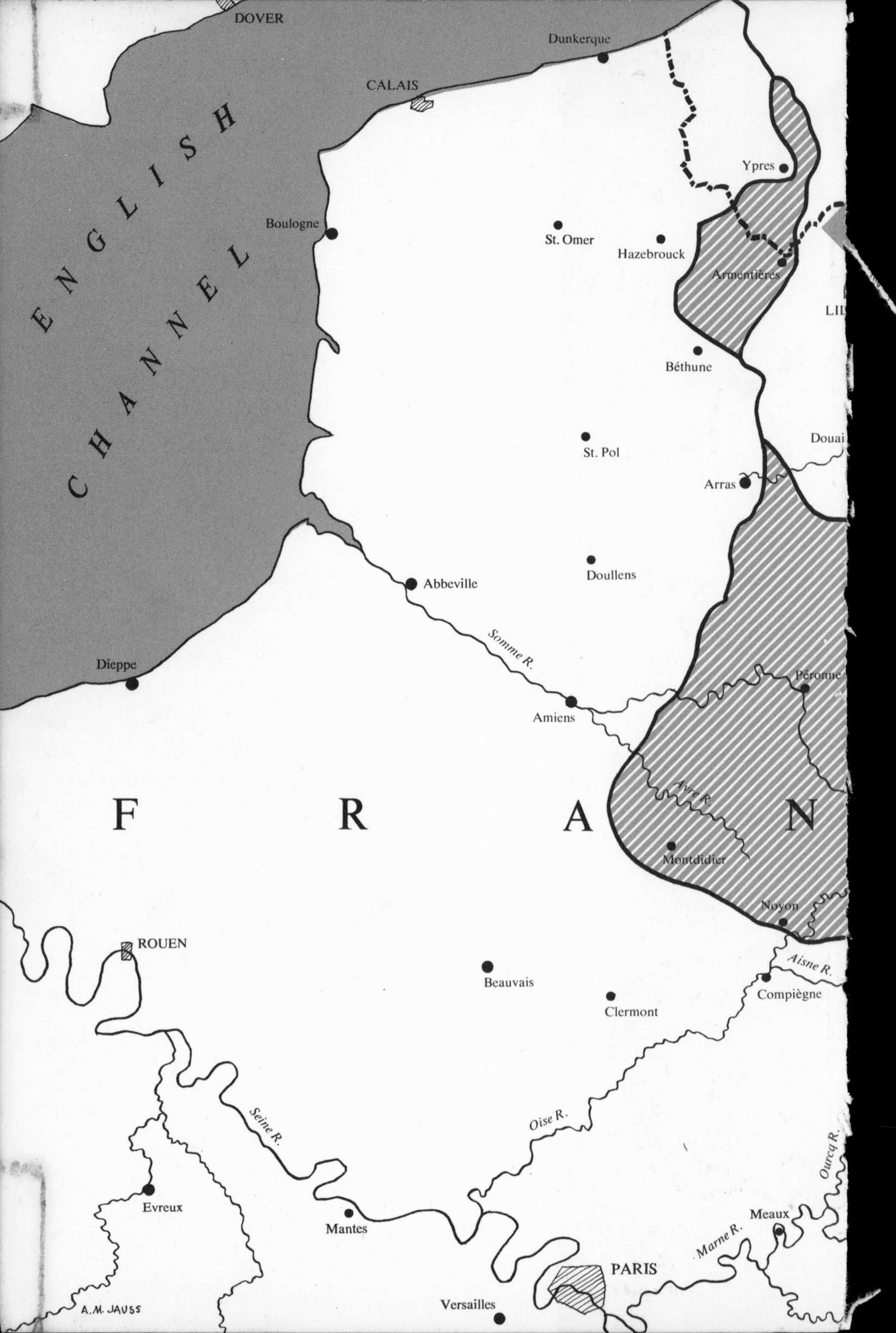
DOVER
Dunkerque
CALAIS
ENGLISH
CHANNEL
Boulogne
Ypres
St. Omer
Hazebrouck
Armentières
LIL
Béthune
St. Pol
Douai
Arras
Doullens
Abbeville
Somme R.
Dieppe
Péronne
Amiens
Avre R.
F R A N
Montdidier
Noyon
ROUEN
Aisne R.
Beauvais
Compiègne
Clermont
Seine R.
Oise R.
Ourcq R.
Evreux
Mantes
Meaux
Marne R.
PARIS
A.M. JAUSS
Versailles